Dear Sister Jonathan, OSBM,

May the warm love of the Infant of Bethlehem fill your heart this Christmas and throughout your lifetime!

Merry Christmas, and a Blessed New Year!

In Christ,
Father John M. Fields

CONFESSOR BETWEEN EAST AND WEST

CONFESSOR
BETWEEN
EAST AND WEST

*A Portrait of Ukrainian Cardinal
Josyf Slipyj*

by

Jaroslav Pelikan

WILLIAM B. EERDMANS PUBLISHING COMPANY
GRAND RAPIDS, MICHIGAN

Library of Congress Cataloging-in-Publication Data

Pelikan, Jaroslav Jan, 1923–
      Confessor between East and West: a portrait of Ukrainian Cardinal
Josyf Slipyj / by Jaroslav Pelikan.
          p.   cm.
      Includes bibliographical references.
      ISBN 0-8028-3672-0
      1. Slipyï, Íosyf, 1892-1984.   2. Catholic Church—Byzantine rite,
Ukrainian—Bishops—Biography.   3. Cardinals—Ukraine—Biography.
4. Catholic Church—Byzantine rite, Ukrainian.   5. Ukraine—Church
history—20th century.   I. Title.
BX4711.692.S45P44   1989
281'.5—dc20
[B]   89-27536
                                                                                          CIP

988 – 1988
TO COMMEMORATE THE MILLENNIUM
OF THE BAPTISM OF RUS',
AND
TO HONOR THE MEMORY OF MY EPONYM
JAROSLAV MUDRYJ OF KIEV

Будучи з вами, не можу не згадати про великого мужа, ісповідника віри, Верховного архиєпископа й кардинала Йосифа Сліпого, якого Господь покликав до вічности. Його смерть обгорнула нас усіх великою жалобою. Він був гідним наслідником праведного мигрополита Андрія Шептицького. Однак, прийшли гіркі часи для української католицької Церкви. Перейшов він іще раз через хресне пережиття і терпіння, подібно як Христос на Голготі. Не міг кардинал Сліпий виконати свого уряду, але засудили його на 18 років заслання, терпіння. Він не заломився, але як герой достойно витримав. Коли вийшов на волю та жив у Римі, то не спочивав, але посвятно працював для добра Церкви та свого народу. Верховний архиєпископ відвідував українські католицькі громади по всьому світі, дбав про науку, заснував університет святого Климента, видавав документи та багато іншого.

В наших молитвах просім Господа, щоб Господь гідно його винагородив за його терпіння, вірність Богові й Церкві та всю його працю. Вічна йому пам'ять!

—Папа Іван-Павло II з промови до Українців у Вінніпегу
16 вересня 1984

While I am with you, I cannot forebear recalling that great man, the Confessor of the Faith, Major Archbishop and Cardinal Slipyj, whom the Lord has called into eternity. His death has filled all of us with great sorrow. He was the worthy successor of the sainted Metropolitan Andrej Šeptyc'kyj. But there came bitter times for the Ukrainian Catholic Church. Once again he passed through the tortures and svfferings of the Cross, similar to those of Christ on Golgotha. Cardinal Slipyj was unable to carry out his office, because they condemned him to eighteen years of imprisonment and suffering. He did not crack, but like a hero he resisted with dignity. When he emerged to freedom and lived in Rome, he did not rest, but labored with a dedication to the welfare of the Church and of his nation. As Major Archbishop, he visited the Ukrainian Catholic colonies all over the world. Because he cared about scholarship, he founded the University of Saint Clement and published many documents and other materials.

In our petitions I pray the Lord to reward him amply for his sufferings, for his faithfulness to God and the Church, and for all his labor. Everlasting be his memory!

—Pope John Paul II to the Ukrainians of Winnipeg,
16 September 1984

Contents

CONTENTS

Preface

I met Josyf Cardinal Slipyj in person only once. Yet the impression created by that brief but unforgettable encounter has been confirmed and deepened during the past several years by the countless hours of research in archives and libraries that have gone into the drawing of this "profile," so that I feel I have come to know him very well indeed. As a historian of the very traditions, doctrinal and liturgical, in which he was steeped and on which he drew; as a native of the New World who has deep roots in the Old and constant contact with it; as a Slav with close ties to both East and West, who is nevertheless not a Ukrainian; as an orthodox and catholic Christian who is denominationally neither Orthodox nor Catholic—I have, I hope, brought to this task a preparation, scholarly as well as personal, that represents a happy combination of love and objectivity.

Yet I could not have carried out the research and writing had it not been for the generosity and kindness of those who have accepted the Ukrainian origins of my Christian name as a kind of passport, granting me access to their own expertise, answering my countless questions and correcting my mistakes, reading successive drafts of my manuscript in whole or in part, suggesting lines of inquiry and yet respecting the integrity of my project, and in the course of time becoming my friends and cherished colleagues: His Beatitude Myroslav Ivan Cardinal Lubachivsky, Slipyj's successor as Metropolitan of L'viv-Halyč; His Excellency Maxim Hermaniuk, Archbishop of Winnipeg and Metropolitan for Ukrainian Catholics in Canada; Bishop Michael

Hrynchyshyn, Apostolic Exarch for Ukrainians of the Byzantine Rite in France; Hieromonk Lubomyr Husar of "Studion" Monastery in Rome, built by Josyf Slipyj, where I have spent many happy hours; Reverend Professor Petro B. T. Bilaniuk of Saint Michael's College in Toronto; and Professor Leonid Rudnytzky of LaSalle University in Philadelphia, who originally broached the proposal that I write a book about the Metropolitan. I must reserve a special word of thanks for Reverend Professor Ivan Choma of the Ukrainian Catholic University in Rome, Director of the *Archivum Patriarchale Sanctae Sophiae;* without his encyclopedic knowledge of the Slipyj materials, which he shared with me in unfailing courtesy and warm hospitality during my repeated visits as his guest in Rome, I would have been overwhelmed or baffled or both. The Saint Sophia Association generously subsidized the research. Among the many others whose encouragement and knowledge were of help, I should also mention His Excellency, Italian Minister of Foreign Affairs Giulio Andreotti, who, as a longtime friend and admirer of Cardinal Slipyj, granted me the opportunity to converse with him in 1986.

Some of the material in Part One was presented in lectures and papers at several international conferences in the United States, Canada, and Western Europe, and, in other forms, has appeared in publications coming out of those conferences. But it was the invitation of President Leonard I. Sweet to deliver the Heck Lectures for 1989 at the United Theological Seminary in Dayton, Ohio, that provided me with precisely the forum I needed to set forth the conception of the work as a whole, as well as the opportunity to work with my colleagues at Eerdmans in the publication of *Confessor between East and West.*

A Note on Languages, Translations, and Transliterations

This book is written chiefly for readers who do not know Ukrainian and the other Slavic languages in which the majority of its sources, both primary and secondary, have been written and printed. The needs of such readers have moved me to adopt the practice that whenever a source already exists somewhere in a translation into some Western language—English, French, German, Italian, or Latin (to list them in alphabetical order, as well as in order of preference)—I have cited it also according to that translation (in parentheses), and in some cases only according to that translation when it is safe to make the assumption that those readers who do have Ukrainian can easily locate the original from my reference. The linguistic complexity of the sources has likewise made it seem desirable for me to follow with almost total consistency (except that I use "ch" rather than "x" for the Cyrillic "x") the system of transliterating the Cyrillic alphabet—or, rather, alphabets—prescribed by the *Slavic and East European Journal*; this system of transliteration has the additional advantage of easy movement and comparison between those Slavic languages that use a Latin alphabet with diacritical marks and those that use a Cyrillic alphabet. In transliterating the Cyrillic character "Г," therefore, I have used "h" if the name or word is Ukrainian or Byelorussian, but "g" if it is Russian, Serbian, or Bulgarian; a "g" in a Ukrainian word or name indicates that the original used a "Ґ." That situation is made even more complex by the linguistic-political circumstance that in the course of their careers some Ukrainians have Russified the pronunciation of their names—including the poet N. V. Gogol and the politician N. V. Podgorny (Pidhornyj), to whom Josyf Slipyj addressed two long epistles from captivity (see pp. 149-50 below).

Abbreviations used in the Notes

AAS	*Acta Apostolicae Sedis.* Rome: Tipografia Poliglotta Vaticana, 1909–.
Alberigo	Alberigo, Joseph, et al., eds. *Conciliorum oecumenicorum decreta.* 3rd ed. Bologna: Instituto per le scienze religiose, 1973.
Ann.Pont.	*Annuario Pontificio.* Vatican City: 1716–.
Arch.Pat.	*Archivum Patriarchale Sanctae Sophiae,* Università Cattolica Ucraina, Rome.
ASS	*Acta Sanctae Sedis.* 41 vols. Rome: Tipografia Vaticana, 1865–1908.
Denzinger	Denzinger, Heinrich, ed. *Enchiridion symbolorum definitionum et declarationum de rebus fidei et morum.* 32d ed. Freiburg im Breisgau: Herder, 1963.
DTC	*Dictionnaire de théologie catholique.* 15 vols. and indexes. Paris: Letouzey et Ané, 1909–50.
LTK	*Lexikon für Theologie und Kirche.* 2d ed. 10 vols. and index. Freiburg im Breisgau: Herder, 1957–67.
NCE	*New Catholic Encyclopedia.* 15 vols. New York: McGraw Hill Book Company, 1967.
Oss.Rom.	*L'Osservatore Romano* (cited by date).
Prav.Slov.	*Polnyj pravoslavnyj bogoslovskij enciklopedičeskij slovar'*

[Complete Eastern Orthodox encyclopedic dictionary of theology] (1913). London: Variorum Reprints, 1971.

Slipyj, *Spomyny* Josyf Slipyj. *Spomyny* [unpublished memoirs]. Colophon dated: "Napysano pid čas ferij 1963 i 1964 r. v monastyri Otciv Pasionistiv v Nettuno [Written during vacation time 1963 and 1964 in the monastery of the Passionist Fathers at Nettuno]."

Slipyj, *Tvory* *Tvory Kard. Josyfa Verchovnoho Archyjepiskopa [Opera omnia Card. Josephi (Slipyj Kobernyckyj-Dyčkovskyj) archiepiscopi maioris]*. Rome: Universitas Ucrainorum a S. Clemente Papa, 1968–.

TCE *The Catholic Encyclopedia*. 15 vols. New York: The Encyclopedia Press, 1913.

Part One

The Heritage of Josyf Slipyj

Three Churches of Saint Sophia

By jet plane the journey between Istanbul and Rome now takes about two hours. Thus on the same day a traveler can (as indeed the author did, on 29 July 1986) see old Saint Sophia in New Rome at sunrise, and then at sunset new Saint Sophia in Old Rome—an exquisite little adaptation of that massive basilica. The historic link connecting these two Churches of Saint Sophia is the Church of Saint Sophia in Kiev, built to copy Constantinople's and represented in a mosaic on the wall of Rome's "miniature Kievan Sophia Church."[1] The third Saint Sophia, a "continuation [*prodovžennja*]" of the one in Kiev,[2] was built in Rome by Josyf Cardinal Slipyj, exiled Ukrainian archbishop and metropolitan of Kiev-Halyč, in the twentieth century; and he marked the day of its consecration on 27 September 1969.[3] The first Saint Sophia in Constantinople—the city he called the "Paris" of the Middle Ages[4]—was built in its present form by Justinian the Great, emperor of the Romans, in the sixth century. Slipyj had long admired it.[5] "Having seen all the cathedrals and the greatest churches of Europe and of Asia" (including Saint Peter's in Rome, the Cologne Cathedral, Notre Dame in Paris, and Saint Paul's in London), Slipyj declared in 1966—echoing the ancient words about Hagia Sophia[6] of the *Primary Chronicle* of Nestor, whom he elsewhere called "our genial and great chronicler and historian, Nestor"[7]—"we can say that upon entering that church something sacred, holy, and mysterious envelops the human soul and incites it to prayer."[8]

The second Saint Sophia was built by Jaroslav the Wise, prince of Kiev, in the eleventh century, as "the high point of Ukrainian architecture."[9] Slipyj idealized the memory of Jaroslav the Wise, and he frequently referred to his reign as a high point of Ukrainian religious and

---

1. Slipyj to Joseph Frings, 7.vi.1964, *Arch.Pat.* 30:290.
2. Slipyj, *Tvory* 14:175.
3. Slipyj, *Tvory* 10/11:143 (144).
4. Slipyj, *Tvory* 2:107.
5. Slipyj, *Tvory* 2:114.
6. "The Russes were astonished, and in their wonder praised the Greek ceremonial. . . . 'We knew not whether we were in heaven or on earth. For on earth there is no such splendor or such beauty, and we are at a loss how to describe it. We only know that God dwells there among men, and their service is fairer than the ceremonies of other nations. For we cannot forget that beauty.'" *The Russian Primary Chronicle* (988), Cross (1953) 111.
7. Slipyj, *Tvory* 12:19.
8. Slipyj, *Tvory* 12:227.
9. Slipyj, *Tvory* 13:17.

cultural life as well.[10] It was a mark of the investiture of the metropolitan of Kiev when he assumed charge of Saint Sophia.[11] To Ukrainians, therefore, it was, together with the monastery at Pečerska Lavra, a cherished symbol of "our holy tradition."[12] Slipyj came through Kiev, as a prisoner, on the morning of 12 April 1945,[13] and he glimpsed Saint Sophia on his final visit to Kiev but was not permitted to go in.[14] Yet he was able to remind the First Secretary of the Ukrainian Communist Party of an icon of Pope Saint Clement I that Jaroslav the Wise had ordered to be placed there.[15] And when it came time to build a church appropriate to the situation of Ukrainians in exile, the Saint Sophia of Jaroslav the Wise served as the obvious model.[16] The Saint Sophia in Rome would be "as though a sister" to the Saint Sophia in Kiev.[17] Of those three churches bearing the name "Saint Sophia," only the little one in Rome still functions as a Christian church, instead of having been "transformed into a museum" by the state.[18] It also functions as a memorial to Josyf Slipyj, who in his "Testament [*Zapovit*]" asked that he be buried there, and then eventually at L'viv or, God willing and the Ukrainian nation consenting, at Saint Sophia in Kiev;[19] his mummified body lies in a crypt beneath the church.

Josyf Slipyj took pleasure in applying to the church he had built the words of Proverbs 9:1: "Wisdom ['H σοφία] has built her house."[20] The building symbolized and honored a divine Wisdom that transcended human thought and speech, but that had endowed the human race with reason—which made the Church of Saint Sophia the fitting architectural crown for the Ukrainian Catholic University.[21] For in the Eastern theological tradition, Greek and then Slavic, Sophia as the personification of the divine Wisdom has always played a far more prominent rôle than it has in the Latin tradition. In various Byzantine, Russian, and Ukrainian thinkers, Sophia has been identified sometimes

---

10. See, for example, Slipyj, *Tvory* 13:233; 237-38.
11. Slipyj, *Tvory* 12:120 (125).
12. Slipyj, *Tvory* 13:29 (30).
13. Slipyj, *Spomyny* 111.
14. Slipyj, *Spomyny* 193.
15. Slipyj to N. V. Podgorny, i.1961, *Arch.Pat.* 28:35 (69).
16. Slipyj, *Tvory* 13:24-25.
17. Slipyj, *Tvory* 14:196.
18. Slipyj, *Tvory* 12:227.
19. Slipyj, *Tvory* 14:487.
20. Slipyj, *Tvory* 8:178; again, Slipyj, *Tvory* 12:225-28; and yet again, Slipyj, *Tvory* 13:16-23.
21. Slipyj, *Tvory* 13:109-10.

with the preexistent Logos, sometimes with the Holy Spirit, sometimes with Mary the Mother of God; and sometimes, in the more speculative systems, it has seemed to critics to have become a distinct divine being, whose veneration threatened to turn the divine Trinity into a quaternity. But even in the strictest and most orthodox construction, Sophia is a fitting object of Christian worship—and, ever since Constantine and Justinian, a worthy patron for the major houses of Eastern Christian worship.

Upon entering the Roman Saint Sophia for the first time, a visitor, even a fairly knowledgeable one, might suppose it to be an Eastern Orthodox church of Slavic provenance. The two parts of the church are divided by an iconostasis, through which the celebrant of the Divine Liturgy comes for the Great and the Little Entrance. On the iconostasis[22] and in the mosaics on the walls are many of the figures familiar from the Eastern patristic and hagiographic traditions—Saint Nicholas of Myra ("Santa Claus"); Saints Constantine the Great and his mother Helena; the Cappadocian fathers of the fourth century (Saint Basil the Great, Saint Gregory of Nazianzus, and Saint Gregory of Nyssa); Saint John Chrysostom [*Ivan Zolotoustyj*]; Saint Romanos "Melodus," the Byzantine poet and hymnographer; Saint Maximus Confessor, cherished by the East but revered also in the West;[23] Saint Ol'ha/Olga and her grandson Volodymyr/Vladimir the Great, together with his son Jaroslav the Wise (without an aureole, though he is sometimes designated "Saint [*Svjatoj*]," at any rate in Russian Orthodox tradition);[24] even "Saint" Clement of Alexandria, whose claim to that title is considerably more ambiguous.[25] But the mosaics also contain some surprises, for closer inspection reveals at least two major figures whom one would not expect to encounter in any Orthodox church, whether Greek or Slavic: Saint Augustine of Hippo and Saint Thomas Aquinas. And in the apse, between the haloed figures of the two "apostles to the Slavs," Saint Cyril (in monk's garb, with the alphabet) and Saint Methodius (in bishop's garb), who are for understandable historical reasons venerated as saints in Eastern far more than in Western Christendom, is the figure (like Jaroslav, without an aureole) of Josyf Slipyj's predecessor as Greek Catholic metropolitan of L'viv-Halyč, Andrej Šeptyc'kyj.[26]

---

22. See *Ikonostas Soboru Svjatoji Sofiji v Rymi* (1979) in the bibliography below.
23. See pp. 100-101 below.
24. *Prav.Slov.* 2:2405 (s.v.: Jaroslav Georgij Vladimirovyč).
25. *DTC* 3:140-42 (André de La Barre, s.v.: Clément d'Alexandrie).
26. Slipyj, *Tvory* 13:229.

1

A Church between East and West

In 1974, as an exile in Rome, far away from his Ukrainian homeland, and as an old man of eighty-two (although he actually still had ten more years to live, during which those parallels would continue to suggest themselves to him),[1] Josyf Cardinal Slipyj spoke about some of the remarkable coincidences between the crucial dates in his own life and "the turning points in our church life and our national life: 1892, 1911, 1917, 1925, 1939, 1944, 1945, 1963, and 1965."[2]

Reviewing the historical atlas together with a chronological table will help to document the ways some of those dates had coincided.[3] When Slipyj was born in Zazdrist', Galicia (Halyčyna) on 17 February 1892, that village was part of the Austro-Hungarian Empire; Ternopil', on the other hand, where he attended *Gymnasium* between 1903 and 1911, from age eleven to age nineteen, had for a brief time at the beginning of the nineteenth century been part of Czarist Russia. With the breakup of the Austro-Hungarian Empire at the end of the First World War, when Slipyj was twenty-six, the city of L'viv (Lwów in Polish, Lemberg in German, and Leopolis in Latin), where he attended seminary and later functioned as professor, rector and metropolitan, was the site of the proclamation of a "West Ukrainian People's Republic" on

1. Slipyj, *Tvory* 14:139 (at eighty-five); and Slipyj, *Tvory* 14:80-81 (at ninety-two).
2. Slipyj, *Tvory* 9:230.
3. In Maps 20-24 Magocsi (1985) has graphically presented this evolution; Horak (1957) provides a detailed chronology.

1 November 1918; two months later that republic announced its union with the "Ukrainian National Republic" at Kiev, but this failed to become a stable and recognized state. Instead, in July 1919 the military forces of a newly revitalized Poland succeeded in annexing Galicia. As part of "Eastern Little Poland [*Małopolska Wschodnia*]," therefore, it had become Polish territory when the thirty-year-old Slipyj came back in 1922 from his studies at Innsbruck and Rome to serve as professor of the major seminary at L'viv; it was to remain Polish throughout the 1920s and 1930s, during most of the metropolitanate of Andrej Šeptyc′kyj.

But L'viv fell on the Soviet side of the line of demarcation agreed upon by Nazi Germany and Soviet Russia as part of their nonaggression pact of August 1939; this obtained until the German invasion of the Soviet Union on 21 June 1941, when Slipyj was forty-nine.[4] For the next three years L'viv and its Galician territory were occupied by the German armies as *"Distrikt Galizien"* of the *"Generalgouvernement"* of the Third Reich. L'viv was recaptured by the Red Army on 27 July 1944, but not without continuing resistance from Ukrainian nationalists, whose principal military force was the "Ukrainian Insurgent Army [*Ukrajinska povstanska armija*]," led by General Roman Šuchevyč.[5] During the second half of 1944 and the first half of 1945, the political and military forces of the Ukrainian Soviet Socialist Republic, of which L'viv was now a part, were engaged in a campaign to consolidate control, one step of which was the arrest of Josyf Slipyj on Wednesday, 11 April 1945, two months after his fifty-third birthday. He was in his seventies when he was set free in 1963, and in 1965 he was made a cardinal of the Holy Roman Church by His Holiness Pope Paul VI.

"At the center of your glorious pontificate," Josyf Slipyj declared to Pope Paul in Saint Peter's on 15 November 1963, "stands the East, and above all the Slavic East."[6] As is clear from such a statement, as well as from the capsule summary just recited of external events in Ukrainian history during his lifetime, Josyf Slipyj was a confessor between East and West who presided over a church that had been positioned, both by geography and by history, between East and West. As Robert Conquest, a leading scholar of twentieth-century developments in the Soviet orbit, has put it,

A major reason why the events we shall be describing never truly gripped the Western mind appears to be a lack of understanding

4. Prokop (1981) 1:94-147.
5. See Slipyj's tribute to him: Slipyj, *Tvory* 14:225.
6. Slipyj, *Tvory* 12:112 (111).

or knowledge of the power of Ukrainian national feeling, of Ukrainian nationhood. In this century an independent Ukrainian state only lasted a few years, and then with interruptions, and was never able to establish itself either physically or in the world's consciousness. In fact the Ukraine, as large as France and more populous than Poland, was by far the largest nation in Europe not to emerge as an independent entity (except briefly) in the period between the two World Wars.

Conquest goes on to declare: "The Ukraine's long independent cultural tradition was little known in the West. . . . Historically the Ukrainians are an ancient nation which has persisted and survived through terrible calamities."[7]

The phrase "between East and West," which forms part of the title of this book, is one that unavoidably comes to mind in any consideration of the Ukrainian nation, of the Ukrainian church, and of the Ukrainian metropolitan. Slipyj took the occasion of his appointment as a cardinal to remind the pope that the Ukrainian church stood on the crossroads "between East and West."[8] Gregor Prokoptschuk made that the title of one of the longest chapters in his informative, if somewhat hagiographic, biography of Metropolitan Andrej Šeptyc'kyj,[9] going on later in the book to speak of "the Ukrainian minority in Poland" as "always standing, both culturally and religiously, on the boundary between East and West."[10] Hryhor Lužnyc'kyj entitled his church history of 1954 (written in Ukrainian) *The Ukrainian Church between East and West.*[11] And Johannes Madey called his highly esteemed[12] church history of 1969 (written in German) *Church between East and West.*[13] For the Slavs understand better than most other Europeans—and the Ukrainians understand better than most other Slavs—the price of living on both sides of that great divide, "between two world views . . . between two churches . . . two spiritualities."[14] Josyf Slipyj was able to boast to a Communist official, and then years later to a congregation of Ukrainian faithful in Rome, that he had been persecuted by the Bolsheviks, by the Poles, and by the Gestapo—quite

7. Conquest (1986) 25-26.
8. Slipyj, *Tvory* 12:176 (177).
9. Prokoptschuk (1967) 179-97.
10. Prokoptschuk (1967) 214.
11. See the full details of publication in the bibliography below.
12. See Janiv (1984) xvii.
13. Madey (1969).
14. Slipyj, *Tvory* 14:260.

indiscriminately.[15] And during the Second World War, as Slipyj reported with a touch of irony, there were bombardments, sometimes simultaneously, "from one direction . . . and from the other," from the Nazis and from the Soviets.[16] The library of the Theological Society of L'viv was destroyed by German bombs, and then the Red Army finished the job.[17]

For, in the epigram of Metropolitan Andrej Šeptyc'kyj, "Now the card of history has been turned over,"[18] and as usual the Ukrainians were caught between the players in the global card game. Like many other Slavs before him and after him, Josyf Slipyj was forced throughout his life to explain to representatives of other ethnic traditions just who the Slavs were—and, within the Slavic community between East and West, just who the Ukrainians were. The terminology of the history books and the nomenclature of the atlases did not help such explanations a great deal. Thus in many accounts, and in the practice of the Roman Catholic Church, the usual name for the Ukrainians was "Ruthenians." Protesting against the use of this "ethnic terminology," a Ukrainian archbishop, writing to the pope while Metropolitan Josyf Slipyj was still in Soviet prison, objected that in common Ukrainian pronunciation the name "Ruthenian" came out as "Russian [Ruskyj]." Besides, "the use by the Roman curia of the antiquated appellation 'Ruthenian, Ruthenians' makes it very difficult for Ukrainian Catholics to achieve any rapprochement or understanding with the Ukrainian Orthodox."[19]

While the name "Ruthenian" was, therefore, objectionable and highly charged, the Old Church Slavonic name Rus' was extremely confusing, and its translation as "Russia" was even more objectionable. As a recent study has observed, "seventeenth-century ancestors of the modern Ukrainians, Belorussians and Russians all used variants of the term 'Rus'' when referring to themselves. . . . Both Ukrainians and Belorussians called themselves 'Ruthenians' (Rusyny)."[20] Rus' is the term that appears in the ancient chronicles, including The Primary Chronicle bearing the name of "Nestor." And there it is usually translated into English and other Western languages as "Russia," so that Nestor becomes (as, for example, in the standard English version) The Russian

15. Slipyj to N. V. Podgorny, 17.ii.1961, Arch.Pat. 28:89 (123); Slipyj, Tvory 13:151.
16. Slipyj, Spomyny 100.
17. Slipyj, Spomyny 70.
18. Slipyj, Spomyny 83.
19. Ivan Bučko to John XXIII, 30.ix.1959, Arch.Pat. 28:4-7.
20. Sysyn (1985) 27.

Primary Chronicle.[21] Slipyj was determined not to surrender the name to the Muscovites.[22] Seeking to explain the meaning of *Rus'* to Eugène Cardinal Tisserant of the Sacred Congregation for the Eastern Church, Slipyj cited a number of the ancient chronicles to prove that in those documents *Rus'* was synonymous with what was now called "Ukraine." The term "Russia," he went on to explain, was a neologism that had come into usage only with the rise of Muscovite Russia many centuries later.[23] Presumably on the basis of Slipyj's explanation, that understanding of the name was often reflected thereafter in Vatican usage. An interesting example of such usage can be found in two letters written to Josyf Slipyj on 19 March 1979 by Pope John Paul II, who before his election as pope had been Karol Cardinal Wojtyła, archbishop of Kraków. In the first letter the term "Rus'" appears in quotes throughout, but the second letter consistently refers to *"'Rus' (Ucraina)."*[24]

In their various letters back and forth[25] (to which there will be repeated references in subsequent chapters of this book) as well as in the pope's memorial tribute of 16 September 1984, a week after Slipyj's death (which serves as the epigraph for this book), Karol Wojtyła/John Paul II and Josyf Slipyj wrote to each other in Polish, in Ukrainian, in Italian, or in Latin. Indeed, Slipyj took obvious glee at being able to append a postscript in Polish to an official letter for the pope that he had written "in the language of the members of the Roman curia," that is, in Italian.[26] On other occasions he would write to the pope in Ukrainian and then send along an official Italian version for the files.[27] Such polyglotism is interesting and important not only because each of them was an accomplished linguist—though that is, of course, eminently true—but because each of them belonged to what Slipyj called "the great family of Slavic nations"[28] and had a Slavic language as his mother tongue. As John Paul II wrote to Cardinal Slipyj in March 1979, "through the inscrutable design of Providence, the Holy See is occupied for the first time by a Slavic pope."[29] Or, as he declared at Gniezno three

21. Cross (1953).
22. Slipyj, *Tvory* 14:139.
23. Slipyj to Eugène Tisserant, 12.vi.1963, *Arch.Pat.* 28:395-98.
24. John Paul II to Slipyj, 19.iii.1979, *Arch.Pat.* 118:75-86.
25. The first of these as one Slavic cardinal to another seems to have been a Christmas greeting: Slipyj to Karol Wojtyła, 23.xii.1967, *Arch.Pat.* 36:402.
26. Slipyj to John Paul II, 23.xi.1983, *Arch.Pat.* 118:292-93.
27. Slipyj to John Paul II, 3.vi.1979, *Arch.Pat.* 118:99-100 (Ukrainian); Slipyj to John Paul II, 15.vi.1979, *Arch.Pat.* 118:102-5 (Italian).
28. Slipyj to Władysław Rubin, 15.vi.1979, Slipyj, *Tvory* 14:374.
29. John Paul II to Slipyj, 19.iii.1979, *Arch.Pat.* 118:83.

months later, on the Sunday of Pentecost, 3 June 1979, during his first visit to his homeland after being elected pope,

> These languages cannot fail to be heard especially by the first Slav Pope in the history of the Church. Perhaps that is why Christ has chosen him, perhaps that is why the Holy Spirit has led him. . . .
>
> Is it not Christ's will, is it not what the Holy Spirit disposes, that this Polish Pope, this Slav Pope, should at this precise moment manifest the spiritual unity of Christian Europe? Although there are two great traditions, that of the West and that of the East . . . , our lands were hospitable [also] to those wonderful traditions which have their origin in the new Rome, at Constantinople.[30]

The Slavs are the only European people to have received both of those "two great traditions" as a permanent heritage, but that means that they are also the only people for whom conversion to the Christian faith has meant cultural division rather than cultural unification and who have therefore lived between East and West throughout their history. For while over the centuries the gospel has been responsible for giving many nations their alphabet, to the Slavs it has given three—the Glagolitic, the Cyrillic, and the Latin. Even a Soviet historian of Kiev is obliged to acknowledge that "the adoption of Christianity was unquestionably a fact of primary importance"; "Christianity, as the generally accepted religion in Europe," he adds, "served to draw the state of Ancient Rus closer to the rest of Europe," while at the same time "the efforts of the Byzantine Church to draw Rus into the sphere of age-long Byzantine culture served to raise her cultural level."[31]

This heritage of the Ukrainian Church between East and West, or between Europe and Byzantium, as the context for Josyf Slipyj's successive vocations, may become clearer through the enumeration, on the basis of his own statements (some of which will appear again later in our account, particularly in our final chapter), of four pairs of positive and negative implications that come out of this separation of Eastern Christianity from much of the rest of Christendom: the preservation of tradition, but the danger of a traditionalism that stifles creativity; the centrality of liturgy, but the danger of a ritualism that cannot distinguish between the important and the trivial; the profound affinity between cultus and culture, but the danger of a cultural impoverishment

30. Levi (1982) 1:4-5.
31. Grekov (1959) 636, 639.

that neglects critical scholarship; the fostering of national identity in each Eastern Church, but the danger of equating that identity with the life-style of the Old World at the eventual cost of both Catholicity and particularity.

I. On 18 February 1981, the feast day according to the Julian calendar[32] of Pope Saint Leo I (one of the popes whose memory was venerated in the East as well as in the West[33]), Josyf Slipyj, signing himself as "Josyf I, Patriarch Archbishop of Kiev-Halyč, Metropolitan of L'viv, and Bishop of Kamjanec'Podil's'kyj," announced his intention of continuing to follow the "custom of the Eastern Churches" rather than that of the Latin West in his garb as a prelate; specifically, he would wear the *kamilavka* (Greek καμηλαύχιον), a hat which was, for an archbishop, covered with white wool.[34] To support this somewhat less than momentous decision, he invoked the entire massive authority of the Eastern Christian tradition: "The church of Christ has always regarded it as important and has taught us to preserve the traditions of our Church of *Rus'*-Ukraine, even though they may have been neglected or forgotten for various reasons in a time of difficult historical experiences for our nation."[35] And when he had to discuss the proposal of a Ukrainian eparchy for Passaic, New Jersey, his approach was to request "permission for a historical digression" and then to proceed to discuss, as though they were recent or even contemporary, situations that had arisen between 1281 and 1321, as well as others from the fifteenth, seventeenth, and nineteenth centuries.[36]

It has been evident to Western observers since the Middle Ages that Eastern Christianity has affirmed the authority of tradition more unambiguously than has the West. Repeatedly, therefore, it has been the vocation of Eastern Christendom to come to the rescue of the West by drawing out from its memory the overlooked resources of the patristic tradition. So it was in the beginnings of the Renaissance in Italy, when the scholars of Constantinople fled to Venice and Florence before the invader, bringing their Greek manuscripts with them, and taught Western thinkers to read not only Plato and Homer (instead of merely Cicero and Vergil), but the Cappadocian fathers, John Chrysostom, and the Greek New Testament.[37] And so it has been again in the twentieth

---

32. *Prav.Slov.* 2:1515 (s.v.: Lev').
33. Slipyj, *Tvory* 12:37.
34. *Prav.Slov.* 2:1174-75 (s.v.: Kamilavka).
35. Message of 18.ii.1981, *Arch.Pat.* 74:262.
36. Slipyj to Angelo Dell'Acqua, 24.ii.1967, *Arch.Pat.* 36:74-75.
37. Geanakoplos (1962).

century. One of the most striking differences between the First Vatican Council and the Second—and a difference that helps to provide an explanation for many of the other differences—is that between 1870 and 1950 the Western Church had once more discovered how much it had been ignoring in the liturgy and spirituality, the theology and culture, of Eastern Christendom. Thus on one point after another in the decrees of the Second Vatican Council, from ecclesiology itself to the collegiality of bishops and the centrality of the liturgy, the one-sidedness of Western ways has been counterbalanced and corrected by characteristically Eastern emphases; and those emphases had often found their most effective voice in Josyf Slipyj.[38]

At the same time Slipyj was sensitive to the charge that his elevation of the authority of tradition made him and other Eastern theologians (in the phrase of Horace, which he transliterated into Cyrillic) *"laudatores antiqui [acti] temporis."*[39] It was, he insisted, an "insinuation that did not correspond to fact" when Western polemists charged "that Eastern Christians are so stubborn and tenacious about the *status quo* that they exclude any progress *a priori.*" Their reverence for the patristic era, which had itself been a time of "immense progress," could also be the basis for further "evolution."[40]

In answer to Western critics who charged the East with living in the past and lapsing into an arid and sterile traditionalism, Slipyj, in a Polish essay published in 1934, made the following observations about Byzantine literature and theology:

> Literature and scholarship are the most powerful expression of the Byzantine spirit. The power of its literary creativity lies in its aesthetic achievements, in the wealth of its contents, and in its beauty of language. Byzantine monuments, which stand in the succession of ancient Greek literature, were the models by which Eastern, Slavic, and other nations were educated. . . . The ancient tradition did not decline in Byzantium as it did in the West, and therefore its literary creativity did not have such a period of neglect. . . .
>
> Of all the areas of scholarship, it was theology that developed the most magnificently. Amid an "extreme traditionalism," which manifested itself in a great dependence upon the church fathers, there arose a large number of original creations, especially in ascetic and mystical theology.[41]

38. See chapter 10, pp. 207-15 below.
39. Slipyj, *Tvory* 13:108.
40. Slipyj, *Tvory* 1:400.
41. Slipyj, *Tvory* 2:225.

In a sense, then, Byzantine traditionalism needed to be rescued from it-self in order to resume the creativity that had always been present in it.

II. The primary locus of that creativity was liturgical. As Slipyj fre-quently suggested during and after the Second Vatican Council, a major element in the genius of Eastern Christianity in comparison with the West has been that "its scientific theology has often developed from a highly original point of view [because of its characteristic emphasis on] the contemplative life" and on the liturgy.[42]

Reformers of Western liturgy have repeatedly acknowledged that "highly original point of view." For example, the monumental *Litur-giarum Orientalium Collectio*, published in two volumes at Paris in 1716 by the French scholar Eusèbe Renaudot, was a work of painstaking scholarship and great devotion intended to enrich post-Tridentine Western worship by infusing a better knowledge of the Greek and Near Eastern rites.[43] The Latin Church has sometimes given the impression that the fundamental meaning of the Christian faith is institutional. "It is altogether necessary to salvation for every human creature to be sub-ject to the Roman pontiff [*subesse Romano pontifici omni humanae creaturae . . . omnino esse de necessitate salutis*]," Pope Boniface VIII declared in his bull *Unam sanctam* of 1302.[44] On the other hand, many of the Protestant churches, especially the Lutheran, have emphasized doctrinal theology as the normative force in the church, producing in such tomes as the *Book of Concord* of 1580 a corpus of official doctrine whose total length surpasses by a factor of ten or more the entire dog-matic legislation of the seven ecumenical councils of the ancient and undivided church. According to the primary document in the *Book of Concord*, the *Augsburg Confession* of 1530, "consensus on the doctrine of the gospel [*consentire de doctrina evangelii*]" was, together with the proper administration of the sacraments, essential to the unity of the church.[45]

But Eastern Christianity, while not indifferent to such institution-al questions as the authority of the episcopate and while certainly vigorous in its espousal of dogmatic and creedal orthodoxy (including the creedal integrity of the only truly ecumenical creed, the Nicene, which it has defended against the Western addition of the *Filioque*), has nevertheless put worship rather than institution or doctrine at the cen-

---

42. Slipyj to Lucca Di Schiena, 24.viii.1963, *Arch.Pat.* 29:122.
43. *DTC* 13:2381-83 (J. Carreyre s.v.: Renaudot, Eusèbe).
44. Denzinger 875.
45. Tappert et al. (1959) 32.

ter of the definition of the church. Thus it is illuminating to note that although Roman Catholics and Protestants have both laid claim to the label "orthodox" for the fidelity of their doctrinal formulations to the doctrine of the Trinity as formulated by the First Council of Nicea in 325, the "Sunday of Orthodoxy" observed in the East is a commemoration of the Second Council of Nicea, that of 787, and of an "ὀρθο-δοξία" that is defined as the right way of rendering "δόξα," the praise of God. And the Slavic languages have preserved this definition in the very term *pravo-slavie* (*pravo* meaning "right" and *slava* meaning "praise"), which Slipyj, citing the precedent of his predecessor Metropolitan Andrej Šeptyc'kyj, repeatedly and vigorously insisted on keeping in the liturgy, also when it was broadcast on Vatican Radio to Ukrainian audiences, despite the identification of the term with those Eastern Orthodox Slavic churches that did not have communion with Rome.[46]

Once again, however, this richness of worship has run the danger of putting all liturgical issues on the same level. It was understandable when Slipyj spoke of "ritual confusion" among Ukrainian Catholics in the diaspora as "the greatest disaster" facing his church.[47] But when he used the same word "disaster" to describe the compulsory introduction of the Gregorian calendar,[48] even some among his supporters found this reaction somewhat exaggerated.

Western churches have frequently been divided over doctrine: justification *sola fide* versus justification by faith and works at the Council of Trent, or verbal inspiration of the Bible versus the historical-critical method in the debates of the nineteenth and twentieth centuries. And sometimes they have been divided over systems of polity and church administration: it is illuminating to note that in Anglo-Saxon Protestantism the nomenclature of many of the major denominations—Episcopalian, Presbyterian, Congregational—has been based on how they have claimed that the church should be organized. But in the East, as the history of Christianity in Ukraine demonstrates, many of the most bitter conflicts have come over the forms of worship, so that even questions of church administration and of doctrine have focused on such issues as the "Latinization" of the liturgy. Another example of this tendency is the statement of Protopop Avvakum, as he himself set it down in his *Žitie* during the 1670s, about

---

46. To select only two of the many references: Slipyj to Angelo Dell'Acqua, 10.i.1965, *Arch.Pat.* 34:23-24; Slipyj to Paul VI, 2.x.1966, *Arch.Pat.* 35:345.

47. Slipyj to Amleto Cicognani, 8.ii.1965, *Arch.Pat.* 32:145-48.

48. Slipyj to Amleto Cicognani, 16.ix.1964, *Arch.Pat.* 31:381-82.

what was at stake in the Raskol of the Orthodox Church of Russia in the seventeenth century:

> In our Russia before Nikon the Apostate, the orthodox faith of devout princes and tsars was always pure and spotless, and the Church was not mutinous. That wolf Nikon, in league with the devil, betrayed us through this crossing with three fingers. But our first shepherds, just as they crossed themselves with two fingers, so did they bless others with two fingers according to the tradition of our Holy Fathers.[49]

Even without seeking to impose on such a statement the Western theories of the distinction between symbol and reality, between *signum* and *signatum*,[50] it does pose the dilemma of Eastern Christianity in the area of worship and ritual.

III. Slipyj recognized that worship and ritual were a question of more than strictly ecclesiastical concern: "cultus" and "culture" are ultimately the same word in Latin and its derivatives. Therefore he could say that "the millennium of our baptism is at the same time the jubilee of our Ukrainian culture [*nauka*]."[51]

This identification of cultus and culture, though universal, has taken markedly different form in Eastern and in Western Christianity, with the Slavic lands as the crucible. For as the next chapter will suggest in more detail, the two missionary methods of the two traditions have been reflected in the two Christian cultures.[52] On the other hand, this view of culture as cultus could lead to an intellectual impoverishment. Josyf Slipyj once pointed out in a report to Pope Paul VI that most of the churches of the East did not cultivate their own religious art and architecture, nor carry on scholarly studies of their own liturgy, but were leaving these fields to scholars trained in the West.[53] Part of the price that the East has paid for its preservation of tradition is a tendency toward the archaic and a corresponding poverty in the area of critical historical scholarship. For even as we measure the contributions that the Eastern tradition of spirituality and patristic theology has made to Western thought, we must recognize that when it has come to making the monuments of Eastern spirituality and patristic theology available in modern critical editions, Western scholars have very fre-

---

49. Brostrom (1979) 92.
50. Pelikan (1986) 123-39.
51. Slipyj, Tvory 9:324-25.
52. See chapter 2, pp. 34-36 below.
53. Slipyj to Paul VI, 26.xii.1964, Slipyj, *Tvory* 12:165.

THE HERITAGE OF JOSYF SLIPYJ

quently had to take the lead. It was not some Byzantine scholar, but Desiderius Erasmus, who first edited Chrysostom, Basil of Caesarea, and Origen. Harvey on Irenaeus, Opitz on Athanasius, Schwartz on the Greek *Acta* of the ecumenical councils, Jaeger on Gregory of Nyssa, Holl on Epiphanius—there was not a single Eastern scholar on this list of indispensable editions of the Eastern Christian tradition. The Byzantine historians did not become available through the publications of Russian scholars, but through the Bonn editions. For the progress of scholarly studies in the Christian East, it was necessary to look to the Oriental Institute founded by Pope Benedict XV in 1917, as well as to Adolf von Harnack and the Berlin corpus of the *Griechische christliche Schriftsteller*. Thus the scientific methodology and devoted research of Western scholars, both Protestant and Roman Catholic, has often borne the principal share of the burden for sorting out the genuine from the spurious in the Eastern heritage and for publishing the results of philological and historical research in a form that both Eastern and Western scholars could use.

Nevertheless, both Slipyj's own early scholarship and the scholarship for which he later served as patron[54] are evidence that it is unfair to ignore the genuine achievements of various Eastern individuals and institutions. One of the many tragic consequences of the momentous events of the Bolshevik Revolution is that they came just as theological and historical scholarship was beginning to blossom in Czarist Russia, and with special richness in Ukraine. For example, one of the most important items on the bibliography of scholarly works on the philosophical-theological apologia for images that underlay their recovery in the eighth and ninth centuries is the massive dissertation of Aleksandr Pavlovič Dobroklonskij,[55] *Prepodobnyj Feodor, ispovednik i igumen studijskij* [Saint Theodore, confessor and Studite abbot], on the theological and monastic leader Theodore of Studios, whose *Antirrhetica against the Iconoclasts* must be recognized as a major statement of the Byzantine apologia; Dobroklonskij's monograph was published at Odessa in 1913/1914. Those two years were likewise the dates of publication for such works as N. F. Kapterev's[56] *Charakter otnošenij Rosii k pravoslavnomu vostoku* [The character of the attitudes of Russia to the Orthodox East], A. Spasskij's[57] *Istorija dogmatičeskich dviženij* [History of dog-

---

54. See chapter 7 below.
55. *Prav.Slov.* 1:749 (s.v.: Dobroklonskij, Al. Pavl.).
56. *Prav.Slov.* 2:1209 (s.v.: Kapterev, Nikolaj Feodorovič).
57. *Prav.Slov.* 2:2106 (s.v.: Spasskij, Anatolij Alekséevič).

matic movements], the *Polnyj pravoslavnyj bogoslovskij enciklopedičeskij slovar'*,[58] and the *Trudy Kievskoj duchovnoj akademij* [Works of the theological academy of Kiev], which began publication in 1913 and contains some of the most illuminating articles available on many patristic subjects. In Europe and North America, the heirs of that scholarly tradition, both Orthodox and Catholic, have striven to carry it on under the conditions of repression or exile and have made valuable contributions, but it does seem clear that the shattering interruption of ecclesiastical and religious life in the Revolution has had a profoundly traumatic effect on scholarship as well. Therefore, by one of the ironies that have always marked the history of Eastern Christendom, Western scholarship has continued to have the primary responsibility for making Eastern identity understood—perhaps even to itself.

IV. To Josyf Slipyj, the achievement and preservation of such Eastern identity among the Ukrainians was a matter of the utmost urgency. "The welfare of the Eastern Catholic Church is the highest law," he affirmed. "Everything that tends to its favor and welfare, in accordance with the Eastern tradition, is to be embraced; everything that is detrimental to it is to be eliminated."[59] Especially in his later years he came to believe that for the sake of that Eastern identity, the recognition of the patriarchate as the distinctive polity of the East, also when a particular church was in communion with Rome, represented the highest ecumenical priority, or, as he felt entitled to call it in 1971, "the center of our present worldwide yearnings and strivings."[60]

Despite the contrast referred to earlier between East and West with regard to the relative importance of church organization, therefore, Slipyj was—without in any way compromising his loyalty to the Holy See—striving to articulate here the Eastern principle that autochthony in culture has as its corollary some sort of autocephaly in church structure.[61] In opposition to the pyramidical system of the Latin West, where a centrality of authority has also meant a uniformity of practice, each church of Eastern Christendom has, at least in theory, been free to evolve many of its own forms of culture and life, forming a bond with the total life of the people that neither Muslim nor Marxist nor militarist governments have succeeded in breaking. There is nothing intrinsically necessary in Western polity or doctrine that would re-

58. See "Abbreviations," pp. xv-xvi above.
59. Slipyj, *Tvory* 12:129.
60. Slipyj, *Tvory* 13:107; further comments, pp. 108-9.
61. See chapter 3, pp. 38-39 below.

quire an equation of unity with uniformity; but in practice, as Eastern Rite Catholics especially in the Ukrainian tradition have had ample occasion to learn, such an equation of unity with uniformity has frequently been the outcome even when it was not the policy. As we shall have occasion to note several times in subsequent chapters, the encyclical *Orientalium dignitas ecclesiarum* promulgated by Pope Leo XIII on 30 November 1894 was for both Josyf Slipyj and Andrej Šeptyc'kyj the central document on this issue, protecting as it did the integrity of Eastern liturgy.[62]

But all such adherence to Eastern definitions of identity and to the bond between church and people in the Old World confronted new and grave challenges in the situation of the Ukrainian diaspora, especially in the New World. When Metropolitan Slipyj spoke about the threat of "deritualization" posed by the position of his church between East and West, he would sometimes link with it, as a parallel threat, the danger of "denationalization."[63] Alternately, he could even associate "deritualization" with "Americanization."[64]

For autocephaly in Eastern Orthodoxy and autochthony in Eastern Rite Catholicism were able to express the genius of each of the Eastern peoples, and specifically of the Slavic peoples, but in the New World they raised anew the dilemma of how the particularity of any single tradition was to be related both to the universality of a church that confessed itself to be *una, sancta, catholica, et apostolica*[65] and to the new reality of the context of a new people, of which those standing in an Eastern Christian tradition also wanted to be a genuine part. The anguished struggles of Eastern Christians in Canada[66] and the United States, whether in communion with the Holy See or not, over this dilemma (including the liturgical and jurisdictional status of the smaller groups, such as those from Jugoslavia) played themselves out in Slipyj's peculiar vocation as a metropolitan-in-exile.[67] But all of this had profoundly political implications as well. Eastern churches that did not have communion with the See of Peter have, as a result of that, sometimes been able to play a part in the political developments of their nations that seemed embarrassing or even dangerous to Rome; conversely, Western churches have often sought a similar power, as they

62. See chapter 4, pp. 58–60 below.
63. Slipyj to Guglielmo Gaudreau, 1.iv.1963, *Arch.Pat.* 28:197–99.
64. Slipyj to Gustavo Testa, 16.x.1963, *Arch.Pat.* 29:238.
65. See also chapter 3, pp. 49–52 below.
66. Yuzyk (1981) is an account of some of these struggles.
67. See chapter 9, pp. 176–79 below.

did most articulately in *The Four Gallican Articles* of 1682[68] or in the German *Kulturkampf* of the nineteenth century. By contrast, Slipyj's theology and churchmanship were based on the recognition that when a benevolent despot has been replaced by a hostile despot—sometimes by one who is less despotic, sometimes by one who is more despotic, but by one who is hostile to Christianity in either case—that very identification of the church with the native culture and with the political order has often meant that there was no Archimedean point of leverage beyond the borders, and hence no recourse to an interdict or other supranational jurisdiction. When one of his Soviet captors exclaimed, "Rome, Rome!"[69] that was a recognition of this stark reality. Indeed, the Soviets sometimes seemed to him to see it better than his fellow Christians did; hence the constant pressure on him to renounce the authority of the pope.[70]

If, according to hallowed Eastern teaching, the authority of the church resided ultimately in an ecumenical council, which ever since Constantine I at Nicea had been convoked by a Christian emperor, it was not clear how the church could have convoked a council to deal with the crisis of "the year 1453, that terrible date for the East, not only for the Greeks but for all the other Christian nations of the East,"[71] when the Turkish sultan occupied the throne of Constantine. Or if, between councils, it was the principle of pentarchy, the authority of the five apostolic patriarchates, that was to be invoked, Slipyj's "Overview of the United and Separated Churches of the East," delivered in December 1936 and published in 1937, demonstrated the implications of the political predicament for that authority.[72] For in the seventh century three of those patriarchates (Jerusalem, Antioch, and Alexandria), and then in the fifteenth century the fourth (Constantinople), had been deprived of any freedom of action.[73] Meanwhile, as the Ukrainian diaspora illustrated, there were many millions of Christians now living beyond at least the geographical borders of any of the patriarchs.

All of these issues in the history of Eastern Christianity have special relevance to the Ukrainian religious experience between East and West, in the diaspora as well as in the Ukrainian motherland. More perhaps than any other churchman of the twentieth century, His Beatitude

68. See chapter 3, pp. 44-46 below.
69. Slipyj, *Spomyny* 138.
70. See also chapter 8, pp. 156-59 below.
71. Slipyj, *Tvory* 12:187 (189).
72. Slipyj, *Tvory* 5:107-45.
73. Slipyj, *Tvory* 1:393.

Josyf Cardinal Slipyj was in many striking ways the embodiment of these issues, whether as a scholar, as a national leader, as a political prisoner, or as a confessor between East and West. And yet, as Cardinal Slipyj would have been the first to insist, he was all of this not principally as an individual but as the beneficiary of a rich and varied heritage. The heritage of Josyf Slipyj—both his heritage as he received it and his heritage as he perceived it (which are not necessarily the same)—will occupy us in the next chapters.

2

The Disputed Legacy of Cyril and Methodius

The beginnings of Christianity in the territories now occupied by the Ukrainians extend back to the earliest traditions of the mission and expansion of the church. According to the first historian of the church, Eusebius of Caesarea in the fourth century—who based his account in turn on "tradition [ἡ παράδοσις]," apparently as Origen of Alexandria in the third book of his *Commentary on Genesis* had transmitted this from still earlier sources in tradition, whether oral or written—the apostle Andrew, brother of Saint Peter, was sent to "Scythia."[1] "Scythia" roughly corresponded to modern Ukraine.[2]

On that basis Josyf Slipyj, when as a prisoner he undertook to write his history of the Ukrainian Church at the behest of his Soviet interrogators, "began with Saint Andrew, and not with Saint Vladimir, as our historians have customarily done."[3] Although he was aware that there were "legends" interspersed with reliable historical materials,[4] his researches had confirmed him in the opinion that the founding of the Ukrainian Church by Andrew "must now be regarded as having been historically confirmed."[5] When he returned from prison to Rome,

1. Eusebius *Ecclesiastical History* iii.1.
2. Rostovtzeff (1931).
3. Slipyj, *Spomyny* 177.
4. Slipyj, *Tvory* 14:112-13, including a discussion of the iconographic evidence.
5. Slipyj, *Tvory* 12:19.

23

he seemed to make increasing use of that tradition.[6] "Although he may not have been in Kiev," Slipyj granted, "Andrew did lay the foundations for Christianity among us."[7] Perhaps because of the increasing confrontations with the authorities of the Western, Latin Church, Slipyj also made a point of referring to Andrew as "the first one called [*Pervozannyj*]."[8] That was a Ukrainian translation of the Byzantine title for him, "Πρωτόκλητος," a reference to John 1:40-42, where Andrew is the one through whom Peter, later to be denominated "occupant of the prime see in the church [Πρωτόθρονος]" and first bishop of Rome, comes to Christ.[9] First there was Andrew—and only then, as Slipyj pointed out in 1977, came Peter, James, and John.[10] By that reading of the history of Ukrainian Christianity, Pope Saint Clement I of Rome, who was to be the patron saint of the Ukrainian Catholic University in Rome, was identified as the one who as an exile had continued Saint Andrew's work in Ukraine.[11] And from various scattered references in patristic sources and later accounts, Slipyj felt able to tell the fathers of the Second Vatican Council that Ukraine had been represented at all five of the first ecumenical councils of the church: Nicea in 325, Constantinople in 381, Ephesus in 431, Chalcedon in 451, and Constantinople II in 553.[12] The history of the Ukrainian Church went back "two thousand years."[13] Slipyj was sensitive to the need to keep up with the changing interpretations of history by scholars.[14] Yet those very changes of interpretation provided him with justification for claiming that the traditional interpretation was now "conceded by historians to be highly probable."[15]

Nevertheless, at the same time that he was making these various claims, Slipyj did recognize that for the history of Ukrainian Christianity, as for that of all the Slavic churches, the crucial events were those associated with the history of the "apostles to the Slavs," Saints Cyril and Methodius.[16] It is suggestive of the entire situation that one of the medals struck for the millennium of the baptism of *Rus'* shows

6. Slipyj, *Tvory* 12:47-48 (53); 178.
7. Slipyj, *Tvory* 13:200.
8. Slipyj, *Tvory* 9:161, 296.
9. Dvornik (1958) 138-299.
10. Slipyj, *Tvory* 14:149.
11. Slipyj, *Tvory* 13:48.
12. Slipyj, *Tvory* 12:86.
13. Slipyj, *Tvory* 12:168.
14. Slipyj, *Tvory* 13:333.
15. Slipyj, *Tvory* 13:37.
16. Slipyj, *Tvory* 12:44-45.

Olga and Vladimir on one side but Cyril and Methodius on the other—all four called "equals to the apostles [*rivni apostolam*]."[17] The Cyrillo-Methodian tradition has stood in the memory of the Slavic nations as a reminder simultaneously of what has bound them together and of what has separated them.[18] There has been a dispute not only between Roman Catholicism and Eastern Orthodoxy (which is our primary interest here), but also between Roman Catholicism and Protestantism, over that Cyrillo-Methodian legacy.[19] Even Russian Communist scholars have felt obliged to take sides in the dispute.[20] Scholarly research into the literary remains and archeological investigation of the sites have become a lively focus both of historical and of ecumenical interest.[21] As a consequence of the encyclical of Pope Leo XIII, *Grande munus* of 30 September 1880, Cyril and Methodius became for Roman Catholics, and especially for Roman Catholics among the various Slavic peoples, the saints of East-West unity. A fraternity led by Archbishop Anton Cyril Stojan (1851-1923) of Olomouc in Moravia—whom Slipyj called "the most worthy and meritorious champion of the union" between the Eastern and the Western Churches[22]—was designated "the Apostolate of Saints Cyril and Methodius."[23] A series of union congresses was inaugurated in Velehrad. "The ecumenists of Velehrad," as Petro Bilaniuk has said, "were truly pioneers."[24] Velehrad had been traditionally regarded as the site of the episcopal see of Greater Moravia, although twentieth-century excavations there have uncovered ruins of a monastery and a church from the Greater Moravian period, but not of an episcopal cathedral.[25] The union congresses were held there in 1907, 1909, and 1911, while Velehrad belonged to the Austro-Hungarian Empire, and again after the First World War in 1924, 1927, 1931, and 1936, when it was part of the Czechoslovak Republic.[26]

When, in 1936, Josyf Slipyj participated in this seventh and last congress on church union held in Velehrad, representing Metropolitan

17. In the possession of the author, by the generosity of Father Ivan Choma.

18. Nahajevs'kyj (1954) 39-54.

19. Krčméry (1935) has presented a survey showing that in the eighteenth and nineteenth centuries Roman Catholic writers such as Ján Hollý and Protestants such as Jozef Miloslav Hurban vied with one another in claiming the legacy.

20. Migovič (1985) 88-94.

21. Nahajevs'kyj (1967), especially 183-86.

22. Slipyj, *Tvory* 1:193.

23. Nemec (1983) 27-30.

24. Bilaniuk (1984) 31.

25. Cibulka (1958).

26. See the bibliography in *LTK* 10:1019 (Franz Machilek s.v.: Welehrad).

Andrej Šeptyc'kyj, he expressed his gratification at being able to come as a "pilgrim" to the lands consecrated by the memory of Cyril and Methodius; the occasion celebrated at the Congress was the one-thousand-fiftieth anniversary of the death of Methodius.[27] Most of the papers at the congress, as reported by Slipyj, dealt with one or another aspect of the Cyrillo-Methodian tradition. Among them was, for example, an investigation of "the sources of the theology of SS. Cyril and Methodius," delivered by František Grivec; these sources were, in Slipyj's summary, "Holy Scripture, the liturgy, the works of St. Gregory Nazianzus, and other works of the Eastern tradition."[28] The interaction of East and West in the missionary work of Cyril and Methodius, and therefore in the dispute over their spiritual and cultural legacy, makes itself visible also in the artifacts of early Slavic Christianity, as unearthed during recent archeological excavations. One of the crosses that have been found at Mikulčice "undoubtedly belongs to the horizon which was directly influenced by the work of the Irish and Scottish missionaries," while on the other hand "the bronze crosses from Mača near Sered and from Trnovec nad Váhom are of distinctly Byzantine origin, even though excavational circumstances place them at the beginning of the tenth century"; in the case of the latter cross, found at Trnovec nad Váhom, there are Greek initials on the transverse arms of the reverse side, but "we cannot rule out the possibility that this was only a native [i.e., Slavic] imitation of a more valuable Byzantine work."[29]

In 1963, on the occasion of the eleven-hundredth anniversary of the mission of Cyril and Methodius, Josyf Slipyj took the opportunity to define with some specificity what he regarded as the legacy of Saints Cyril and Methodius.[30] The anniversary was celebrated at the Church of San Clemente in Rome, named for the first-century Pope Saint Clement I, whose relics, which repose at San Clemente, had been brought to Rome from the Crimea in the ninth century by Cyril and Methodius. Clement was "the patron saint of the Ukrainian Catholic University of Pope Saint Clement," which Slipyj was beginning to found at that very time in Rome.[31] Speaking for that anniversary in that church, Slipyj singled out three characteristics of the apostles to the Slavs that were worthy of notice and emulation: their heroic virtues; their Catholic convictions; and their method of apostolic work. The second of these

27. Slipyj, *Tvory* 5:88.
28. Slipyj, *Tvory* 5:90.
29. Dekan (1981) 19-21, with plates 121-27.
30. Slipyj, *Tvory* 12:44-45.
31. Slipyj, *Tvory* 12:257.

qualities, symbolized by their having carried the relics of Pope Clement I to Rome, was all the more remarkable, Slipyj noted, "in view of their having been attacked in Moravia by bishops of the Roman Rite." They were attacked for the very "method of apostolic work" about which Slipyj spoke in the third and final section of his homily, which he entitled "the Slavonic language." Yet it was to their translations of the Bible and the liturgy into Slavonic that Christianity in the Slavic lands—"Bohemia, Slovakia, Hungary, Slovenia, Croatia, even Poland"—ultimately owed its origins. "Therefore," Slipyj concluded, "Byzantium spread Christianity in Ukraine from the South, but so did Cyril and Methodius and their disciples from the West, from Moravia."[32]

Slipyj was, of course, especially interested in the significance of Cyril and Methodius for the Ukrainian Church. Noting that "the cultus of the holy apostles [Cyril and Methodius] was translated by the South Slavs together with the liturgical books,"[33] Slipyj was conscious as well of the rôle of Cyril and Methodius as a symbolic force that bound together the divided Slavic peoples who shared their legacy even as they disputed the conflicting claims to it.[34] Cyril and Methodius belonged to an entire catalogue of neglected Eastern saints who deserved a place in Western Catholic life and thought.[35] Many years later, on 1 October 1979, Slipyj was to describe the impact of the Christian mission on his own people this way: "In the first place, obviously, for us as Christians it was an event of supernatural significance. We were born again in Christ to eternal life, we became members of the mystical body of Christ here on earth and heirs of his eternal kingdom. . . . 'We entered into Christ's epoch of God's blessing.' "[36] The occasion for this statement by Cardinal Slipyj was, in fact, the preparation for the jubilee of Ukrainian Christianity, for he continued: "The millennium of our baptism is at the same time the jubilee of our Ukrainian culture."[37] And a year earlier, in 1978, when Karol Cardinal Wojtyła was elected pope as John Paul II, Slipyj wrote to him (in Polish):

> This has happened precisely at the time when the Polish nation is observing the millennium of its Christianity and when the

32. Slipyj, *Tvory* 12:45.
33. Slipyj, *Tvory* 1:384.
34. Slipyj, *Tvory* 1:387.
35. Slipyj, *Tvory* 2:123.
36. The closing sentence was a quotation from Metropolitan Ilarion.
37. Slipyj, *Tvory* 9:324-25.

Ukrainian nation is also preparing to commemorate a similar event in its history.

An additional reason for our happiness is this, that in your person, Holy Father, the Slavic East [*Wschód słowiański*] and in a personal way the Ukrainian Church and nation obtain a firm defender.... Who can better succeed in understanding the Slavic soul than a son of the nation, the great family of nations, which had its apostles Cyril and Methodius, who found understanding and aid for their work only in the successor of Peter in Rome?[38]

The letter was acknowledged in cordial terms by Pope John Paul II.[39]

A few years later, writing again to Pope John Paul II (but this time in Italian), Slipyj recalled that Cyril and Methodius had been pupils of the "schismatic" patriarch of Constantinople, Photius—about whose trinitarian theology, in contrast with Western Augustinian and Thomistic trinitarianism, Slipyj had written at considerable length in 1920/1921[40]—and were "sons of the East and of Byzantine culture," but that they had manifested "the true Catholicity of the church." Thus they were "the precursors of authentic ecumenism."[41] It was part of "the Cyrillo-Methodian idea," Slipyj declared, to emphasize in the spirit of Pope John XXIII that "there is more that unites us than there is that separates us."[42] In reviewing the language of a projected papal encyclical in 1963 on Cyril and Methodius, therefore, it was appropriate that the language of the draft about separated Christians "returning to" the Apostolic See of Rome be changed to a statement about "recovering the integrity [*redintegrare*]" of their communion[43]—a striking anticipation of the language that was to open the Decree on Ecumenism of the Second Vatican Council, *Unitatis redintegratio*. Later that year, on 29 October 1963, Slipyj celebrated for the participants of the Second Vatican Council a Liturgy of the Byzantine Rite in the Basilica of Saint Peter; the program notes for the celebration explained that the translation of the liturgy into Church Slavonic "constitutes even now the most precious heritage of the apostles [Cyril and Methodius] among the Eastern and Southern Slavic peoples, both Orthodox and Catholic."[44]

38. Slipyj to John Paul II, 19.x.1978, *Arch.Pat.* 118:51.
39. John Paul II to Slipyj, 12.xi.1978, *Arch.Pat.* 118:54.
40. Slipyj, *Tvory* 1:91-158.
41. Slipyj to John Paul II, 10.ii.1981, *Arch.Pat.* 118:200-201.
42. Slipyj to Giovanni Battista Scapinelli, 20.iii.1963, *Arch.Pat.* 28:177-81.
43. Alphonsus Raes to Slipyj, 19.iii.1963, *Arch.Pat.* 28:171-74.
44. "Divina Liturgia iuxta Ritum Byzantino-Ucrainum coram Sacrosancto Concilio Oecumenico Vaticano II," *Arch.Pat.* 29:189-94.

Slipyj recalled with gratitude that in the encyclical *Grande munus*[45] Pope Leo XIII had acknowledged Cyril and Methodius as saints of the entire Catholic Church, not only of Eastern Christians, and had appointed 5 July as their feast day.[46] Although he was, therefore, dutiful and correct about acknowledging the action of Pope Paul VI in 1964, designating Saint Benedict of Nursia, founder of Western monasticism, as patron saint of Europe,[47] he would wax eloquent when, in 1981, Pope John Paul II joined Saints Cyril and Methodius to Saint Benedict as co-patron saints of Europe: echoing the words of the pope to him in 1979,[48] he declared his certainty that it was part of "the inscrutable plans of Divine Providence" that "the first Slavic pope should have been the one to proclaim the apostles to the Slavs as co-patron saints of Europe."[49] To understand what Slipyj called the "*nauka* [culture]" of *Rus'*-Ukraine,[50] therefore, it is essential to locate, within the larger history of Christian missions, the Byzantine missionary program that brought Christianity to the Slavs and to Kiev, and to identify some of the special characteristics that set it apart from other similar achievements in other periods and other places.[51]

As Karl Holl has said, refuting the conventional wisdom about a lack of missionary interest within Eastern Christianity,

> The territory won by it extends from the Black Sea to the Baltic Sea. And among the nations that she missionized the Greek Church [of Constantinople] accomplished something that the West may well envy: she actually endeared herself to her adherents. Her faithful [in other nations] cling to her with tenderness, indeed, with deep feeling. The modern intellectual may outgrow her, and he may regard her ceremonies as superstition; yet even with the skeptically minded there mysteriously remains something of a love for her.[52]

The disputed legacy of Cyril and Methodius makes sense in the context of Byzantine history in the ninth and tenth centuries, during which the creation of the Carolingian empire in the West, the so-called Photian schism, and the missions to the various Slavic peoples all

45. See p. 25 above.
46. Slipyj, *Tvory* 1:387.
47. Slipyj to Paul VI, 21.x.1964, *Arch.Pat.* 31:389.
48. John Paul II to Slipyj, 19.iii.1979, *Arch.Pat.* 118:83; see chapter 1, p. 11 above.
49. Slipyj to John Paul II, 10.ii.1981, *Arch.Pat.* 118:198-99.
50. Slipyj, *Tvory* 9:324-25.
51. Slipyj, *Tvory* 2:113.
52. Holl (1928) 125-26.

came together to determine for the next thousand years the way (or, rather, the ways) the Slavs have understood their position between East and West, between New Rome and Old Rome.[53] Fundamental to that position was their "rejection of extremist views, both Western and Eastern."[54]

"What Rome was for the West and for the Germans," Slipyj once noted, "that Byzantium was for the East and for the Slavs."[55] The use of the cognomen "the Philosopher" for Constantine-Cyril[56] suggests one of the most far-reaching differences between the Eastern and the Western church: for five centuries the Constantinople from which Constantine and other missionaries came had been a major center of philosophical apologetics. In the *Žitie* [Life] of Constantine we are informed that his education had consisted, in considerable measure, of the philosophical theology of the Greek fathers. Although scholars continue to dispute whether this refers to the Cappadocian fathers or to other, perhaps later thinkers, no one will question the superiority of ninth-century Byzantine thought to its Western contemporaries in sophistication about philosophy. In Slipyj's striking phrase, Constantinople was "the librarian of the human race."[57] Applied to the issue of Christian missions, this sophistication meant that missionaries like Constantine-Cyril brought to their task a far more subtle awareness of the problems involved in the relation of the Christian gospel to the indigenous culture and religion of "pagan" peoples.

It has become almost a cliché in the textbooks of the history of missions to point out that when Pope Gregory I sent Augustine to England, he instructed him not to uproot local religious traditions indiscriminately, but to build Christian churches in the sacred places of pagan shrines. The cultural and religious fruit of that papal policy was the Anglo-Saxon church, English and particular and yet Roman and Catholic, as it has been carefully and lovingly described by the Venerable Bede.[58] But at the end of the sixth century when Augustine sailed to Britain, or even in the ninth century when Cyril and Methodius went to the Slavs, the West was still relying primarily on the schematization of the relation of continuity/discontinuity between paganism and Christianity that had been formulated in the *City of God*

53. Nahajevs'kyj (1954) 109-25.
54. Sobieski (1966) 94.
55. Slipyj, *Tvory* 2:121.
56. See Slipyj's comments on this title: Slipyj, *Tvory* 13:229.
57. Slipyj, *Tvory* 2:123.
58. See chapter 3, p. 41 below.

of Augustine of Hippo.[59] And when, in the ninth century, Latin metaphysical thought produced its first original attempt at a speculative system coordinating natural and revealed knowledge, in the work of John the Scot usually identified as *De divisione naturae*, much of the conceptual apparatus for that work had in fact come from Byzantine sources, as Slipyj pointed out in his outline history of medieval thought.[60] Byzantine thought recognized that the universality of the creating and revealing action of God made every tradition an authentic medium to which the specifically Christian revelation could be attached and through which it could be communicated. Thus when the Second Vatican Council, before going on at its ninth session to discuss the missions, declared already at its seventh session that "the Catholic Church rejects nothing of what is true and holy in these religions [*nihil eorum, quae in his religionibus vera et sancta sunt*],"[61] it was voicing an understanding of nature and grace that came much closer to the Byzantine style of philosophical apologetics than to the traditional accents of Western theology.

By the time it was sending Cyril and Methodius and their successors to the Slavic peoples, Byzantine theology had already been engaged for two centuries not only in dealing with the relation between classical Hellenic philosophy and Christian thought, but in confronting the most formidable alternative ideology Christianity has ever faced (at least until the rise of Marxism), in the faith of Islam.[62] Like Christianity itself, Islam was an ideology that soon acquired, despite its humble intellectual origins, a formidable philosophical theology, one that could address a vigorous challenge to Christian doctrine. It was to be several centuries before Latin theology took on Muslim thought with any comparable thoroughness, for, until Peter the Venerable and Raimond Lull, the West continued to draw upon John of Damascus and other Byzantine interpreters of Islam.[63] In Byzantium the destiny of geography joined with the imperatives of theology—and indeed, over and over, with the realities of warfare—to make the Christian interpretation of the religion of the Prophet an unavoidable intellectual task, and the Christian mission to the followers of the Prophet (whatever form such a mission might assume) an assignment that demanded attention.

59. Pelikan (1986) 34-51, 69-89.
60. Slipyj, *Tvory* 2:52-53.
61. *Nostra aetate* 2, Alberigo 969.
62. Pelikan (1971) 2:227-42.
63. See Southern (1962) and Kritzeck (1964).

As the checkered history of Byzantine attempts to bring the message of conversion to the Muslims suggests, the relation of Christianity to Islam occupies a unique place on the complex map of the world religions. Here again, Byzantine thought led the way, when John of Damascus recognized that it would not do to lump Islam with the pagan religions; instead, he classified it as a Christian "heresy." For it was monotheistic in its central creed, despite its not having received a direct monotheistic revelation as, according to Byzantine and all other Christian theologians, both Judaism and Christianity had. Islam had also—presumably from Christian sources, whether orthodox or heretical—acquired a high estimate of the Virgin Mary (despite the apparent confusion in the Quran between the Mother of Jesus and the sister of Moses). To be sure, both East and West faced the continuing obligation to come to terms with the reality of Judaism, which, despite Christian predictions in every generation, refused to wither away. But for the Christian interpretation of the place of Israel in the plan of God, the Church had the profound, though puzzling, explanation set forth in the ninth, tenth, and eleventh chapters of the Epistle to the Romans— even though the meaning of that explanation, especially of course of the words "All Israel shall be saved," continued to elude it. For the Christian interpretation of Islam, however, the Church was on its own, since neither the New Testament's treatment of Jewish monotheism nor its critique of Graeco-Roman polytheism provided it with a paradigm. This experience meant that the Byzantine Christianity which sent missionaries to the Slavs had for centuries been probing the nuances of the problem of faith in one God in a way and at a depth that the Latin West had not.

The encounter of Greek Christian missions and apologetics with Islam had also served to confirm a long-standing theological propensity that had been a distinctive characteristic of the East since the patristic era: an understanding of the relation between grace and free will that transcended the conventional Western dichotomy between Augustinianism and Pelagianism, by emphasizing both, as in the oft-quoted formula of Maximus Confessor (to whom Slipyj had a special attachment),[64] which defined salvation to be "a reward as a gift to those who have believed Him, namely, eternal deification."[65] It was a distinctive Eastern characteristic of which Augustine himself had been made painfully aware when Pelagius had defended himself before a synod of

64. See pp. 100-101 below.
65. Maximus Confessor *Quaestiones ad Thalassium.*

Greek-speaking bishops held at Diospolis-Lydda in Palestine in the year 415. After hearing him out, these bishops ruled: "Now since we have received satisfaction on the points which have come before us touching the monk Pelagius, who has been present; since, too, he gives his consent to the pious doctrines, and even anathematizes everything that is contrary to the church's faith, we confess him to belong to the communion of the Catholic Church."[66] This implied as well, Pelagius argued, that Augustine's position, as defined in opposition to him, did contain a doctrine contrary to the Catholic faith, specifically as this had been interpreted in the East.[67] In *On the Proceedings of Pelagius* [*De gestis Pelagii*], Augustine strove to refute that implication and to vindicate the Catholic orthodoxy of his doctrine of grace; as Josyf Slipyj was to point out, this statement of Augustine's implied a "mutual respect" between East and West despite differences of language and emphasis.[68]

Now it is notable that, although most of the works of Augustine, with the exception of a few fragments, were unknown in Byzantium until the translations of Maximos Planudes at the end of the thirteenth and the beginning of the fourteenth century,[69] the *Acta* of the Synod of Lydda-Diospolis were known. In fact, they were preserved, and in Greek, in the *Bibliotheca* of Photius, the philosopher and patriarch;[70] Photius was the subject of one of Slipyj's early theological monographs, published in 1920/1921, which included a comparison of Photius and Augustine, but on the doctrine of the Trinity rather than on the relation of nature and grace.[71] The resistance of Photius to what appeared to be the determinism in Augustine's doctrines of grace and predestination became indigenous to Byzantine theology and preaching and was expressed also in its catechisms and hymns. With the need to define the essence of Christianity in reply to what appeared to be an even more thoroughgoing determinism in Mohammedan doctrine, Byzantine teaching was, by the ninth century, asserting the interdependence of grace and freedom with still greater vigor.[72] Thus the version of the gospel that it exported to the Slavs bore that distinctive mark. Repeatedly, as for example on several occasions in the history both of the spiritual academy at Kiev and of the theological academy at L'viv,

66. ap. Augustine *De gestis Pelagii* xx.44.
67. See Augustine's comments on this, *ibid.*, xi.25.
68. Slipyj, *Tvory* 1:401-2.
69. Beck (1959) 686-87.
70. Photius *Bibliotheca* cod. 54.
71. Slipyj, *Tvory* 1:132-38.
72. Hildebrand Beck (1937).

Eastern teachers who have come under strong Augustinian influence have campaigned to correct this apparent imbalance and to make Augustine's doctrine of grace a part of the theological curriculum as well as of the catechism, but over and over that effort has collided with the consensus of the Eastern centuries. At best, as the history of theology within the Ukrainian Catholic Church amply demonstrates, the Augustinian system of the Latin West and the Cappadocian system inherited from Byzantium have existed in an uneasy tension. One need only point to the Thomist orientation with which Cardinal Slipyj came to his own Eastern *réssourcement*,[73] and to his efforts to resolve those tensions within (to cite the most serious theological example) the doctrine of the Trinity, where he adopted the Augustinian *theologoumenon* of the Holy Spirit as the "love [*amor*]" with which the Father and the Son love each other but strove to harmonize it with the Byzantine version of trinitarianism.[74]

It is well known that in addition to such doctrinal and theological emphases, however, the two most immediately striking of the distinctive features of Eastern Christianity that the Byzantine missions brought to the Slavs lay in the areas of polity and of liturgy. Many observers, Eastern as well as Western, have suggested that the differences of doctrine between East and West, including even the celebrated *Filioque* doctrine, could probably have been worked out if the differences in the area of polity had been resolved; and many of these observers would also agree that the differences in liturgy became as decisive as they did primarily because they illustrated and exacerbated the differences of polity. Certainly to the common people, these were the decisive differences of both method and outcome between the Byzantine and the Western (usually German) missionaries, and historically that assessment has been vindicated over and over. Differences in polity and differences in liturgy, moreover, have been closely related to each other, as Eastern Rite Catholics of various traditions have had to discover when they have sought to combine a polity that tied them to the Holy See with a liturgy that set them apart from the vast majority of those who were also in communion with Rome; for that combination Josyf Slipyj found justification in the legacy of Cyril and Methodius.[75]

An oversimplified formula for the description of Byzantine mission policy, but a formula that correctly identifies the central issue, is

73. See chapter 6 below.
74. Slipyj, *Tvory* 1:159–90.
75. Slipyj, *Tvory* 13:270.

to say that while it was the purpose of Western missionaries during the Middle Ages to convert a new people by incorporating it into the *corpus Christianum* of which the pope was the visible head, it was the intention—or at any rate, it was the result—of Byzantine missions to convert a new people by calling into being a new church which would have its life and its administrative structure within that people and which would establish fraternal and federative relations with other churches. Thus although Bede was concerned with the history of the English Church, the conflicts he described had as their theme the choice between an English Church that had authority over its own affairs and an English Church that was "Catholic" in the sense of being obedient— on issues ranging from administrative jurisdiction to the date of Easter to the tonsure of monks—to the See of Rome. Significantly, the Anglican Reformation of the sixteenth century was able to attach itself to a long-standing sense within the English Church that, despite the victory of Bede's definition of "Catholic," the Church *in* England was truly the Church *of* England. In doing so, the Anglican Reformers could appeal to Eastern precedent. Nevertheless, despite this feature of Byzantine mission strategy, there have not been many scholarly studies that would coordinate missiology and foreign policy in the Byzantine Empire, as that policy expressed itself not only in the Christianization of the Slavic peoples but in the military conquest of others and in the establishment of diplomatic relations with yet others.[76]

This difference in missionary policy precluded not only the imposition of a single pyramidical structure in polity, but the program of a single *Kultsprache* in liturgy. For the Slavs to whom the Byzantine missions came, the principle of autocephaly found its most cherished symbol in the Church Slavonic liturgy, to which bishops from various Slavic lands could go on pointing, even at the Council of Trent in the sixteenth century and again at the Second Vatican Council in the twentieth, as evidence that Catholicity and Latinity were not to be equated. In the cultures that have been shaped by *Pravoslavie*, the linguistic inheritance of the Byzantine missions has been transmitted through the special rôle that Church Slavonic has played in relation to the various individual Slavic vernaculars, the vocabulary it has bequeathed to them, and the

76. In the first of the six Andrew W. Mellon Lectures which I delivered at the National Gallery of Art in Washington in the autumn of 1987 under the general title "Imago Dei: The Byzantine Apologia for Icons," to observe the 1200th anniversary of the restoration of the icons by the Second Council of Nicaea in 787, I discussed "Realpolitik and Religion Byzantine Style," as this affected both the abolition of images and their recovery.

link it has sometimes formed between them. As the history of the *Raskol* in Russian Orthodoxy makes clear, attachment to the forms of the Church Slavonic liturgy, even to certain pronunciations of individual sacred words, could become a divisive issue whenever attempts were made at liturgical reform. Less drastic in their outcome, but often more far-reaching in their implications, have been those reform movements within *Pravoslavie* which have pointed out the anomaly of resisting the imposition of Latin but retaining, in the name of "the language of the people," a language that is in fact used only in the liturgy. Campaigns for the vernacular—if not those of the Protestant Reformation, then those of the liturgical reformations coming out of the Second Vatican Council—have heightened that anomaly in Western Slavic lands; and the liturgical evolution of *Pravoslavie* in North America calls attention once more to this distinctive feature of the Byzantine missions.[77]

There is another linguistic consequence coming out of this distinctive liturgical philosophy. The cultural superiority of Byzantium to the West throughout the Middle Ages, which spokesmen for the West had to recognize even when they defensively refused to acknowledge it, was based on a fortunate combination of various economic, political, even military factors. Yet beneath and beyond all these factors, it was the consequence of one factor: the Greek language. Byzantium felt entitled to the Christian culture of Athanasius and the Cappadocian fathers, to the text of the New Testament, to Plato and Aristotle, Aeschylus and Sophocles, and to Homer, as a single, though not uniform, inheritance that was bound together by the simple and powerful fact of its having been written in Greek. Nevertheless, although the heritage of Latin culture could not be compared with all of this and the Latin of the Mass, the Vulgate, and Augustine was not classical, the fact remains that by teaching the nations Latin and imposing it upon them as a condition of their becoming Catholic Christians, Western missionaries did give them also at least some access to the language and the culture of Rome, pre-Christian as well as Christian, to Roman jurisprudence and to Vergil, to Roman rhetoric and to Horace. The Eastern Orthodox heirs of Byzantine culture who lived in Constantinople or in Athens did indeed receive the treasures of Greek culture, but the Slavic peoples did not; for, as Slipyj pointed out, Greek never became as dominant in the East as Latin did in the West.[78] The indigenous Christian culture and language of the Eastern Slavs were, no doubt, often the richer for it, but

77. See chapter 11, p. 223 below.
78. Slipyj, *Tvory* 2:111.

they did not have in that culture the point of contact for a Renaissance in the way that both Byzantium itself and the Latin West did.

As part of the heritage of Josyf Slipyj, Byzantine missions also carried deep implications for the unity of Christendom. The historical contemporaneity of the Byzantine missions of Cyril and Methodius with the alienation between Constantinople and Old Rome made the battle in the Moravian mission field, a battle that was waged over both polity and liturgy, the first and in some ways the most dramatic of a series of conflicts that have torn the Slavs apart. The question came to be seen as a choice between following Cyril-Methodius in maintaining a Slavonic liturgy and a national church or following Cyril-Methodius in preserving the unity of Christendom by affiliation with the Apostolic See. In the history of *Rus'*-Ukraine the question has been not only its political relation to Poland toward the West and Russia toward the East and North, but its ecclesiastical relation between Old Rome and New Rome. The missions to the Slavs came *from* New Rome; in a sense, even those to Poland were the Western heirs of a Byzantine mission. But Cyril-Methodius went *to* Old Rome, and repeatedly the implications of that move have formed the agenda for Slavic Christians in various lands. As became evident at the Second Vatican Council, this duality in the legacy of Cyril and Methodius has continued to be a central component of the ecumenical agenda for the Slavs, whether Eastern Orthodox or Catholic, in the twentieth century.[79]

These issues received further clarification during the generation that preceded Josyf Slipyj in the thought of Vladimir Soloviev.[80] His ecclesiological vision, grounded as it was in his cosmological speculation and incarnationist metaphysics, is an undeniable descendant of the Christian philosophy of Byzantium. And yet it is a vision that carried beyond Byzantium to the universality of the church, which is what the Byzantine mission of Cyril and Methodius itself had done. But if, according to Josyf Slipyj, Cyril and Methodius had manifested "the true Catholicity of the church" and were at the same time "the precursors of authentic ecumenism,"[81] the search for Catholicity among the Slavs and the patterns of ecumenical reconciliation between East and West were fundamental to any understanding of their legacy.

79. Hryn'och (1980).
80. See chapter 4, pp. 67-72 below.
81. Slipyj to John Paul II, 10.ii.1981, *Arch.Pat.* 118:200-201.

3

Particularity versus Catholicity in the History of the Slavs

According to Josyf Slipyj, Cyril and Methodius had manifested "the true Catholicity of the church."[1] In the attempt to claim the legacy of Cyril and Methodius for his concept of an Eastern church in union with the See of Rome, the itinerary of their missionary journeys, from Constantinople to Slavic Central Europe but then from Slavic Central Europe to Rome, took on the quality of a parable for Slipyj's Ukrainians and for other Slavs seeking to find and to articulate "the true Catholicity of the church" between East and West. To the Orthodox East, such a concept seemed a betrayal of the unique tradition of Constantinople as that had been borne to the Slavs by Cyril and Methodius. Therefore Slipyj was concerned to preserve the Eastern idea of "particularity [*pomisnist'*],"[2] a "particular church" with the competence and authority to have jurisdiction over its own internal life, including both liturgy and canon law.[3] The two great themes of the church, then, were Catholicity and particularity.[4] To the Latin West, on the other hand, such a definition of a "particular church" seemed to lay claim to "autonomy" in a manner that was inconsistent with the primacy of the Apostolic See and that was therefore not authentically "Catholic." The

1. Slipyj to John Paul II, 10.ii.1981, *Arch.Pat.* 118:200-201.
2. Slipyj, *Tvory* 14:119 (118).
3. Slipyj to Jean Villot, 21.x.1972, *Arch.Pat.* 41:218-25.
4. Slipyj, *Tvory* 14:65.

abortive attempt at a "Ukrainian Autocephalous Orthodox Church [*Ukrajinska Avtokefal'na Pravoslavna Cerkva*]"[5] at the end of the First World War made the term "autocephalous" all the more suspect. Consequently, Slipyj was no less concerned to define the Catholicity of the church under the authority of the Holy See in a way that would not fall victim to the pressures of "Latinization."[6] And he quoted an anonymous cardinal who had said to him about the Ukrainian Church and people: "It is amazing that this people, which has had to endure so much from Latin Catholics and has been treated so badly and unjustly, has nevertheless remained Catholic."[7]

The widely accepted term for this Slavic brand of Catholic particularity was "Greek Catholic." Although he had used the term quite regularly himself, Slipyj did not find it especially appropriate or accurate. The usage went back to the days of the Hapsburgs, when L'viv-Halyč had been part of the Austrian and Austro-Hungarian Empire; but now Slipyj preferred the designation "Ukrainian Catholic Church."[8] Karol Cardinal Wojtyła, too, regarded "Greek Catholic" as an old-fashioned and inaccurate term for this Eastern rite within Catholicism; for "although it is Greek as far as its liturgy is concerned, it is nevertheless Slavic as far as its language is concerned."[9] The problem of identifying and following the path of an "authentic ecumenism," which has certainly proved to be difficult enough for Christians of every denominational persuasion, has taken a very complicated form in the tangled history of relations between the Christian East and the Christian West.[10] But, as Slipyj had noted already in 1933, "in recent times, especially among Catholic writers and theologians, there has been a greater and deeper consciousness of the universality of Catholicity and of its transcendent character,"[11] by contrast with the dominant trends of Roman Catholic theology around the time of the First Vatican Council. In that attempt to find "the universality of Catholicity" and "its transcendent character," but to give it a form that would at the same time preserve local particularity and linguistic-liturgical uniqueness, the situation of the Slavs, and above all that of the Slavs in Central Europe between East and West, has had to face special challenges.

5. Polons'ka-Vasylenko (1964) 94-109.
6. Jean Villot to Slipyj, 29.ix.1972, *Arch.Pat.* 41:203-4.
7. Slipyj, *Tvory* 13:123.
8. Slipyj, *Tvory* 9:66.
9. Karol Wojtyła to M. Denko, 5.xi.1972, *Arch.Pat.* 118:24-26.
10. See chapter 4, pp. 53-72 below.
11. Slipyj, *Tvory* 2:103.

Indeed, the very concept of "Central Europe" as it is being used here has itself been highly ambiguous. Near the end of his war memoirs of 1925, entitled *Světová revoluce* [World revolution] in Czech but *The Making of a State* in the English translation by Henry Wickham Steed, Tomáš Garrigue Masaryk, the first president of Czechoslovakia, after listing the "new" states that had arisen after the First World War, commented on the ambiguity of the concept of "Central Europe":

> Upon the precise area of "Central Europe," opinions differ. The whole of Germany, Switzerland, and Italy are sometimes reckoned as belonging to it. But if Western culture, not geography alone, be taken as a guide, Western Germany, Switzerland, and Italy belong to Western Europe, as do Bohemia and German Austria. The dividing line of culture runs to the west of the former territory of Russia, and leaves also Galicia [Halič], Hungary, Romania, and the Balkans to the East.[12]

One part of that taxonomy with which everyone would agree would be the opening statement: "Upon the precise area of 'Central Europe,' opinions differ."

There is, however, an additional element in Tomáš Masaryk's analysis with which everyone would probably agree: the distinction between a definition of Central Europe that is determined only by "geography" (in which somehow the rivers, above all of course the Danube and then the Leitha, always seem to be the decisive factor, with the mountains, especially the Carpathians, as an important but secondary factor) and a definition that proceeds also on the basis of "culture." The problem with such a distinction is the identification of any "cultural" lines of demarcation that will be as palpable as the Danube River and the Carpathian Mountains in drawing the map. In some parts of the world, cultural anthropology has been able to invoke a linguistic criterion for such an enterprise. This may be the criterion on the basis of which Masaryk assigned Germany and Italy to Western rather than to Central Europe. But when he went on in the next sentence to link Bohemia with "German Austria," and then in the sentence after that Hungary with Romania, he demonstrated that no map of languages will bring sufficient precision to this murky concept of "Central Europe." A political meaning for "culture" seems at first to be more helpful; for the creation of the Dual Monarchy by the *Ausgleich* of 1867,

---

12. Masaryk (1925) 502 n. (ET [1937] 370); in the English translation, the footnote has been incorporated into the text.

especially if the promise of a third, Slavic kingdom had been realized, appeared to envision a multilingual, multiethnic federation, with its own autonomous commercial, military, and political destiny. The Czech historian František Palacký had contemplated such a vision for a time.[13] Masaryk's polemic against this notion of a Danubian federation, despite his own great debt to Palacký, is an understandable expression of his insistence on ethnic self-determination, but it is also a symptom of why the political methodology for identifying "Central Europe" as a cultural unity broke down in Austria-Hungary, and would presumably have done so even if the First World War had not erupted there.

That leaves religion as another methodology, and the one that is especially appropriate to the present context. The tension between the particularity of the nation and the Catholicity of the church has long been a dominant concern throughout the Judaeo-Christian tradition: "Are you not like the Ethiopians to me, O people of Israel?" was the word of the Lord through the prophet Amos.[14] And using a Greek word which, with its cognates, has "so far been found only in Christian writers,"[15] the apostle Peter is represented in the Acts of the Apostles as declaring: "Truly I perceive that God shows no partiality [προσωπολήμπτης]: but in every nation any one who fears him and does what is right is acceptable to him."[16] Yet, in order to find those who would fear God and do what is right, wherever they were chosen by God to be, the Christian mission went to that "every nation" of which the apostle Peter spoke. There it repeatedly created the conditions that fostered national particularity, often providing the language with its first literary deposit and the nation with the first mark of its historical identity. At the same time, one of the most important monuments of the creation of the historical identity of any nation, *The History of the English Church and People* of the Venerable Bede, is the documentation of the complexity of that process.[17] For while it was helping to create national identity, the Christian mission likewise took it upon itself to relate this national particularity to *una sancta catholica et apostolica ecclesia*, striking down with vigorous force and even with ruthlessness any effort to elevate the requirements of the particular over those of the universal.

13. Kohn (1940) 94-105.
14. Amos 9:7.
15. Bauer (1979) 720.
16. Acts 10:34-35.
17. See also chapter 2, p. 30 above.

In the Western theological vocabulary of several languages during the twentieth century, awareness of that tension has led to the adoption of the term *sobornost'*, best known through its use by A. S. Chomjakov and V. S. Soloviev, as an attribute of the church.[18] *Sobornaja* appears in the Church Slavonic version of the Nicene Creed as a rendering of the Greek "καθολική," which is of course the same as the English word "Catholic." Just how early that term came to be used in the Slavonic text of the creed is a matter of some debate. Chomjakov maintained that it had appeared very early, but his view is contested by others. The domestication of *sobornost'* in the theological vocabulary of the Western churches during the period between the two World Wars was an outgrowth of the ecumenical movement, and especially of the deepening participation of Eastern Orthodox theologians and churchmen in its deliberations. Specifically in the doctrine of the church, it has come to be seen as a way out of a false dilemma between an institutionalism that was in danger of equating the church with a particular historical structure and an individualism or idealism that was in danger of making the Catholicity of the church into an abstraction or an afterthought. For by its emphasis on tradition as a living reality, Eastern Orthodox ecclesiology made the Catholicity of the church visible, but visible as an article of faith; at the same time, it emphasized, more explicitly than Roman Catholicism tended to do, the national particularity of the forms that this church Catholic assumed in particular cultures.

Within the history of the Christian Church, that tension of *sobornost'* and national particularity—and therefore the quest for "the true Catholicity of the church"—has made its presence felt at various times and in various ways. In addition to the metropolitanate of L'viv-Halyč, which is our primary concern here, another movement from the church history of the Slavs of Central Europe warrants examination here in some detail: the Hussite Reformation. Beyond both the Eastern and the Western boundaries of whatever is taken to be "Central Europe," however, every specific manifestation of the tension between national identity and ecclesiological universality has provided a revealing index to the special genius of that unique place and time, but also a helpful insight into the definitions of both Catholicity and particularity. Because they can serve as a context within which to consider the Ukrainian experiment in coping with the tension and because they also help to explain attitudes toward it, it will be useful first to look briefly at one example of the tension in the East and one in the West:

18. Pelikan (1971) 5:282-336.

the jurisdictional concept of "autocephaly" in the canon law of the Eastern Orthodox Church, and the political-national movement of "Gallicanism" in the Church of France, which was, in Slipyj's words, "a phenomenon in the West analogous [to Byzantinism in the East]."[19]

In the definition of "autocephalous church" given by the best-known of the Russian Orthodox theological dictionaries,[20] the paradigm set forth is the relation among the major centers of the church in the first centuries, when the apostolic patriarchates of Rome, Constantinople, Jerusalem, and Alexandria (as well as Antioch) each had autonomous jurisdiction, without a central monarch. Their Catholic unity and *sobornost'* was achieved and maintained by the "ecumenical council [*sobor*]," in which they legislated together on matters of faith and morals. But it is clear from the puzzlement manifest in the interpretation of "autocephaly" even by an extremely learned, if in many surprising ways fundamentally unsympathetic, Western observer like the French Assumptionist Martin Jugie,[21] that any comparison between the canon law of the Western Church and that of the Eastern Church will almost inevitably find the Eastern model of the structure of the church slipshod to the point of being chaotic. Thus despite such a standard volume as the Serbian handbook of Nikodim Milaš,[22] much of the fundamental scholarly work on Eastern Orthodox canon law, even on such questions as marriage and divorce, has in fact been carried out by Catholic historians and canon lawyers, including Ukrainian Catholic canon lawyers, rather than by those who stand in the Orthodox tradition.[23] In addition to the meanings it had in earlier usage, the term "autocephalous" has been defined in another Western encyclopedia as referring to "an Orthodox national church that has become independent of the jurisdictional primacy, though not of the primacy of honor [of Constantinople], and is acknowledged as such by a metropolitan see." This concept, the definition continues, "is connected with the Eastern concept of the church, which is neither monarchical nor federative (both of which require a central authority), but represents an aggregate of national churches that subsist alongside one another, are organized into their own hierarchies, and are independent [of one another]."[24]

19. Slipyj, *Tvory* 2:112-13.
20. *Prav.Slov.* 1:44-45 (s.v.: Avtokefal'naja cerkov').
21. *DTC* 14:1407-20 (Martin Jugie s.v.: Schisme Byzantin); on Jugie, see also chapter 6, p. 119 below.
22. Milaš (1926).
23. See, for example, the works of Victor Pospishil cited in the Bibliography.
24. *LTK* 1:1130 (Perikles-Petros Joannou s.v.: Autokephal).

The reliance of an "autocephalous" polity on each national church to legislate for itself has fostered in Eastern Orthodoxy a flexibility that has permitted it to adapt its structures to local conditions and yet to preserve not only a doctrinal orthodoxy but an orthopraxis. From comparative studies of Eastern Orthodox monasticism now being carried on, for example, it is evident that the freedom from the heavy hand of a "general of the order" with international authority did enable Russian monasteries to respond to the spiritual and moral crises of difficult times in the history of the Orthodox Church of Russia: the institution of the "*starec* [elder]," familiar even to Western readers because of the character of Father Zossima in *The Brothers Karamazov*, frequently brought a sensitivity to human need and a pastoral touch that may sometimes have been absent from the ministrations of the parish clergy. Yet the imperative of a *sobornost'* and Catholicity beyond national borders has proved to be difficult to articulate institutionally, much less to enforce administratively, under the terms of autocephaly. The ancient patriarchates of the church had the ecumenical council as a court of appeal, and at one or another time the particular doctrines held by each of them (including also Rome, in the *cause célèbre* of Pope Honorius I)[25] were reproved by the universal authority of an ecumenical council.[26] But when all four of the ancient patriarchates of the East came under the political sway not of the Christian empire of Constantine and Justinian, but of Islam, the juridical structure of the council seemed to disappear. With it there disappeared a functional way to express, and to legislate for, the *sobornost'* and universal authority of the church; and the national particularity of each autocephalous church was left to its own resources.

The ideal of a church that would be free to embody the national particularity of its own special traditions—not dogmatically, but administratively and perhaps liturgically—was never lost in the West, either, and much of the diplomatic history of the Holy See is set down in the documents coming out of its negotiations with the several national churches and national governments over the right to name bishops. Such negotiations have frequently remained at the political level, but in at least some of them the fundamental doctrinal issues of *sobornost'* and ecclesiastical authority were treated as decisive. Of these latter, "Gallicanism" is in many ways the most intriguing. Many of its

25. Pelikan (1971) 2:150-53.
26. Milaš (1926) 307-13.

most influential proponents, from Jean Gerson at the beginning of the fifteenth century to Jacques Bénigne Bossuet at the end of the seventeenth, distinguished themselves also as the most eloquent defenders of the Roman Catholic tradition against its critics—Gerson through his prosecution of Jan Hus at the Council of Constance in 1415; and Bossuet through his *Histoire des variations des églises protestantes* of 1688, which was, and is, a landmark definition of the meaning of Roman Catholic continuity as *semper eadem* in opposition to the fluctuations of Protestant doctrines since the Reformation a century and a half earlier. Yet both Gerson and Bossuet, functioning (so they believed) as spokesmen for the Catholicity of the church, articulated and defended the historic rights of the particular church of France to self-determination.

The most systematic codification of the Gallican position is set down in the Four Gallican Articles of 19 March 1682.[27] These Gallican Articles were also the form in which Gallicanism was condemned, in the apostolic constitution *Inter multiplices* issued by Pope Alexander VIII on 4 August 1690. They are a fascinating political document and deserve to be studied as such—but not only as such, since for our purposes here they are of interest as an effort, within the doctrinal and jurisdictional context shaped by the development of the papacy in the Western Church, to combine and harmonize the demands of Catholicity and of particularity. This they did by several theological distinctions. One was the reminder, in the very first words of the first article, that Christ had vested power "in the church as such [*ipsi ecclesiae*]," and, for the benefit of the universal church as such, in "Saint Peter and his successors, the vicars of Christ." Therefore there was a *"plena potestas"* over such spiritual matters as belonged to the successors of Peter, but only with a second distinction: that drawn at the fourth and fifth sessions of the Council of Constance between the authority of the pope and the superior authority of the ecumenical council. Legislation by the supreme pontiff in matters of faith, therefore, did not achieve authority as *"irreformabile"* until and unless it was ratified by the *"Ecclesiae consensus"* in the Council. It was the ecumenical council which most fully represented the voice of the universality of the church—and which at the same time safeguarded the prerogatives of the "Gallican Church [*ecclesia Gallicana*]," or, as the Articles call them, the "rules, customs, and institutions received by the Gallican realm and Church [*regulas, mores et instituta a regno et ecclesia Gallicana*

---

27. The Latin text of the Gallican Articles is conveniently edited, together with the condemnatory paragraph of the constitution *Inter multiplices*, in Denzinger 2281-86.

recepta]." On that ecclesiological basis it was necessary to draw a still further distinction, between the "power over spiritual matters and over those that pertain to eternal salvation [*potestas rerum spiritualium et ad aeternam salutem pertinentium*]," which had been entrusted to the successors of Peter, and authority over "civil and temporal matters [*rerum civilium et temporalium*]," which the New Testament had reserved for temporal rulers; the Articles quoted the familiar words of the New Testament about "the governing authorities," which had after all been spoken about the emperor Nero.[28]

Both the principle of autocephaly within Eastern Orthodoxy, "New Rome," and the theory of Gallicanism within Western Catholicism, "Old Rome," were efforts to come to terms with the tension between Catholicity and national particularity. But because of its situation midway between Old Rome and New Rome, Slavic Central Europe has manifested that tension in special forms and with special poignancy. Two of the territories listed by Masaryk in his attempt to draw the boundaries are "Bohemia [*Čechy*]" and "Galicia [*Halič*]." As it happens, the Hussite Reformation among the Czechs and the Catholic metropolitanate of L'viv-Halyč among the Ukrainians—so radically different from each other in origin, development, and outcome—are two especially intriguing case studies in how national particularity and the commitment to universality have interacted in the Slavic quest for Catholicity-*cum*-particularity. An examination of this question—or cluster of questions—in Hussite thought may therefore illumine not only the history of the definition of *una sancta catholica et apostolica,* but the special nature of the problem of Catholic particularity in the Ukrainian context.

As much of the scholarly and theological literature about Jan Hus and the Hussite movement demonstrates, it is almost irresistibly tempting, but also disastrously simplistic, to see the fundamental impulse of that movement as the espousal of national particularity against the universal authority of Roman Catholicism. But it is clear that Hussite ecclesiology struggled to do justice to both elements of the tension, not only to Czech particularity but also to genuine Catholicity, and that in at least three ways.

The first, and in many respects the most fundamental, was the very definition of reform. From an external or institutional definition of the essence of the church, the Hussite reform had to be seen as schismatic: there could be no conceivable reason, under any circumstances,

28. Rom. 13:1.

for severing ties with the Holy See. Not only does such a view overlook the existential crisis in which the very identity of the "Holy See" was caught as a consequence of the Babylonian Captivity in Avignon and then the Great Schism, but it fails to grasp what was at stake in the reform of the church according to Hussite (and not only Hussite) doctrine. Of the four "notes of the church" enumerated earlier, *una sancta catholica et apostolica*, the first and the third expressed the meaning of *sobornost'*. In his conflicts with the Donatist schism, Augustine had, in effect, subordinated the attribute *"sancta"* to the attributes *"una"* and *"catholica,"* arguing that the only context within which the church as a body or the individual believer could strive for holiness was the preservation of Catholic unity.[29] The repeated breakdown of this institutional rationalization during the thousand years between Augustine and Hus seemed to prove that more drastic measures were called for if the unity and Catholicity of the church were to be preserved and/or recovered: it could not be *"una"* in a meaningful sense of the word unless it regained the imperative of holiness, and its Catholicity was nothing more than a juridical description unless it restored the norm of apostolicity, as defined in the apostolic Scriptures, to its proper and primary place. Therefore the Czech Reformation was not, according to Hussite teaching, merely an assertion of national particularity against Catholicity, but an affirmation of Catholicity as this could be achieved through the reform of the church within the Czech nation and then within the whole of the Western *corpus Christianum*.

In a deeper sense, however, it was an error to identify the church with the Western (or even with the Western plus the Eastern) *corpus Christianum*. For the same Augustine who had defended the Catholic unity of the institutional church against the Donatist schismatics had also, both against the Donatists and especially in his *City of God*, pointed beyond any institutional church to the church as it was known to God alone, the company of the elect or *universitas praedestinatorum:*

> Let this City [of God] bear in mind that among her enemies there lie hidden those who are destined to be fellow citizens, so that she may not think it a fruitless labor to bear what they inflict as enemies until they become confessors of the faith. So long, too, as she is a stranger in the world, the City of God has in her communion, and bound to her by the sacraments, some who will not eternally dwell in the lot of the saints.[30]

29. Pelikan (1986) 90-122.
30. Augustine *City of God* 1.35.

In his most important theological work, *De Ecclesia*, Jan Hus, reworking material that he had received from John Wycliffe but giving it his own special emphasis, revived this Augustinian definition of the church.[31] Many people, therefore, were, according to Hus's teaching, *"in ecclesia"* who were not *"de ecclesia"*;[32] this applied, moreover, also to the pope himself. The true church was the body of the predestinate, and in the fullest sense of each of the four attributes listed in the Nicene Creed, only that true and elect church could be said to be authentically "one, holy, Catholic, and apostolic." Conversely, no jurisdictional dispute within the administrative structure of the institutional church and no schism between a national church and Rome (or Avignon or Constance) could ever jeopardize that eternal Catholicity.

The history of the Hussite movement in the two centuries between the execution of Jan Hus in 1415 and the extinction of the Unity of Bohemian Brethren at White Mountain in 1620 provides evidence that this predestinarian definition of the church did not, as it well might have, undercut the imperative of the Hussite national church to realize a greater degree of external and visible unity with the church beyond the Czech borders.[33] Both of the major Hussite groups, the Unity of Bohemian Brethren and the Utraquists, sought to take positive steps toward that ecumenical goal. Seeking to obtain legitimate ordination for their clergy, the Utraquists in 1450 undertook negotiations with the Ecumenical Patriarchate in Constantinople, where they obtained a promise of such ordination; but 1450 was the worst of all possible times for Constantinople to fulfill that promise, since it was caught between its newly assumed rapprochement with Rome, the ill-fated Union of Florence proclaimed in *Laetentur coeli* of 5 July 1439,[34] and the Turkish threat, which ended in its fall in 1453. In 1486 the Unity of Bohemian Brethren sent a delegation to look for ecumenical affiliation, making contact with some Waldensians. A few years later, in 1511, they asked Erasmus for an endorsement of their confession of 1508. But the Hussite quest for some concrete form of unity with like-minded believers produced results only with the emergence of Martin Luther. The Utraquists entered into correspondence with him shortly after he had spoken out on behalf of Hus at the Leipzig Debate of 1519. With the *Unitas Fratrum*, his correspondence and negotiation proved to be more

31. Thomson (1956) 45.
32. Thomson (1956) 15.
33. Pelikan (1964) 106-46.
34. See chapter 4, p. 62 below.

fruitful, and in 1538 he published their statement of faith, the *Confessio Bohemica* of 1535, with a commendatory foreword. These contacts, and the later ones with Calvinist churches, were yet another means of simultaneously demonstrating and achieving the unity of the church Catholic.

These three concepts of the relation between Catholicity and particularity—the Byzantine and Eastern Orthodox concept of autocephaly, Gallicanism as (in Slipyj's formula) "a phenomenon in the West analogous [to Byzantinism in the East],"[35] and the Hussite vision of the church—all contribute to an understanding of a unique way of coping with the tension between Catholicity and particularity that has characterized the Catholic metropolitanate of L'viv-Halyč renewed by Pope Pius VII in 1807, particularly during the twentieth century in the incumbencies of Andrej Šeptyc'kyj and Josyf Slipyj. The special mixture of universal and particular manifested there was a theme to which Slipyj returned often. It was, he was convinced, the lesson of Ukrainian history through the centuries that "the pope has protected our church and ourselves against denationalization" in relation both to the Russians on the East and to the Poles on the West.[36] But the enemies of the church could not comprehend that the concept of "Catholicity" was considerably more subtle than that, as the Ukrainian relation to the Poles made clear:

> The fact that the Poles are our political enemies does not have any substantial significance as far as our Catholic Church is concerned. For in the Catholic Church all nationalities and their interests are cancelled out [*styrajut'sja*] and in time will even clash. But all of them *are in fact harmonized within the total concord of the Catholic Church*, a harmony that you strive to achieve exclusively on a political level. . . . The providence of God in the judgment of history allotted to us the assignment of living under one government with the Poles for several centuries. But this did not do us any permanent damage, and in the course of time it helped us to have been Catholics. The Catholic faith brought us closer to the Poles, and it restrained them in their hostility towards us.[37]

Thus in addition to all the other factors underlying the Union of Brest of 1595/96 and its backgrounds in the participation of Metropolitan

35. Slipyj, *Tvory* 2:112-13.
36. Slipyj, *Spomyny* 194.
37. Slipyj to N. V. Podgorny, 17.ii.1961, *Arch.Pat.* 28:81-82 (116); italics in the original.

Isidore of Kiev in the Union of Florence in 1439,[38] it can be seen, from a theological perspective, as an effort to hold together the two themes of Catholicity and national particularity. That effort made itself visible within a third of a century after the Union of Brest, with the proposal of a joint Orthodox-Catholic synod in 1629[39]—a proposal revived centuries later by Slipyj.[40] The ecumenical "ideal" of such a reunion represented, in the thought and career of both Šeptyc'kyj and Slipyj, several of the issues to which we shall be turning at greater length in subsequent chapters.

For in one respect it was intended to preserve the independence of the Church of Ukraine and Byelorussia from the dominance of the recently established patriarchate of Moscow. Union with Rome gave the Ukrainian Church a religious fulcrum outside the borders of its own nation. And as Eastern churchmen since Saints Athanasius and Maximus Confessor had repeatedly appealed from the political pressures of Eastern monarchs and from the heretical dogmas of Eastern prelates to the authority of Old Rome, so the metropolitans of L'viv-Halyč made use of their Roman connection to secure—or at any rate, to attempt to secure—their national and religious particularity against the demands that came from Poland but above all from Russia. Rome stood as the bulwark of the particularity of the metropolitanate—and at the same time as the guarantee of its genuine Catholicity. What Metropolitan Šeptyc'kyj strove to achieve was the vision described by V. S. Soloviev.[41] For Šeptyc'kyj's ultimate vision was a reunion of Orthodox and Catholic in a single autocephalous metropolitanate of Kiev, in union with Rome. The description of Rome as a fulcrum was to achieve a grim reality with the release of Josyf Slipyj from a Stalinist prison camp in 1963, for it was in Rome that he would spend his remaining years.

But having invoked the authority of Rome to appeal to a Catholicity beyond the borders of his own nation, Josyf Slipyj in fact spent most of those remaining years in a battle against fellow Catholics to preserve the peculiar forms of particularity for which his church stood. He combined the two emphases constantly in his writings and addresses, for example in a public presentation to Pope Paul VI on 24 November 1973, where he spoke of "the unshakeable fidelity to the Apostolic See on the part of our Particular Ukrainian Church" and of

38. On the Union of Florence, see chapter 4, pp. 62-66 below.
39. Choma (1973), with documents.
40. See the editors' comments in Slipyj, *Tvory* 5:36 (37).
41. See chapter 4, pp. 67-72 below.

his sure conviction that "in the bosom of the Catholic Universal Church, our Particular Church [*Pomisna Cerkva*] will preserve its Eastern traditions and its rights."[42] That included such rights as the relation of his authority to that of Ukrainian Catholic bishops in other lands, especially in North America, and at the same time the relation of the Ukrainian Catholic Church on the one hand to the Latin churches and on the other hand to the Ukrainian Orthodox churches there. As he came to see it with increasing force, and (to use his own words) "great preoccupation and bitterness,"[43] that battle was chiefly against Rome; and frequently in his letters and the other personal documents, he lamented that the curia was causing him and his Ukrainian Church more trouble than the Communists had. Of the various areas of church life in which he strove to affirm Ukrainian particularity vis-à-vis the threat of "Latinization," he was probably the most successful in the area of liturgy. He could call on a long succession of papal documents to insist that the integrity of the Eastern liturgies must be preserved in any union of an Eastern church with Rome. He was also able to capitalize on the liturgical mood created by the Second Vatican Council, which was not only more receptive to the traditions of the Liturgies of Basil and of Chrysostom than earlier generations of the Latin Church had been, but which granted a wide range of liturgical self-determination to many churches whose liturgical heritage was far more recent than that of Cyril and Methodius.

With the preservation of Ukrainian particularity in other areas than liturgy, and specifically in polity and in theology, on the other hand, the struggle was much more ambiguous. For reasons that are understandable but that were in many ways unfortunate, the symbol for all of this became the title of "patriarch," to which we shall return at some length later.[44] Slipyj had of course been designated metropolitan; then he was identified as *archiepiscopus major*, which was said to be equivalent to patriarch; he then received the red hat of a cardinal. His letters on each of these "promotions" are, as the protocol of the curia requires, self-effacing to the point of being obsequious, but they always have an edge: he wanted to be called patriarch, alongside the patriarchs of the ancient Near Eastern sees. Petitions poured in from all over the Ukrainian diaspora, and when he did not receive the title officially, he permitted it to be used nevertheless, and he used it himself. He came

42. Slipyj, *Tvory* 13:244-45 (245-46).
43. Slipyj to Mario Brini, 11.x.1966, *Arch.Pat.* 35:310.
44. See chapter 10, pp. 190-96 below.

to see in the patriarchate a primary means of assuring that the Ukrainian Church could maintain its jurisdictional identity and canonical authority—the word "autocephaly" does not seem to have appeared very often in the documents, probably because of its juridical association with Eastern Orthodoxy—and at the same time keep its precious ties with the Holy See. Even the word "particular" could be confusing, if it "suggests a notion of something partial ('part'), incomplete," and it has been suggested that "individual" is a preferable rendering because "it indicates rather a solid ecclesiastical body";[45] but perhaps because of its association with modern Western individualism, that term, too, has its difficulties, while "particularity," especially in conjunction with "Catholicity," seems to have established itself in contemporary usage in a manner that excludes the connotation "partial."

The quest for such a "Catholic particularity" in the area of Eastern Church doctrine took yet another form. Josyf Slipyj had received a Western theological education, at Innsbruck and in Rome, and he wrote one dissertation on the New Testament but another on the doctrinal relations between East and West especially in the doctrine of the *Filioque*.[46] In his exposition of this doctrine, Slipyj took a basically Thomistic position. In his theological lectures, he likewise espoused the theology of Thomas Aquinas.[47] Although Šeptyc′kyj, with his Polish roots, had in many ways come out of a more Western background than had Slipyj, he steeped himself in the Greek fathers and in Eastern liturgies, and his doctrine of the church was in several profound ways more typically Eastern than was Slipyj's.[48] That is, in relation to the present theme, Šeptyc′kyj appears to have recognized, in considerable affinity with Soloviev, that the East had developed a distinctive approach to the very definition of the nature of the church, and not merely to the method of organizing it, and that therefore what he was striving to achieve through the ambiguities of the situation of the metropolitanate of L′viv-Halyč was a *tertium quid* that participated in the traditions of both East and West but transcended them both in a genuine Catholic particularity.

45. Mončak (1987) 55.
46. See chapter 6, pp. 109-10, 119-21 below.
47. See chapter 7, p. 138 below.
48. See chapter 5, pp. 85-86 below.

4

Patterns of East-West Reconciliation

"I have been studying the problem of union for forty years," Josyf Slipyj declared in 1974; and he would go on studying it for ten years more. He had a thorough grasp of the problem in its historical dimension; but he knew it existentially as well, for he saw his years of imprisonment as a "suffering for the cause of the unity of the church" between East and West. His study had convinced him that both sides had to accept their share of the historic responsibility for the division of Christendom.[1] When he arrived in Rome from Moscow in 1963, the first words of Pope John XXIII to him were a commitment to reconciliation between the Eastern and the Western churches, together with a criticism of any Roman Catholic ecumenism that "wants to achieve unity, but does not want to hold dialogue."[2] He quoted Pope John as having, with "heroic humility," blamed the East-West schism on the West: "The guilt for the separation rests upon our shoulders."[3] To change that situation, according to Pope John, "it is necessary to have a dialogue with them," instead of condemning them and withdrawing from them.[4]

Metropolitan Slipyj responded positively to such papal overtures, for they stood in an apostolic succession with his own deepest traditions, as these had been articulated by his predecessor as Metropolitan

---

1. Slipyj, *Tvory* 13:268.
2. Slipyj, *Tvory* 13:298.
3. Slipyj to Lucca Di Schiena, 24.viii.1963, *Arch.Pat.* 29:120.
4. Slipyj, *Tvory* 13:215.

of L'viv-Halyč, Andrej Šeptyc'kyj, who had "anticipated the present ecumenical movement."[5] For if Cyril and Methodius were "the precursors of authentic ecumenism,"[6] it behooved the joint heirs of their disputed legacy to carry on genuine and vigorous dialogue over it. Having come from Constantinople as their intellectual and spiritual matrix and having gone to Rome to certify their ecclesiastical jurisdiction, Cyril and Methodius had reconciled in their own persons and ministry the ancient and seemingly unbridgeable division of East and West. Through his own traditions and through his scholarly investigations, Slipyj recognized, far better than most, just how ancient that division was—how ancient, and how complex. Implacable foe of "Bolshevism" though he was, Slipyj knew that it had not begun with the October Revolution, but much earlier: "The difference between East and West has been present ever since the time of Constantine."[7]

Just when East and West first came apart, and for what reasons, was and is a question that has long engaged historians of Christianity, and historians of Europe as well. If, on a physical map of Europe without political boundaries, one were to draw a line running north to south (presumably in imperial purple) delineating the division of the Roman Empire under Diocletian; and if one were then to draw a second north-south line (this time in Byzantine gold) to indicate the schism between Roman Catholicism and *Pravoslavie* during the Middle Ages and since; and if one drew a third line (in red, of course) to make more precise than Winston Churchill himself did, when he spoke in his Iron Curtain address of 5 March 1946 about a line "from Stettin in the Baltic to Trieste in the Adriatic,"[8] what the border between East and West became after the Yalta Conference (held in the territory of the Ukrainian Soviet Socialist Republic)—the three lines would, to be sure, not be identical, but they would in striking measure be more similar than dissimilar. This does suggest that East-West division has managed to perpetuate itself in pre-Christian Europe, in Christian Europe, and in post-Christian Europe, and that it had already begun when, in the words of Edward Gibbon, "Diocletian had divided his power and provinces with his associate Maximian."[9] As a consequence of Diocletian's action, as Gibbon suggested earlier in his account, "the political union of the Roman world was gradually dissolved, and a principle of division was

---

5. Slipyj, *Tvory* 13:303.
6. Slipyj to John Paul II, 10.ii.1981, *Arch.Pat.* 118:200-201.
7. Slipyj, *Tvory* 5:77.
8. Churchill (1980) 881.
9. Gibbon (1896) 1:441.

introduced, which, in the course of a few years, occasioned the perpetual separation of the eastern and western empires."[10]

Of those three lines of demarcation between East and West, it is the second, the separation between Roman Catholicism and *Pravoslavie* during the Middle Ages and since, that has received the most systematic and sustained intellectual attention (as distinct from political, economic, or military attention), in fact much more attention than the other two combined. It is as well the most pertinent to the present examination of the heritage of Josyf Slipyj—invoking a distinction introduced earlier, both of his heritage as he had received it and of his heritage as he perceived it. This is not the place to recount the history of the division, nor to rehearse "the theological origins of the schism";[11] many of those issues will concern us in subsequent chapters, particularly in chapter 6 and again in chapter 11. But a consideration of Slipyj's heritage does suggest a historical typology of three alternative patterns for the reunification of East and West that have come out of the doctrinal and ecclesiastical schism. To resort to alliteration in English, as he sometimes liked to do in Ukrainian, these patterns are: conquest, compromise, and concord.

The most obvious and direct means of reunification has always been through conquest. At the same time, the relations between East and West are a prime illustration of the principle that as the military or political conquest is going in one direction, the intellectual conquest, and therefore the reunification through conquest, may be going in the opposite direction at the same time. As Slipyj's favorite Latin poet, Horace, had observed in one of his *Epistles*—and as he exhibited in his own poetry—"Greece, once overcome [by Rome], overcame her wild conqueror, and brought the arts into rustic Latium."[12] During the first three centuries or so of the history of Christian doctrine, a similar "conquest" of the West by the East took place in theology. Rome continued to be the political capital of the Mediterranean world until 330 C.E., and it was rapidly becoming the ecclesiastical capital as well, with the primacy of the See of Peter being acknowledged by almost every Christian teacher everywhere. Nevertheless, most of the monumental intellectual achievements of Christian theology during that period (and well beyond it) were written in Greek. In Slipyj's judgment, this mutual incomprehension between those who wrote Greek and those who

10. Gibbon (1896) 1:384.
11. Pelikan (1971) 2:146-98, with bibliography, pp. 308-10.
12. Horace *Epistles*, Book II, Epistle i, line 156.

wrote Latin was the principal reason why "the difference between the two views" was not "settled peacefully, as many another conflict between Easterners and Westerners had been."[13] Of the works of theology that were written in Latin, moreover, many of the most significant did not come from Rome at all but from Roman North Africa. The prominence of North Africa would continue with the arrival on the scene of Augustine of Hippo, who, theological genius though he undoubtedly was, still had to recognize that on the cardinal doctrines of the faith—the Trinity and the Incarnation—the Greeks had been the chief pioneers; it was their creed that he recited with the formula, "This is my faith, since it is the Catholic faith."[14] The first seven ecumenical councils of the undivided church, Josyf Slipyj once reminded an audience on Italian television, "were chiefly a creation of the Eastern Church," with the West playing a largely secondary part.[15] Therefore it was essential not to confuse the various kinds of "conquest."

Sometimes, however, the military conquest and the intellectual domination have in fact coincided, also in the history of the church and of its theology. So it was with the sack of Constantinople by the Venetians in the Fourth Crusade of 1204. "There never was a greater crime against humanity than the Fourth Crusade," Sir Steven Runciman asserted near the conclusion of his *History of the Crusades,*[16] and his graphic description of the pillage of a Christian capital by Christian barbarians bears out the assertion. Undeniably, the Latinization of Constantinople and of Jerusalem by the Crusaders did bring some intellectual benefits. For example, it did make a useful contribution to the historical understanding of the constitutional law of Western feudalism, which was systematized and codified more thoroughly when it was exported to the Near East than it had ever been in the home countries of Western Europe. But applied to the liturgical and theological forms of Eastern Christendom, the reunification of East and West through Latinization was largely a disaster. The Greek patriarch of Constantinople was compelled to flee to Nicea, and his place for the next half-century was taken by a Latin patriarch.[17] Byzantine churches were closed, monks were imprisoned, and characteristically Western formulas of doctrine were imposed on the Greeks. As one scholar has recently described the relations between the two

13. Slipyj, *Tvory* 1:150.
14. Augustine *On the Trinity* I.ix.7.
15. Slipyj, *Tvory* 12:78 (82).
16. Runciman (1951) 3:130.
17. Wolff (1954).

churches between 1204 and 1261, "the discussions all but foundered at the start on matters of protocol. As it was they drifted into a sea of theology in which there was no hope of agreement."[18] For doctrine, the net result of the Latin conquest was an even deeper division of East and West.

Into modern times, the memory of the atrocity of 1204 remains alive in Eastern Orthodox Christendom. An anecdote narrated by Josyf Slipyj in 1974 may serve to illustrate this:

> A Roman monsignor, while visiting the major archbishop of Athens, wanted to understand the mentality of the average priest and therefore expressed the desire to visit a village, in the company of a bishop. After the visit in the church, the prelate met face to face with the priests and the faithful. In the course of the conversation, the Greek understood that the monsignor heard a question from one of those present as to who he was. The bishop replied with the explanation that they were dealing with a representative of the pope in Rome. Several voices responded: "Oh, he's the one who destroyed Constantinople!"[19]

Thus there is much to be said in favor of the position of those who take 1204 as the decisive date for the schism of the Eastern and Western Churches. Most manuals of church history, at least in past generations, have accepted the traditional date for it as 1054,[20] when, in Gibbon's phrase, the patriarch of Constantinople, "Michael Cerularius was excommunicated in the heart of Constantinople by the pope's legates," who "deposited on the altar of St. Sophia a direful anathema"; "from this thunderbolt," Gibbon continued, "we may date the consummation of the schism."[21]

Actually, the break was not as abrupt as the "thunderbolt" metaphor suggests, for there continued to be sporadic fraternal contacts throughout the twelfth century. At one time it was thought appropriate to date the divorce of the two churches from "the Photian schism" of the ninth century. Because of the connections of that schism with the jurisdictional and liturgical dispute over Moravia and the mission of Saints Cyril and Methodius,[22] such an interpretation must be said to have a certain appeal; but closer scrutiny of "the Photian

18. Nicol (1966) 303.
19. Slipyj, *Tvory* 13:268.
20. See Slipyj, *Tvory* 14:261 (263).
21. Gibbon (1896) 6:370.
22. See chapter 2, pp. 34-36 above.

schism," particularly by Francis Dvornik, showed it to be, in his phrase, at least as much "legend" as "history."[23] At about the same time as Dvornik, Josyf Slipyj was also studying the Photian schism, especially as it pertained to dogma, and by his researches into the trinitarian doctrine of Photius he made a significant contribution to the clarification of the doctrinal question that has been cited the most frequently as the point of division.[24] Finally, there are those, primarily it would seem among canon lawyers, for whom the breakdown of the Union of Florence in the fifteenth century is technically the point when East and West finally came apart. But both symbolically and intrinsically—and certainly if conquest through Latinization is the issue—1204 deserves the dubious honor.

Nor are spokesmen for Eastern Orthodoxy the only ones who have lamented and criticized the policy of Latinization. On 30 November 1894 Pope Leo XIII, who a few years earlier, in 1888, had told the youthful Andrej Šeptyc'kyj—then still Count Roman Szeptycky—that it was "the great mission" of the Basilian Order to help bring about "the reunion of the East with the West,"[25] issued his encyclical *Orientalium dignitas ecclesiarum*.[26] Adrian Fortescue, of whom it has been said that "no one in England at that time knew as much about Oriental liturgies as Fortescue,"[27] called this encyclical "perhaps the most important of all documents of this kind."[28] The primary purpose of the encyclical was to lay to rest the long-standing and well-grounded fears of most Eastern theologians and churchmen that "the price of such submission [to the pope] was invariably the Latinization of their rites, the abandonment of their ancient traditions, and acceptance of Latin clergy as supervisors,"[29] because Rome was intent on destroying the particularity of their traditions and on imposing the patterns of scholastic theology and Latin liturgy upon them instead. Leo XIII was, after all, the pope whose encyclical *Aeterni Patris* of 1879 had become the charter of Neo-Thomism in the West, also for such Eastern Neo-Thomists as Josyf Slipyj,[30] just as his encyclical *Rerum novarum* was, in Slipyj's judgment,

23. Dvornik (1948).
24. Slipyj, *Tvory* 1:91-158.
25. Prokoptschuk (1967) 90-93.
26. *ASS* 27 (1894): 257-64.
27. *NCE* 5:1033 (Clifford Walter Howell, s.v.: Fortescue, Adrian).
28. *TCE* 5:239 (Adrian Fortescue, s.v.: Eastern Churches), with a concise summary of its chief provisions.
29. Zernov (1961) 170.
30. Slipyj, *Tvory* 2:42.

the foundation for such social encyclicals of the twentieth century as *Quadrigesimo anno* of Pope Pius XI and *Mater et Magistra* and *Pacem in terris* of Pope John XXIII.[31]

This made *Orientalium dignitas* all the more effective as a critique of reconciliation through conquest. In it Leo XIII rejected Latinization on the grounds that many of the traditions embodied in the Eastern liturgies which it would displace were actually older and more solemn than the Latin Mass. In fact, some of the noblest elements in the intellectual and liturgical life of the Western Church had come to it from the East, as the very vocabulary of the West demonstrated through the use of such terms as "liturgy" and "Eucharist." In addition, Leo XIII repudiated, as alien to the authentic Catholic tradition, any effort at homogeneity. Despite the theological oxymoron "Roman Catholic," the truly Catholic Church was "Catholic" only if it was not exclusively Latin and did not adhere merely to one liturgical tradition. To be Catholic, it had to be, in the phrase of the Psalm (at any rate of the Psalm in Latin), "surrounded with variety [*circumdata varietate*],"[32] embracing particularity as well as Catholicity.[33] Josyf Slipyj was echoing that formula of Leo XIII when, in introducing his overview of the Christian churches of the East, Orthodox and Catholic, and of the dogmatic differences separating them, he reminded his audience that "from the very beginning there was a variety of rites, not only in the East but also in the West," of which the "Roman" had been only one among several.[34] And he denounced the widespread idea that "it would be better if the church observed a single rite and followed the same discipline," as a notion to which the practice of the church throughout the entire "patristic millennium" had been opposed.[35] Instead, the church was called to be an example to secular society of how to manifest an essential unity amid a variety of observance.[36]

On the basis of these theological presuppositions, Pope Leo XIII set out concrete educational and canonical provisions for the preservation of Eastern rites in those churches, such as the Ukrainian, that undertook reunification with Rome, and he threatened with suspension any Western proselytizer who would strive to Latinize an adherent of one of these churches. For Metropolitan Andrej Šeptyc'kyj of Kiev-

31. Slipyj, *Tvory* 12:252.
32. Ps. 45:10 (44:10 according to the Vulgate numbering of the Psalms).
33. See chapter 3, pp. 38-52 above.
34. Slipyj, *Tvory* 5:107.
35. Slipyj, *Tvory* 1:396-97.
36. Slipyj, *Spomyny* 73.

Halyč, who was dedicated to the ideal of a fraternal reunification of the Ukrainian Orthodox Church and the Ukrainian Catholic Church into a single autocephalous, Eastern church in union with the Holy See, *Orientalium dignitas* was the Magna Charta of a program for the reunification of East and West that would not merely not require, but would prohibit, "hybridism" and the sacrifice of Eastern identity for the sake of unity.[37] As his successor Josyf Cardinal Slipyj continued the policy of Šeptyc'kyj in making appeals to the Orthodox for reunion;[38] his editors have suggested that the paper which Slipyj delivered at the ecumenical congress in L'viv in 1936 was "the first time in half a millennium that the idea of a common council of Catholics and Orthodox is mentioned,"[39] although there had been a proposal for such a council on Ukrainian soil in 1629.[40] But before his career was ended, he was obliged to invoke *Orientalium dignitas* even more vigorously in his defenses against the Latins.[41] Concerned as he was especially with the status of Ukrainian Catholics in the diaspora of North America,[42] Slipyj battled for the integrity of Eastern liturgy and Eastern canon law, and at the Second Vatican Council he found the opportunity to make his case for a reunification that did not resort to conquest.[43]

A second path to the reunification of East and West, and one often taken in reaction against the first, has been compromise. It has not been accidental that proposals of doctrinal compromise as a means of achieving the intellectual reunification of East and West have frequently been inspired by *raisons d'état* and have come at a time when one or the other or both of the sides stood under severe political or even military pressures. For more than a thousand years the most troublesome dispute over dogma between the Latin West and the Greek East has been the *Filioque:*[44] Does the Holy Spirit in the Holy Trinity proceed eternally from the Father only, as the Nicene Creed originally seemed to imply and as the East went on teaching, or does the Holy Spirit proceed eternally "from the Father and the Son [*ex Patre Filioque*]," as the West eventually confessed in its unique version of the Nicene Creed? At the deepest metaphysical level, what Slipyj called the "subtle and dry

37. Korolevskij (1964) 323-48; see also p. 239.
38. See especially chapter 11, p. 220 below.
39. Slipyj, *Tvory* 5:37.
40. Choma (1973).
41. Slipyj, *Tvory* 12:80 (84).
42. See chapter 9, pp. 174-76 below.
43. See especially chapter 10, pp. 206-15 below.
44. Pelikan (1971) 2:183-93.

metaphysics"[45] of this seemingly abstruse, ultimately perhaps unanswerable, question involved two different ways of affirming the oneness of the Godhead as the essential presupposition for the trineness of the Godhead. For the Western position as it received its classic formulation in the trinitarianism of Augustine, God as the Trinity of Father, Son, and Holy Spirit was nevertheless one because both the Father and the Son participated in the procession of the Holy Spirit. For the East, on the other hand, as its trinitarianism was worked out by the three Cappadocian church fathers of the fourth century, God as the Trinity was still one because both the Son and the Holy Spirit came from the Father, who remained the sole "origin [ἀρχή]" within the Godhead.[46]

Like many theological questions, the *Filioque* in part resolved itself, also for Josyf Slipyj, into the issue of authority. To Slipyj, the primacy of the pope was both theologically and personally a foundation of his faith and of his theology, and he would have nothing to do with any effort to cast any doubt upon it at all.[47] His loyalty to it had been put to the test in the repeated efforts of his Soviet captors to make him renounce it, and he had heroically withstood them all.[48] Even in a discourse whose opening theme was "the history and the importance of Eastern Christianity in various ecumenical councils," therefore, he concluded by warning against the idea that the jurisdiction of the church was "collegial"; for "the jurisdiction of the pope is supreme, and the jurisdiction of the bishops is subordinated to it, as the apostles were subordinated [*pidčyneni*] to Saint Peter."[49] On the other hand, it was the Byzantine view, and then the Eastern Orthodox view in general, that by adding this phrase to the Nicene Creed (though only, it must be recalled, after considerable hesitation[50]), Rome had set itself apart from the other four historic patriarchates of the church—Constantinople, Jerusalem, Alexandria, and Antioch—and had arrogated to itself the right on its own to legislate "new" doctrine for the church as a whole, and to do so without a church council. There were literally hundreds of treatises from both sides catapulted over the line of battle between East and West. As the twelfth chapter of the *Žitie* [Life] of Saint Methodius shows, he was obliged to clarify his position on this ques-

45. Slipyj, *Tvory* 1:93.
46. On Slipyj's "graphic" diagrams of the various trinitarian alternatives, see chapter 6, p. 120, n. 146 below.
47. Slipyj, *Tvory* 12:105.
48. See chapter 8, pp. 156-60 below.
49. Slipyj, *Tvory* 12:78-82 (82-85).
50. Pelikan (1971) 2:186-87.

tion;[51] and some of the earliest monuments of Slavic literature include discussions of *Filioque*.[52]

"In the history of dogma," Slipyj once observed, "it is not possible to find many examples where the opponents understood one another as little as they did in the battle over the *Filioque*."[53] But at the union councils of the later Middle Ages the delegates from both sides looked for some way out of the impasse. Slipyj lamented that the untimely death of Thomas Aquinas in 1274, just before the Council of Lyons, meant that the theologians of the East had not been given the opportunity to hear him out on the question.[54] But a century and a half later, at the Council of Florence in 1439, the representatives of the East, including the Byzantine Emperor John VII Palaeologus and Patriarch Joseph II of Constantinople, did accept and sign a compromise formula.[55] As the bull of reunification, *Laetentur caeli* of 6 July 1439, explained in both its Greek and its Latin versions, the compromise proceeded on the basis of the study of "many authorities from the holy doctors both Eastern and Western, some of whom say that the Holy Spirit proceeds from the Father and the Son but others of whom say [that the Holy Spirit proceeds] from the Father through the Son." But the formula concluded that "in diverse ways of speaking [ἐν διαφόροις ταῖς λέξεσιν, *sub diversis vocabulis*]" the phrase "from the Father and the Son [*ex Patre Filioque*]" meant the same as "from the Father through the Son [*ex Patre per Filium*]." The Greeks, it explained, had been reassured that the Latins agreed with them about a single "origin [ἀρχή, *principium*]" in the Godhead; the Latins, for their part, now acknowledged that when the Greeks spoke (as had the Creed of Nicea) about a procession "from the Father," they "did not do so with the intention of excluding the Son."[56]

As it stood, the solution of the *Filioque* set forth by the Council of Florence represented a considerable degree of intellectual sophistication, and it was not devoid of promise for an authentic meeting of minds; therefore it has continued to serve as a point of reference for the discussion of East-West reunion, especially among the Slavs.[57] Slipyj

51. See Dvornik (1970) 163-65.
52. Popov (1875) 84.
53. Slipyj, *Tvory* 1:158.
54. Slipyj, *Tvory* 2:87.
55. Geneakoplos (1966) 84-111.
56. The portion of the text, both Greek and Latin, dealing with the *Filioque* appears in Alberigo 524-27.
57. Choma (1981) 29.

held the Council of Florence itself in very high regard, and he took the occasion of a visit to Florence in 1964 as an opportunity to celebrate a Church Slavonic requiem [*panachyda*] for Patriarch Joseph II of Constantinople, who is buried there.[58] *Laetentur coeli,* Slipyj asserted, stood as "a foundation and a guide for future centuries [*osnovoju i dorohovkazom na majbutni stolittja*]."[59] But for its own century it did not in fact succeed in addressing the fundamental and underlying issues which the *Filioque* had come to symbolize in the theology of both sides, leaving the basic philosophical and theological presuppositions largely untouched; and "the union of the churches attempted at the Councils of Lyons (1274) and Florence (1437) did not lead to any permanent actuality."[60] Even Slipyj himself had considerable misgivings about the adequacy of the compromise formula "from the Father through the Son," which he found "speculatively unclear."[61] In addition—and more importantly—the time was too short to overcome "the age-old hostility of Moscow to the Catholic Church," a hostility that was, Slipyj suggested, even greater in Constantinople than in the Slavic East.[62]

When the political and ecclesiastical situations on both sides shifted, therefore, the intellectual reunification collapsed. It must be acknowledged from the history of the church that some formulas of reconciliation which might be labeled as "compromises" and which have come into being under particular political circumstances have then gone on to outlive those circumstances: the creed of the Council of Nicea in 325 and the confession presented at the Diet of Augsburg in 1530 are both examples of that. But to do so, they had to have the time to acquire an intellectual integrity of their own that did not depend on the *Realpolitik* in whose context they originally arose. Neither in the East nor in the West did the existential situation at the middle of the fifteenth century allow such processes of maturation to develop for the compromise formula of the Union of Florence. Less than fifteen years after *Laetentur caeli* there came, in Slipyj's words, "the year 1453, that terrible date [*žachlyva data*] for the East, not only for the Greeks but for all the other Christian nations of the East."[63] Constantinople fell to the Turks; and the papacy, already beleaguered at the Council of Basel which was moved to Ferrara which was moved to Florence, was lurch-

58. Slipyj, *Tvory* 12:140.
59. Slipyj, *Tvory* 12:120 (125).
60. Slipyj, *Tvory* 1:391.
61. Slipyj, *Tvory* 1:144-49.
62. Slipyj, *Tvory* 12:120 (125).
63. Slipyj, *Tvory* 12:187 (189).

ing toward the crisis of the Protestant Reformation, which largely over-shadowed the desire for the reunification of East and West, whether intellectual or ecclesiastical, for several centuries. The Church of Russia repudiated the Union of Florence, and so did the Church of Constantinople. It has stood as a cautionary tale ever since, as the use of it in subsequent negotiations toward the intellectual reunification of East and West in Europe demonstrates; for example, one standard account in English about the ambiguities of the Union of Brest-Litovsk in 1595/1596 bears the title *From Florence to Brest*.[64]

But it was specifically on account of the Union of Brest that Slipyj regarded the Council of Florence as "a foundation and a guide for future centuries,"[65] because Florence had made possible an eventual reconciliation in which, beyond both conquest and compromise, concord became a third path to the intellectual reunification of East and West. Two fifteenth-century patriarchs of Constantinople became for Slipyj living embodiments of that method, and therefore also in themselves "a guide for future centuries": Bessarion of Constantinople and Isidore of Kiev. As archbishop of Nicea, Bessarion had come to the Council of Florence in 1438 with the Byzantine emperor, John VII Palaeologus.[66] There, in the words of the miniature biography of him that Slipyj prepared in 1972 for the quincentenary of Bessarion's death, he

> ... showed himself to be the greatest theologian at the Council of Ferrara and Florence and an eloquent defender of the unity of the church. There was no one capable of being compared with him. He gave solutions and explanations of the points of difference between East and West, the *Filioque*, primacy, purgatory, and the other questions, solutions and explanations that have remained valid to the present day.[67]

Bessarion's defense of the use of Greek philosophy in Christian theology can still be studied as a classic statement of the case for Christian Hellenism.[68] As a theologian and churchman, Bessarion therefore articulated the kind of humanistic scholarship and ecumenical loyalty to both the Greek and the Latin traditions that Slipyj himself sought to

64. Halecki (1958).
65. Slipyj, *Tvory* 12:120 (125).
66. *DTC* 2:801-7 (Aurelio Palmieri, s.v.: Bessarion), with extensive bibliography of primary and secondary sources.
67. Slipyj, *Tvory* 13:187.
68. Pelikan (1971) 2:250-51.

espouse. He was "the most Greek of the Latins, the most Latin of the Greeks [*Latinorum Graecissimus, Graecorum Latinissimus*]."[69]

While less universally known and celebrated than Cardinal Bessarion, Cardinal Isidore of Kiev was an incarnation of the same qualities.[70] Indeed, the two of them had been elevated to the cardinalate at the same time for their unionistic service.[71] As a Ukrainian prelate who represented the separation between Kiev and Moscow, moreover, Isidore held a special place in Slipyj's catalogue of patrons.[72] On 8 March 1964, at the Church of the Holy Apostles in Rome, Slipyj celebrated a special memorial for Isidore's quinquecentenary, to which he invited not only Ukrainians and other Eastern Catholics such as Gregory Peter Cardinal Agagianian, but Latin churchmen as well.[73] His panegyric on that occasion took as its basis the discussion of the *Summa* of Saint Thomas Aquinas on the relative merits of the active and the contemplative life.[74] Combining the active and the contemplative in his own career as a monk and a prelate, Isidore had served both the East and the West. He was "a lion in all directions as a defender of the unity of the church against attackers." The cause of effecting concord and reunion between Rome and Constantinople had brought him to the Council of Basel-Ferrara-Florence, and in turn it was he who brought the Union of Florence to Moscow. As metropolitan of Kiev and All Rus', he linked the Slavic Christian community both to New Rome and to Old Rome. And although he and the Union of Florence were repudiated by both Constantinople and Moscow, his achievement stood. In Josyf Slipyj's view of church history, the concord for which Isidore had striven until his death in 1463 found its fulfillment in the Union of Brest in 1596, almost a century and a half after his death, and in the Union of Užhorod in 1646, almost two centuries after his death.[75]

For those events, too, Slipyj found anniversary opportunities, both of them in 1971.[76] The Union of Brest was a consequence of the Union of Florence; Moscow had repudiated Florence, but there was a "survival of the Florentine tradition among the Ruthenians."[77] In the

---

69. Slipyj, *Tvory* 13:189.
70. *LTK* 5:788-89 (Joseph Gill, s.v.: Isidoros v. Kiew).
71. Slipyj, *Tvory* 13:187, n.
72. Slipyj to Maximilian de Furstenberg, 28.iii.1972, *Arch.Pat.* 41:115.
73. Augustin Bea to Slipyj, 7.iii.1964, *Arch.Pat.* 30:149.
74. Thomas Aquinas *Summa Theologica* II-IIae Q. 179-82.
75. Slipyj, *Tvory* 12:121 (126).
76. Slipyj, *Tvory* 9:155-58.
77. Halecki (1958) 123-40.

decades leading up to the Union of Brest, the metropolitanate of Kiev, for both political and ecclesiastical reasons, continued to look for ways to recover that Florentine tradition.[78] The Union of Brest, however, differed fundamentally from the Union of Florence, which "was understood and interpreted by the popes and western theologians as a subjection of a separate local church to the 'universal' Latin church of Rome."[79] The Union of Florence did grant to the East as well as to the West the integrity of its own liturgical tradition, but as drawn it did not appear to rule out the Latinization of Eastern Rite churches, especially those that constituted a minority within the territory of Latin Rite churches, where those whom a recent monograph calls "uniformitarians" took it as a license for Latinization.[80] In fact, "all subsequent 'reunions' were clearly formulated as an unconditional surrender of each of the Eastern Churches to the Roman Church."[81] For the Ukrainians that was a fundamental, indeed a fatal, drawback. Therefore the official papal proclamation of the Union of Brest, the bull *Magnus Dominus et laudabilis nimis* issued by Pope Clement VIII on 23 December 1595, took pains to specify that the special liturgical practices of the Eastern Rite churches, including the retention of the Julian calendar, were to be respected by the Latins.[82] The "critical times for the Union"[83] in the early seventeenth century proved that none of those concessions could ever be taken for granted. Nor did conditions improve in the eighteenth century.[84]

In his defense of the Union of Brest, Metropolitan Josyf Rutskyj, "a man of dedication and piety ... sought to buttress the position of his church by securing a papal edict against transferring rites, by establishing a Ruthenian seminary, and by requesting the elevation of the Kievan see to a patriarchate"[85]—the very steps that were at the center of Metropolitan Josyf Slipyj's grand strategy, too, which was why he strove to identify his stand with Rutskyj's.[86] The preservation of Eastern rites was retained in the Union of Užhorod of 1646.[87] There is

78. Choma (1976).
79. Bilaniuk (1975) 11.
80. Mončak (1987) 226-35.
81. Bilaniuk (1977) 3:124.
82. Text in Welykyj (1970) 217-26.
83. Choma (1974) 99-102.
84. Macha (1974).
85. Sysyn (1985) 55.
86. Slipyj, *Tvory* 14:113.
87. Lacko (1966) is an instructive account; see pp. 43-46 on the relation of the Union of Užhorod to the Union of Brest.

some question about lines of jurisdiction at the time of the Union of Brest.[88] The diocese of Mukačevo—which was part of Hungary, then of Czechoslovakia, then of Hungary again, and now of Soviet Ukraine—was the base for the "Ruthenians" adhering to the Union of Užhorod.[89] The diocese of Prešov was its nineteenth-century heir in Eastern Slovakia.[90] Because they combined recognition of the authority of Rome with the inviolability of the integrity of Eastern liturgy and custom, the Union of Brest and the Union of Užhorod articulated, at the end of the sixteenth and the beginning of the seventeenth centuries, the principles of authentic reconciliation that Josyf Slipyj was espousing in the twentieth century. Therefore he celebrated them together as "the beginning of a new era in the church life" of Ukrainians in "Subcarpathian Rus' " as well as of those in L'viv-Halyč.[91]

The most brilliant formulation of those principles of reconciliation in the nineteenth century came in the thought of Vladimir Sergejevič Soloviev, who counted a Ukrainian family among his forebears.[92] His exposition of the Eastern Christian understanding of the gospel in his *Lectures on Godmanhood* [*Čtennija o Bogočelovečestve*] of 1878 is an indispensable historical key to understanding not only what Georges V. Florovsky called the "paths" of Russian theology, but the intellectual worldview of the Greek church fathers in their distinction from the Latin tradition. Yet the work of Soloviev in which his position on the reconciliation of East and West has been stated most fully was not in fact published in Russian, but in French: *La Russie et l'église universelle* in 1889. In this context it is not necessary to enter into the mooted questions about Soloviev's own personal resolution of the tension between East and West and the form of his private reconciliation with Rome, but rather to look at the problem he poses in *La Russie et l'église universelle* as it describes this third way of reunification. Soloviev was to become an inspiration for Slipyj's mentor, Andrej Šeptyc'kyj, who met him in 1886 and who was to make his own Soloviev's vision of East-West reconciliation.[93] But, as Šeptyc'kyj said in 1939,

> If we speak of the Slavic East, which includes the greatest number of [Eastern] Christians, the well-known Russian philosopher

88. Pekar (1956) 25-30.
89. *LTK* 7:671-72 (Jozef Tomko, s.v.: Mukačevo).
90. *LTK* 9:125-26 (Michael Lacko, s.v.: Ruthenen).
91. Slipyj, *Tvory* 9:156.
92. Herbigny (1934) is a useful introduction for readers who do not have Russian.
93. Prokoptschuk (1967) 92.

Vladimir Soloviev has often been compared with [John Henry] Newman. Soloviev was certainly a powerful thinker, and a thinker possessing originality, and he bequeathed a certain school to Russian literature. But unfortunately, Soloviev's pupils hardly became heirs of his Catholic outlook. To be sure, he did have various followers in this respect, that is, in the affirmation of his Catholic thought, but it is unfortunately impossible to speak about a movement that took a friendly position toward the Catholic Church.[94]

It is intriguing to note that sometime after coming to Rome from his imprisonment Josyf Slipyj took out of the library of the *Russicum* a copy of the Russian edition of Soloviev.[95] Sometime thereafter he linked the names of Soloviev, Strossmayer, and Šeptyc'kyj as the Eastern leaders who had moved the church out of its "stagnation" on the issue of unity.[96]

Like the Slavophils,[97] to whom he has a complex relation on many aesthetic and theological questions, Soloviev strove to distance himself from much of Western thought, secular as well as religious, as his youthful thesis "against the positivists" already made clear. Toward Western Christian thought he took a polemical stance for its rationalism: he attacked Protestant theologians, especially German Lutherans, for their excessive individualism, and Roman Catholic prelates and scholastics for their simplistic identification of the church as body of Christ with the church as papal institution; and he professed to see Roman Catholicism and Protestantism, for all their mutual recriminations, as having in common the fatal flaw of Western theology. Even in its most radical expressions, Russian sectarianism had retained a sense of community that Soloviev found lacking in the Pietist forms of Protestant theology and devotion. He likewise saw in the Roman Catholic Inquisition—as did, of course, a more famous Russian literary friend of his in those same years—the embodiment of an ecclesiastical tyranny that would not suffer even the figure of Christ to interfere with its thought control. In his work on "theocracy" Soloviev examined closely the biblical metaphor of "the kingdom of God," seeking to come to terms with its eschatological-apocalyptic connotations while at the same time probing for an identification of the concrete

94. Prokoptschuk (1967) 181.
95. Attestation by Ludwig Pichler, Librarian of the *Russicum,* 24.iii.1972, *Arch.Pat.* 117:198.
96. Slipyj, *Tvory* 13:267.
97. See Gratieux (1939).

structures, political as well as ecclesiastical, in which it might be able to find embodiment. Thus Soloviev was one of the most eloquent among Eastern critics of the endemic Western proclivity for using the devices of conquest to resolve intellectual and spiritual differences, and in this Slipyj followed him.

He was at the same time set against the device of theological compromise, because it was an evasion of the fundamental source of such differences; and like Slipyj after him,[98] he was correspondingly critical of the theological imprecision that he took to be all too characteristic of much of Eastern thought, especially in its modern and Russian phases. That criticism did not extend to the Greek church fathers and the ecumenical councils of the church, where Soloviev, and then Šeptyc'kyj and Slipyj, frequently found corroboration for their ideas. Sometimes, therefore, Soloviev appears to have joined himself to the Westernizing repudiation of those features in *Pravoslavie* that tended toward obscurantism and superstition, especially when these manifested themselves in works that made intellectual and scholarly claims. He likewise faulted the East for having manifested too little of the very tendencies that had been manifested to excess in the West, the emphasis on church structure and order. When Alexander Schmemann spoke about the "ecclesiological silence" of Eastern Orthodox theology in the modern period, referring to a Byzantinism "which shaped the 'historical consciousness' of Orthodoxy, and which still constitutes the essential context for the Orthodox experience of the Church, of the World, and of their relationship with one another,"[99] he was, with significantly different conclusions in mind, sharing the diagnosis of Eastern thought that Soloviev had set forth.

What Soloviev proposed as an alternative was, to use a term made familiar by Pavel Florenskij, a "universalizing concord [*vseedinstvo*]" that would be based on an acceptance of the dialectical character of Christian doctrine and therefore on the interdependence of the Eastern and Western versions of it. In this he consciously patterned himself after what he took to have been the methodology of intellectual reunification in the dogmatic decrees of the seven ecumenical councils from Nicea I in 325, which affirmed the Trinity, to Nicea II in 787, which reaffirmed the icons. At none of those councils, by Soloviev's reading at any rate, had one of the contending parties simply conquered the other; nor, on the other hand, was the emerging doctrinal formulation simply

---

98. Slipyj, *Tvory* 1:144-50.
99. Schmemann (1978) 236-37.

a compromise between two or more positions. On the contrary, both the party which had stressed the oneness of God at the expense of the distinction among the ὑποστάσεις of the Trinity and the party which had emphasized the distinction but in a way that threatened the oneness were making a valid point, but it was a point that needed to be set into polarity with the other. Therefore the Nicene Creed opened with: "We believe in one God," but went on to make the Son and the Holy Spirit objects of faith in their own right. At work in this process was a principle of truth as complementarity, and a corollary definition of reunification as concord. So it had been above all, according to Soloviev, in the debates over the person of Christ, where either His authentic humanity or His total deity or the genuine integrity of the relation between the two appeared to be in jeopardy, but where the formulas of the Council of Ephesus in 431 and above all of the Council of Chalcedon in 451 had gone beyond the supposed alternatives, but had gone on to concord rather than to compromise. *Bogočlovečestvo* was a doctrinal truth about the two natures in Christ—and therefore also a metaphysical truth about human nature and about the very nature of being.

It appears to be consistent with Soloviev's interpretation of both East and West to see in this understanding of concord the key to the intellectual reunification of the two. Each of the two, in his judgment, needed what the other possessed in isolation, but the exchange and the concord had to be reciprocal. Speaking to a Polish Roman Catholic audience in 1933, Slipyj urged that Byzantine culture and theology could be a "counterweight" to those of the West.[100] Throughout the modern period there has been a continuing Western influence on Eastern Orthodox theology in its methods and even in its theological categories. In examining, for example, the curriculum of Russian Orthodox "spiritual academies" in the nineteenth century, one must be struck by their adoption of courses and of texts that came from the Latin tradition.[101] The same is true of works in dogmatics and catechetics. Not only Feofan Prokopovič, who had for some time adhered to the Latin obedience, but such enormously influential Russian theologians as Filaret (Drozdov) and Makarij of Moscow organized their presentations of Orthodox doctrines on the basis of distinctions borrowed from Latin scholasticism. Despite his own heavy borrowing from Western intellectual sources, especially from German Idealism, however, Soloviev did not see such Thomism as the primary contribution of West

100. Slipyj, *Tvory* 2:120.
101. Makarij (1843) 69-74.

to East; and in this extremely important respect Slipyj, as a faithful Thomist, diverged fundamentally from him.[102] According to Soloviev, that contribution was to come, as he argued in *La Russie et l'église universelle,* from the Western sense of the need for a Catholic order that transcended local and particular traditions. Through his conversations with the Croatian "father of the fatherland," Bishop Josip Juraj Strossmayer—"this dazzling creature," as Rebecca West once called him[103]—Soloviev came to believe that the principle of authority needed an institutional representation, which the historic concept of "pentarchy"—the authority of the five "apostolic" patriarchates— could no longer provide. Rome was the only one of the five able to function as a viable authority and leader.

But Soloviev's and Slipyj's constant refrain was that Rome and the West could not do so by ignoring the Eastern heritage. For although the Latin West in the first five centuries owed much of its intellectual and theological patrimony to the thought of the Eastern church fathers, its relation to Eastern thought had now for a millennium been one of ignorance, as the bibliographies and library catalogues of Western theology, whether Roman Catholic or Protestant, made evident. As a consequence, it had become an occupational disease of Western theologians to turn complementarity into disjunction. The rationalism of such disjunctions had shaped Western doctrinal controversy. Thus in the sixteenth century the question was: Is the presence of the body and blood of Christ in the Eucharist a "real presence" or a "mystical presence"? As Slipyj's exposition of the Roman Catholic Tridentine doctrine of the Eucharist in an Eastern liturgical context also strove to demonstrate,[104] the historic Eastern answer to such Western questions was that it was not a matter of either/or but of both/and. Moreover, according to Soloviev it was not only this or that Western answer that was wrong; the question was wrong, and it would remain wrong until the *Fragestellung* was shaped not by scholasticism but by the liturgy, where both poles of such controversies had come to voice. Concord between East and West, and therefore intellectual and theological conciliation, had to come through the use of a method that would sound the differences to their depths in a common tradition, in which apparently antithetical teachings had existed side by side, not because previous generations of believers and theologians had lacked our

102. See chapter 6, pp. 103-22 below.
103. Rebecca West (1982) 104.
104. Slipyj, *Tvory* 6:353-64.

acuity in recognizing the antithesis but because, while recognizing it, they had possessed—or been possessed by—what the New Testament called "the unity of the Spirit in the bond of peace."[105] Josyf Slipyj learned the deeper meaning of that "unity of the Spirit in the bond of peace"[106] between East and West above all from his spiritual father, Metropolitan Andrej Šeptyc'kyj.

105. Eph. 4:3.
106. Slipyj, Tvory 3/4:79.

5

The Far-Seeing Plans of Andrej Šeptyc'kyj

The most influential figure in the life of Josyf Slipyj was Metropolitan Count Roman Andrej Šeptyc'kyj.[1] He was, Slipyj and his episcopal colleagues of the Ukrainian Synod would declare in 1977, "the initiator, the renewer, the inspirer, and the tireless worker" for all of Ukrainian church life and national life.[2] Šeptyc'kyj has been an object of admiration, but also of puzzlement, throughout the twentieth century.[3] The foreword of Ludwik Bazylow of the University of Warsaw to a recent hostile book about Šeptyc'kyj, written by Edward Prus and published in Poland, expresses that puzzlement in pointed fashion: "A Pole who became a Ukrainian could not, even with his iron nature, avoid being subject to powerful (as it is said nowadays) 'stresses [*stresami*].' "[4] Bazylow goes on to list some of the paradoxes in the long political and

1. Although most of the literature on Šeptyc'kyj, whether scholarly or popular, is in Ukrainian or in Polish, at least two full-length monographs about him have been published in Western languages: Korolevskij (1964) and Prokoptschuk (1967). In addition, I have benefited greatly from Husar (1972), a dissertation that is, unfortunately, still unpublished.

2. Slipyj, *Tvory* 9:299.

3. As is probably evident from my exposition in this chapter, I hope eventually to place a study of Šeptyc'kyj alongside this study of Slipyj, even though the exigencies of my research schedule have dictated that the book on the disciple come before the one on the mentor. Therefore I have, with great reluctance, refrained from using here the materials from his writings that I have been gathering.

4. Prus (1985) 5.

ecclesiastical career of Šeptyc'kyj, charging him with having addressed, at various stages of that career, "obsequious" letters to (among others) Czar Nicholas II, Joseph Stalin, and Adolf Hitler.

Šeptyc'kyj was born not as a Ukrainian Greek Catholic, but as a Polish Roman Catholic aristocrat of Ukrainian blood, who eventually became a Ukrainian metropolitan; even Slipyj, who was concerned to make him out to be as much of a Ukrainian as possible, acknowledged that the Šeptyc'kyj family had "become Polish."[5] Slipyj explained, somewhat defensively, that Metropolitan Andrej's father, "Ivan Šeptyc'kyj, although he had been reared in a Polish spirit [*v pol's'kim dusi*], nevertheless lived according to the traditions of his Ukrainian forebears" and identified himself as a "Ruthenian [*Rusyn*]" (which was a name for the Ukrainians who lived in Galicia and elsewhere in Polish-speaking territories); but even Slipyj acknowledged that the metropolitan's mother Sofija came from the Polish nobility, and that Roman (Andrej) was baptized in a Latin Rite Roman Catholic church.[6] He was born Roman Maria Alexander Szeptycki on 29 July 1865, to a noble family that had for centuries been giving leaders to church and civil state, including two metropolitans of Kiev.[7] After beginning his education at home and at the *Gymnasium* as well as putting in a year of military service, he studied law at the Universities of Kraków, Breslau (today, again, called Wrocław), and Munich, earning the degree of *Doctor Juris.* But his true vocation lay elsewhere, and during the later years of his university study he was already pressing toward a monastic vocation. A parchment in his hand, dated 23 May 1888, preserved in the family archive and quoted by Josyf Slipyj, articulated his sense of that vocation: "In Thy law send forth out of my family in every generation some of its members to serve at Thine altars. Grant the Spirit of love . . . poverty . . . apostleship."[8] In the monastery he adopted the name of Andrej. He took solemn vows as a Basilian monk on 14 August 1892 and was ordained a priest on 22 August of the same year. A scant seven years later, having meanwhile become *ihumen* (prior) of the Basilian monastery in L'viv and then briefly professor of moral theology and dogmatics at Krystynopil', he was appointed bishop of Stanislaviv in 1899, and in the following year (at the age of thirty-five) metropolitan of Halyč and archbishop of L'viv. This position he

5. Slipyj, *Tvory* 13:297.
6. Slipyj, *Tvory* 2:201-3.
7. Nazarko (1960) 89-95, 108-9.
8. Slipyj, *Tvory* 2:218.

held, through several changes of political régime and despite various kinds of imprisonment and harassment, until his death on 1 November 1944.

Arguably, Metropolitan Andrej Šeptyc'kyj was the most influential figure not only in the life of Josyf Slipyj but in the entire history of the Ukrainian Church during the twentieth century, more influential in some ways than Slipyj himself; and there are some who would regard him as the only twentieth-century Ukrainian prelate deserving to be ranked alongside Metropolitan Ilarion of Kiev in the eleventh century and Metropolitan Petro Mohyla of Kiev in the seventeenth.[9] Josyf Slipyj, writing almost two-thirds of a century later, recalled that when he was a schoolboy, his elementary school was visited by Metropolitan Šeptyc'kyj, who undertook to catechize the pupils. The instructor of the class, Father Pljaton Karpins'kyj, pointed to young Josyf, and Šeptyc'kyj asked him for the meaning of the phrase "the communion of saints" in the Apostles' Creed.[10] (He seems to have asked Slipyj the same question a decade or so later at the entrance exercises of the Theological Academy in L'viv.)[11] And when Šeptyc'kyj died on 1 November 1944, it was Slipyj, by then his hand-picked successor, who recited the Church Slavonic "requiem [called *Panachyda* in Ukrainian]" for him.[12]

During the nearly half a century between that first encounter with the metropolitan and that final encounter with him, Slipyj's life was throughout decisively shaped by Šeptyc'kyj. In a highly revealing personal statement Slipyj once said of him:

Already in the *Gymnasium* and after that in the University I dreamt of becoming a university professor, except that I thought that this could be an impediment to my priestly vocation. But when my predecessor, the Servant of God Metropolitan Andrej Šeptyc'kyj, to whom I disclosed the intimate secrets of my soul, sent me to pursue higher studies in Innsbruck, that decided the destiny of my life as a priest. For this I am grateful to him from the depths of my heart, as much as I am to my own parents. And from then on I entered, at least to some extent, into the far-seeing plans and gigantic works [*nei lungimiranti piani e nelle gigantesche*

9. Such is the judgment of Prokoptschuk (1967) 105-7.
10. Slipyj, *Spomyny* 13.
11. Slipyj, *Spomyny* 48; it is, of course, possible that Slipyj's memory was unreliable and confused about the relation between the two events, but since the *Spomyny* were gone over and corrected in his own handwriting it would seem that if there were any such mistake, it should have been corrected in that process.
12. Slipyj, *Spomyny* 103.

opere] of Metropolitan Andrej Šeptyc'kyj in both the ecclesiastical and the social field.[13]

Elsewhere he spoke of Šeptyc'kyj's life as one "full of suffering and difficulty, but high in creativity."[14] He was outstanding not only for his mind, but for his sanctity and for his accomplishments.[15] He was "an ascete and a genius."[16] It was a gratitude that was to stay with Slipyj all his life, as he pointed out in a letter he addressed to Šeptyc'kyj's nephew, Count Jan Szeptycki (who had retained the Polish spelling of the family name), many years later.[17] And on his own eightieth birthday in 1972, he paid eloquent tribute to Šeptyc'kyj.[18] "There was," he said elsewhere, "no area of our life to which he did not put his hand, where he did not help, where he did not create something new, where he did not elevate and accomplish."[19] He was the Moses who had led the Ukrainian people out of captivity.[20]

In 1926, Slipyj published a study which dealt with the most complicated and the most sensitive point of dogmatic difference between the Eastern and the Western churches, the question of whether the Holy Spirit proceeds from the Father only, as the original text of the Niceno-Constantinopolitan Creed seemed to imply when it confessed, "who proceeds from the Father [τὸ ἐκ Πατρὸς ἐκπορευόμενον]," or from both the Father and the Son, as the Western recension of that creed asserted when it declared "who proceeds from the Father and the Son [*qui ex Patre Filioque procedit*]." He dedicated that publication to Šeptyc'kyj in honor of the twenty-fifth anniversary of his episcopate: "To the most worthy metropolitan, and most ardent protagonist of the union of the churches, Count Andreas Szeptyckyj."[21] It was likewise in 1926, for the silver anniversary of Šeptyc'kyj's elevation to the metropolitanate, that Slipyj published in the journal *Bohoslovija* an account of Šeptyc'kyj's early life.[22] And Šeptyc'kyj, in turn, was the one who provided the *imprimatur* (in

13. Slipyj, "Brevi note autobiografiche scritte dal Cardinale Jozyf Slipyj nel 1965," *Arch.Pat.* 32:162.

14. Slipyj, *Tvory* 13:232.

15. Slipyj, *Tvory* 13:299.

16. Slipyj, *Tvory* 14:154.

17. Slipyj to Jan Szeptycki in Johannesburg, 7.v.1963, *Arch.Pat.* 146:14-15; Jan Szeptycki died on 4 June 1980.

18. Slipyj, *Tvory* 13:149.

19. Slipyj, *Tvory* 13:297.

20. Slipyj, *Tvory* 13:337.

21. Slipyj, *Tvory* 1:211; I have kept the spelling of the name as given in that Latin dedication.

22. Slipyj, *Tvory* 2:197-219.

Ukrainian) for Slipyj's monograph of 1925 in observance of the 650th anniversary of the death of Thomas Aquinas.[23] In 1935, for the observance of Šeptyc'kyj's seventieth birthday, Slipyj was the celebrant of the Divine Liturgy at the Theological Academy in L'viv.[24]

Thus when one of Slipyj's captors was to tell him that he was in prison as a replacement for Šeptyc'kyj,[25] that was, somewhat ironically, an acknowledgment of precisely what Slipyj wanted to be—and what he wanted to be acknowledged as being, also by the Soviet authorities:[26] "a worthy successor to the great Metropolitan *Kyr Andrej*."[27] Many years later, the challenges to the legitimacy of his position as metropolitan were still making it necessary for him to seek official documentation from the Vatican to substantiate his appointment.[28] That was a problem that his colleague Bishop Lakota had anticipated when, directly after Šeptyc'kyj's death, he advised Slipyj to secure the pallium from the pope as soon as possible.[29] Therefore when he spoke of "entering, at least to some extent, into the far-seeing plans and gigantic works of Metropolitan Andrej Šeptyc'kyj in both the ecclesiastical and the social field,"[30] he meant that Šeptyc'kyj was to be both his mentor and his model. We cannot rehearse all of Šeptyc'kyj's career and thought in the present context, but must concentrate on those characteristics, actions, and experiences of Šeptyc'kyj that were to prove decisive for Slipyj as his disciple and successor. Many of these were enumerated in the memorial tribute of Pope John Paul II to Josyf Slipyj delivered (in Ukrainian) in Winnipeg, Manitoba, a few days after Slipyj's death, and reprinted (in Ukrainian, with an English translation) as the epigraph to this book. (Many of them are as well the themes for the second part of the present volume.) No less revealing are the contrasts in style and approach between the two metropolitans of L'viv-Halyč, some of them due to differences between the personalities and outlooks of the two men, including differences in their theological outlooks, and others to the exigencies of the constantly changing political and ecclesiastical position of the Ukrainian Church before and after Šeptyc'kyj's death in 1944.

23. Slipyj, *Tvory* 2:35.
24. Slipyj, *Tvory* 3/4:654-55.
25. Slipyj, *Spomyny* 115-16.
26. Slipyj, *Spomyny* 165-66.
27. Laba (1972).
28. See Jean Villot to Slipyj, 26.ii.1972, *Arch.Pat.* 41:74.
29. Slipyj, *Spomyny* 104.
30. Slipyj, "Brevi note autobiografiche," *Arch.Pat.* 32:162.

Slipyj pointed out in his introduction to one of the volumes of the *Monumenta Ucrainae Historica*—a collection of source material patterned after the celebrated *Monumenta Germaniae Historica*, and originally planned and to a considerable degree edited by Šeptyc'kyj—that both he and Šeptyc'kyj contrasted themselves simultaneously with the Latin Roman Catholic West and with the Russian Orthodox East, by engaging in a lifelong campaign of advocacy for distinctively Ukrainian and Eastern Catholic forms of liturgy, of polity, and to some extent even of doctrine.[31] But that polemical stance, for all the vigor with which they both espoused it, must not be permitted to obscure the Western, indeed Germanic, flavor of their upbringing and especially of their formal education and theological-historical scholarship. German thought and German scholarship were highly influential throughout Slavic Europe during the nineteenth century.[32] In his own tribute to Šeptyc'kyj, Professor Adolf W. Ziegler of Munich attests that "he spoke German as only a German could, from Munich, which he knew very well, having studied jurisprudence at the University of Munich in the years 1889-1890."[33] It was a background that would enable him to deal skillfully with the German authorities during the Nazi occupation of Ukrainian territory from 1941 to 1944, and thus to extend the protection of the metropolitan of Halyč to Ukrainian Jews who were threatened by the beginnings of the Nazi Holocaust.

There was, as Władysław Bartoszewski has pointed out, "a group of Lvov's Polish intelligentsia which had its roots in democratic and socialist circles and in the Home Army, and which had been involved in helping the Jews in Lvov since 1941."[34] The members of that group came from various backgrounds, and of course by no means all of them were Greek Catholics. It is nevertheless in that context that Šeptyc'kyj's rescue of Jews is to be viewed. Metropolitan Šeptyc'kyj undoubtedly saved the lives of many Jews, as unsolicited Jewish testimonies to him have declared.[35] (Such testimonies are paralleled by the later tributes of various Jewish fellow prisoners to Metropolitan Slipyj.)[36] One of the testimonies to Metropolitan Andrej deserves to be quoted *in extenso:*

31. Slipyj, *Tvory* 10/11:109 (111).
32. Berlin (1979) 136-49.
33. Prokoptschuk (1967) 9.
34. Bartoszewski (1987) 62; on Lvov, see also pp. 82, 101.
35. The most reliable study of the entire development is Friedman (1980) 176-208.
36. See chapter 8, pp. 166-67 below.

I am a survivor of the Lemberg (Lwow) ghetto and I am familiar with activities of Archbishop Sheptyckyj during the 2nd World War period.

He was one of the greatest men of his time. I know, from the accounts of the people who knew him well, that he did everything in his power to save as many Jews as he possibly could. He also appealed on many occasions (with little success) to the Ukrainian collaborators not to participate in the Jewish holocaust. . . .

Were Archbishop Sheptyckyj alive, after the creation of the State of Israel, he would have [been] hailed there as one of the greatest gentiles, and trees would have been planted in Jerusalem, in his memory.[37]

Yet even that experience was not without its own ambiguities.

Despite his great admiration for Šeptyc'kyj, therefore, even Cyrille Korolevskij felt obliged in his biography to speak of Šeptyc'kyj's "illusions" about the German occupation.[38] Although Šeptyc'kyj in February 1942 addressed a strong and courageous letter to Heinrich Himmler, protesting vigorously against the Nazi persecution of the Jews,[39] it was, unfortunately, not his only communication with the German authorities. Thus Gregor Prokoptschuk described as "shocking [erschütternd]" a letter addressed to Adolf Hitler by a group of Ukrainian leaders, with Šeptyc'kyj's signature as "President of the Ukrainian National Council" at the head of the list.[40] In another letter, addressed this time to Pope Pius XII and from himself alone, Šeptyc'kyj felt moved to declare: "By the victory it has won over Russian Communism, the German Army has rendered a signal service to Christianity, perhaps to all of humanity. . . . If the victory of the Germans remains definite and certain to the end, Bolshevism will cease to exist."[41] One reason for this attitude was certainly the initial posture of tolerance toward the Ukrainian Church manifested by the occupying German forces. That treatment was soon to change to a persecution by the National Socialist West matching any that had come from the Communist East, bringing about what even a somewhat criti-

37. Richard M. Rindner to Leonid Rudnytzky, 16.iii.1979 (copy in the author's possession).

38. Korolevskij (1964) 373.

39. Lewin (1960).

40. Prokoptschuk (1967) 272-74.

41. The text of the letter is reprinted in French in Korolevskij (1964) 373-75. Because he could not decipher the number of the year in the manuscript, next to 29 October as its date, Korolevskij conjectured that the letter was written in 1942; but in the light of Šeptyc'kyj's letter of 29-31 October 1942 (see p. 80, n. 44 below), it may be preferable to assign this letter to 1941.

cal author has called "a sharp change in Sheptyts'kyi's attitude."[42] As Šeptyc'kyj courageously declared to the German military authorities, "Germany is even worse than Bolshevism, [although] National Socialism has more attractiveness for the masses and more power among the youth than Bolshevism does."[43] Or, as he said in another letter to the pope, only recently made public, "gradually the government has instituted a reign of terror and of corruption that is truly incredible ... almost diabolical. ... The Jews are its primary victims."[44]

If Slipyj shared any of the criticisms of the "illusions" of Šeptyc'kyj about the relative threats from Bolshevism and from National Socialism, the available documentation suggests that he apparently kept these to himself. While he did, for example, ascribe "naïveté" to a Ukrainian priest who had unwittingly brought an informer with him when he visited Slipyj's cell,[45] and did criticize Golda Meir for her "naïveté" in giving a list of Jewish dissidents to Soviet foreign minister Vyacheslav Molotov in the hope that he would permit them to emigrate to Israel,[46] he does not seem to have found similar fault with Šeptyc'kyj for his naïveté in dealing with the Germans. On the other hand, his slightly comic account of Šeptyc'kyj's having been taken in by the impostor "Carivna Tatjana [Romanov]," who claimed to have survived the execution of the Russian imperial family at Ekaterinburg on 16 July 1918, does clearly imply a certain naïveté on the part of Šeptyc'kyj, who "received her with open arms" but said nothing to Slipyj "because he knew that I would not be enthusiastic about it."[47] And indeed Slipyj was not the least bit "enthusiastic about it" (to put it mildly), and later on his captors were to use it as part of their case against him.[48]

Yet the positive side of Šeptyc'kyj's Germanic connection was his continuing appreciation for German theological scholarship, which had prompted him to send the young Josyf Slipyj to Innsbruck for postgraduate theological study.[49] That appreciation for learning, which was in Slipyj's words his great "merit [zasluha],"[50] was part of Šeptyc'kyj's profound respect for the place of scholarship and educa-

42. Armstrong (1955) 172.
43. "Unterredungen mit Monseigneur Szepticki, Metropoliten der griechisch-katholischen Kirche zu Lemberg," 19.ix.1943 (copy in the author's possession).
44. Šeptyc'kyj to Pius XII, 29.-31.viii.1942, in Muzyčka (1988) 10-14.
45. Slipyj, Spomyny 182.
46. Slipyj, Spomyny 154.
47. Slipyj, Spomyny 100.
48. Slipyj, Spomyny 197.
49. Slipyj, Spomyny 53.
50. Slipyj, Tvory 10/11:128 (132).

tion in the life of the church and of his commitment to it as a key to the future of the Ukrainian Church.[51] "He collected a great variety of ancient materials of our culture," Slipyj said of him in 1974, and "the creation of the Theological Academy brought about a high level of enlightenment among the clergy."[52] And Metropolitan Šeptyc'kyj was, of course, an honorary member of that Theological Academy.[53] It was, moreover, an adaptation of the characteristically German system when Šeptyc'kyj sought to supply the intellectual and scholarly needs of the church by establishing not only the Theological Academy, but an entire Ukrainian university at L'viv. In an effort to recoup the losses brought about by the Reformation—which had begun in a university—and to bring both the teaching of theology and the training of the clergy under closer church control, the Council of Trent had, in one of its most important reform decrees, mandated the establishment of seminaries in all the dioceses of the church.[54] "With the establishment of the seminary," Slipyj once declared, speaking as a church historian, "begins the rebirth of the Catholic Church."[55] But by a special arrangement in Roman Catholic Germany, theological education there continued to be carried on in the universities, where the faculty of theology stood alongside those of law, medicine, and philosophy rather than in isolation from them, as it evolved in the seminary system elsewhere.[56] Indeed, the deleterious intellectual and professional consequences of such academic isolation were felt in Protestant theology and church life no less than in those of Roman Catholicism.

For Šeptyc'kyj, as later on for Slipyj, the ideal of incorporating the theological faculty in the university was also tied closely to the cultivation of a distinctively Ukrainian national culture.[57] In a remarkable address to the Austrian Parliament in Vienna on 28 June 1910, and then in his memorandum of 15 August 1914 to the Austro-Hungarian government,[58] Šeptyc'kyj affirmed the cultural and religious identity of the Ukrainians. In that address he also stated the case for "the creation of an independent university in L'viv [Lemberg]."[59] Contrasting

51. Slipyj, *Tvory* 14:29.
52. Slipyj, *Tvory* 9:219.
53. Slipyj, *Tvory* 3/4:742.
54. Text of the decree in Alberigo 750-53.
55. Slipyj, *Tvory* 2:265.
56. Merkle (1905).
57. Slipyj, *Tvory* 13:112.
58. Isajiv (1968).
59. The address is reprinted in Prokoptschuk (1967) 133-37. All the quotations that follow in this paragraph are from that address.

the situation of the Ukrainians ("Ruthenians") of Galicia-Halyč within Austria-Hungary—numbering at that time a population of three and one-half million people, they were, after the German-speaking Austrians, the Hungarians, and the Czechs, the fourth largest national group in the Hapsburg Empire—with that of the other national minorities, he found that they lacked even that "minimum of the means for their cultural development" conceded to other groups; the Czechs, for example, still had "Charles University [*Karlová universita*]" in Prague, founded in 1348, at which the German and the Czech faculties existed in uneasy symbiosis. Universities were, Šeptyc'kyj asserted, "the greatest and the most important centers in modern times for cultural and national life," and therefore any nation with cultural aspirations was entitled to have one of its own. He acknowledged with thanks the "genuine religious toleration and assurance of freedom for the development of their culture" that his nation and church had enjoyed in the empire under the Roman Catholic House of Hapsburg.

But Šeptyc'kyj reminded the Austrian authorities that the empire contained the largest group anywhere of adherents to the Union of Florence, who "preserve the worthiest ancient traditions of early Christianity, namely, the principle of the union of the Western and Eastern Churches." A university was, therefore, essential for "the cultural and Catholic-religious development of the Ruthenian nation under the Hapsburg scepter." It was essential as well for its theological development. Josyf Slipyj knew from his study of the history of medieval thought that the University of Paris had played the decisive role in that history.[60] Therefore he prepared himself to become a university professor, in the hope that the government in Vienna would allow the creation of a Ukrainian university.[61] Throughout his life, moreover, he continued to pursue Šeptyc'kyj's ambition of a Ukrainian university, or perhaps a special university for Eastern Rite Catholics.[62] He was convinced that anyone who pondered the state of the Ukrainian Church at home and in the diaspora would have to agree that "the establishment and organization of a Ukrainian Catholic University" was the *summum desideratum*.[63] When it proved impossible to establish (or reestablish) one in L'viv, he would go on to call one into being in Rome—by a

60. Slipyj, *Tvory* 2:64-71.
61. Slipyj, *Tvory* 13:151.
62. Slipyj, *Tvory* 1:407-8.
63. Slipyj, *Tvory* 7:5.

miracle of life out of death that he himself would liken to the word addressed by Jesus to the son of the widow at Nain in the Gospel, "Young man, I say to you, arise!"[64]

In Šeptyc'kyj's own career, but not in Slipyj's, this academic commitment existed alongside, and occasionally in tension with, a monastic vocation; and Šeptyc'kyj somehow managed to combine them.[65] Although Slipyj encouraged, supported, and personally supervised (often in minute detail) the monastic communities of the Ukrainian Church in exile,[66] the contrast between him and Šeptyc'kyj represented by Šeptyc'kyj's monastic profession was perhaps the most striking personal and professional difference between the two. Šeptyc'kyj's decision to become a member of the Basilian Order was closely tied to the program for closer East-West relations that formed a major element of the twenty-five-year pontificate of Pope Leo XIII. According to a transcript of the interview of the Šeptyc'kyj family with the pontiff at a papal audience, written down immediately afterward by Šeptyc'kyj's mother, the pope asked young Roman Šeptyc'kyj: "Are you the one who wants to become a religious?" to which he replied, "Yes, Holy Father, a Basilian," indicating that this had been his intention since childhood. The mission of the Basilians for recovering the relation of the Western Church with the Eastern, Pope Leo declared, was "great and beautiful," and it would now become young Šeptyc'kyj's task in life.[67] According to another account—which was repeated by Slipyj in 1926, during Šeptyc'kyj's lifetime, and which therefore would seem to have been verified by Šeptyc'kyj or even to have come from him— when Roman Šeptyc'kyj communicated that decision to Pope Leo, the pontiff responded, paraphrasing the Vulgate of Luke 10:42, "*Optimam partem elegisti, quae non auferetur a te* [You have chosen the best part, which shall not be taken away from you]."[68] It was as a Basilian that Šeptyc'kyj was transferred to the Eastern, Greek Catholic Rite, from the Latin, Roman Catholic Rite in which his Polish family had reared him.

Slipyj, by contrast, had grown up in the Greek Catholic Rite, and he did not need a monastic vocation to make him part of it. What he did need was a way to realize his long-standing scholarly ambitions, and to put them into the service of the church. Slipyj was, he would admit somewhat sheepishly years later (and after he had in fact become

64. Slipyj, *Tvory* 13:279 (Luke 7:14).
65. Slipyj, *Tvory* 10/11:109 (111).
66. See chapter 9, pp. 186-89 below.
67. Transcribed from family documents in Korolevskij (1964) 28-29.
68. Slipyj, *Tvory* 2:216-17.

a pastor on a global scale), "afraid to become a pastor [*ja nevtoropno bojavsa dušpastyrstva*]" and wanted rather to be a professor, "an aristocrat of the spirit."[69] On the other hand, as the Jewish refugees whom Šeptyc'kyj sheltered from the Nazis also repeatedly observed, Šeptyc'kyj even in his final years retained much of the manner and appearance of a monk. By contrast, when Slipyj was in the concentration camps, he was indeed sometimes recognized as a priest,[70] although he was also sometimes taken to be a high-ranking military officer, perhaps because of his soldierly bearing.[71] But in the camp at Novosibirsk, "when they asked who I was, I said I was a professor"—telling the truth and nothing but the truth, if not quite the whole truth.[72] Slipyj recalled with pleasure the comparison that Thomas Aquinas had drawn between the vocation of the professor and that of the pastor in the church, "to the advantage of the former," and (writing in 1925, when he himself did not yet hold any position in the church hierarchy) he noted that although other scholastics had gone on to appointments in the hierarchy—Peter Lombard was named bishop of Paris, Albert the Great also became a bishop, and Bonaventure was created a cardinal—Thomas had been content to remain a professor.[73]

For Šeptyc'kyj and even more for Slipyj, the combined vocation of professor and prelate decisively shaped their churchmanship. It is clear that Šeptyc'kyj saw the scholarly impoverishment of the Ukrainian Church as a major obstacle to its future development, and he urged the necessity of learning and scholarship, for without it the church would accomplish nothing.[74] Therefore he set Ukrainian scholars, above all the Ukrainian Basilians, to work on rectifying the situation by editing and publishing many volumes of source materials; he worked on these projects personally as well, particularly in connection with the *Monumenta Ucrainae Historica*.[75] Although that work was interrupted by the outbreak of the Second World War, the commitment of the metropolitanate to the scholarly enterprise, identified with the work of Šeptyc'kyj, was honored and even deepened by his successor. The continuity between Šeptyc'kyj and Slipyj in the promotion of theological and historical scholarship was evidenced in the volumes of the journal

69. Slipyj, *Tvory* 13:151.
70. Slipyj, *Spomyny* 132.
71. Slipyj, *Spomyny* 134.
72. Slipyj, *Spomyny* 128.
73. Slipyj, *Tvory* 2:70, 83.
74. Slipyj, *Tvory* 13:237.
75. Slipyj, *Tvory* 10/11:107-65.

Bohoslovija [Theology]: it was established by Šeptyc'kyj in 1924, it was edited by Slipyj until its suspension in 1943, and it was resumed by him in Rome in 1963, soon after his liberation. *Bohoslovija* was intended to become one of the primary vehicles for the development of an indigenous Ukrainian Catholic theology. Although some of the articles published in it during the early years of Slipyj's editorship were not, by any scholarly standards, what Šeptyc'kyj and Slipyj, as products of Germanic theological *Wissenschaft*, would have found acceptable, their commitment to such standards did prevail. It should perhaps be added that some of Slipyj's own articles helped to document what the professional and scholarly aims of Šeptyc'kyj had been in founding the journal. Slipyj deplored what he called "a defect of erudition and an ignorance of their own history" among Ukrainian and other Eastern clergy (including Eastern Orthodox clergy), blaming it for their "proclivity for an alien tradition and a rejection of their own traditions."[76] This made them excessively dependent on scholars who had received their training in Western institutions.[77] He was convinced that "unless we create a scholarly center, one of our own, we shall never attain to a position of our own in philosophical and theological scholarship."[78] Even under the trying circumstances of the Nazi occupation of L'viv in 1941, Slipyj insisted on the enforcement of strict scholarly standards for the theological faculty, and some permanently valuable scholarly publications came out of this period as well.[79]

As the next chapter will suggest, however, the contrast between Šeptyc'kyj and Slipyj as theologians and scholars was not confined to the differences stemming from the distinct vocations of the monk-scholar and the priest-scholar. There is a subtle but unmistakable development in the thought of Metropolitan Andrej Šeptyc'kyj, as a result of which his hold on the special qualities and spirit of Eastern Christendom was steadily deepened. It seems clear that a major component of that development was aesthetic.[80] Šeptyc'kyj had an admiration for the Byzantine religious art of icons and mosaics, and for its transmission and adaptation in Russian Orthodoxy. This is all the more understandable in the light of the surprising art-historical connection between Halyč and the Byzantine tradition; as even Russian art historians have

76. Slipyj, *Tvory* 1:393. See also his later comments in the same essay, *Tvory* 1:395; 407.

77. Slipyj to Paul VI, 26.xii.1964, Slipyj, *Tvory* 12:165.

78. Slipyj, *Spomyny* 68.

79. Slipyj, *Spomyny* 95.

80. See Korolevskij (1964) 337-39.

observed, "the illuminations of the Galich-Volynian Principality are closer to those of Byzantium than similiar examples from northern and central areas of Russia."[81] That admiration was deepened through Šeptyc'kyj's studies and through his travels. He recognized, moreover, that in its fundamental inspiration this Orthodox artistic tradition was liturgical. To be able to claim, in substance and not only in propaganda, that it truly was an Eastern Christianity as Eastern as was Russian *Pravoslavie*, the Ukrainian Church needed to purge itself of the "Latinisms" in ritual that made it a "hybrid." But that was necessary not only, not even primarily, for tactical but for theological reasons: Šeptyc'kyj recognized the leitmotif of the Eastern Orthodox liturgy, as well as of the tradition of Byzantine monasticism embodied in the spirituality and theology of Theodore of Studios, as an expression of the downward movement of the incarnation of the Logos as divinity becoming human, and the upward movement of the new humanity becoming divine through God's gift of "divinization [θέωσις in Greek, *oboženie* in Russian]." These dogmas as such were, of course, not denied in Western doctrinal theology; but the Latin understanding of such theological themes as law and grace, righteousness and justification, had—in the theology of Augustine, of Thomas Aquinas, and for that matter of Martin Luther—taken preeminence over them, so that the incarnation of the divine Logos was affirmed as that which made the atonement possible and divinization was seen as a particularly vivid way of speaking about salvation and forgiveness. Slipyj identified Šeptyc'kyj, together with several Russian Orthodox theologians, as a leader in the neo-Byzantine school of Eastern theology.[82] Conversely, those who attacked Šeptyc'kyj's (and Slipyj's) way of doing theology were identified as anti-Byzantine.[83] Despite his own "Thomism with a Slavic accent," therefore, Slipyj would make Šeptyc'kyj's program of both liturgical and monastic reform his own and would strive to continue and intensify the campaign of purging the "hybridism" out of Ukrainian observance.

For Slipyj also inherited from Šeptyc'kyj the profound conviction that the integrity of Ukrainian Catholicism, and ultimately of Ukrainian Christianity as a whole, both Eastern Orthodox and Catholic,[84] had been, and would continue to be, preserved against all its enemies foreign and domestic only through the dual bond of its loyalty to the Holy See, as af-

81. Popova (1984), Plate 9.
82. Slipyj, *Tvory* 1:397.
83. Slipyj, *Spomyny* 76, 83.
84. Lencyk (1971).

firmed in the Union of Brest-Litovsk, and of its adherence to the Eastern ritual—and through neither of these without the other,[85] since the first had kept it from being absorbed by Russian Orthodoxy and the second had prevented its being swallowed up by Polish Roman Catholicism. Pope Benedict XV, whom Slipyj gratefully remembered as "my personal benefactor,"[86] pointed to the inseparability of the two when, in expressing the pastoral concern of the Papacy for the suffering of the "Ruthenians" in the First World War, he said that the reason for their martyrdom was "their adherence to their own rite."[87] But the Ukrainian or "Ruthenian" rite as Šeptyc'kyj had encountered it at the beginning of his ministry as metropolitan of L'viv-Halyč had been corrupted by "hybridism," and the external pressures were almost totally on the side of still further adaptation of Eastern forms to Western piety and Latin practice. Therefore any attempt to interpret that rite as an authentic expression of the Eastern liturgical tradition faced insurmountable obstacles; for it stood as proof that despite Rome's assurances that it truly was interested in achieving and preserving a Catholic Church that was genuinely "Catholic," not merely "Roman Catholic,"[88] the Latinization of rites continued to be its long-range goal and hidden agenda.

"The disputed legacy of Cyril and Methodius" served as a cautionary tale for Šeptyc'kyj, as it would for Slipyj; for to the detractors of the Union it proved that once the centralized authority of Rome was acknowledged, the distinctive liturgical observances of the Eastern and Church Slavonic patrimony would be surrendered one by one, until there was none left. Except for the actual commemorations of the memory of Saints Cyril and Methodius every year, there was very little of their liturgy surviving in the worship of the Moravia to which they had come. In an effort to reverse that Latinizing tendency, Šeptyc'kyj's liturgical reform, shaped by his own highly refined understanding of Eastern Christian worship, constituted one of his most "far-seeing plans." Indeed, it was in many ways an anticipation of the liturgical legislation incorporated into *Sacrosanctum Concilium*, the Constitution on the Sacred Liturgy promulgated almost twenty years after his death, on 4 December 1963, as the first Constitution published by the Second Vatican Council.[89] Because Metropolitan Slipyj's release from his Soviet

85. Slipyj, *Tvory* 14:94.
86. Slipyj, *Tvory* 13:51.
87. Benedict XV, reprinted in Prokoptschuk (1967) 155-56.
88. On the encyclical *Orientalium dignitas* of Pope Leo XIII, see chapter 4, pp. 58-59 above.
89. See Pelikan (1966) 179-82.

imprisonment had taken place early in the same year, he had not had the opportunity to participate in the initial deliberations and debates over the Constitution on the Sacred Liturgy, but some of his most important subsequent interventions at the Council were concerned with the issues raised in that Constitution as they affected the vital liturgical and spiritual interests not only of the Ukrainian Catholic Church, but of all the Eastern communities in fellowship with the Holy See. And in those interventions it was the liturgical heritage of Andrej Šeptyc'kyj that Slipyj was presenting, even when he did not make explicit reference to his predecessor as metropolitan of L'viv-Halyč. Similarly, Slipyj began already in 1963 to cite the authority and precedent of Šeptyc'kyj in support of his campaign for a recognition of the special "Oriental Code" of canon law for the Eastern Rite churches.[90] At the Synod of Ukrainian Bishops in 1972, Slipyj also invoked the precedent of Šeptyc'kyj's practice of nominating new bishops as a thousand-year-old right of the metropolitan of Kiev-Halyč, which needed to be asserted against the assumption of centralized authority over the Ukrainian Church by "the Apostolic See."[91]

At the same time, the other plank of Šeptyc'kyj's (and Slipyj's) platform for the Ukrainian Church was union with Rome. Between 1914 and 1917 Metropolitan Andrej, who was arrested on 19 March 1914, discussed with various spokesmen for Russian Orthodoxy the grounds for reconciliation between them; in a letter of 24 May 1917 he recorded his impression that discussions of "the Union [of Brest]" (as well as of other divisive issues) were proceeding "better than we had hoped, but slowly."[92] To this Union of Brest the metropolitan (and his successor) clung, in spite of punishments for holding to it and blandishments for deserting it. The unsuccessful attempt to create a "Ukrainian Autocephalous Orthodox Church" after the First World War[93] included the proposal that Šeptyc'kyj become its patriarch. Because of the independence of action accorded to each sovereign church under the principle of autocephaly,[94] this could have become an opportunity to unite all of Ukrainian Christianity and then eventually to lead the united Ukrainian Church back into the Union with Rome, but Šeptyc'kyj would not desert the Union even temporarily.

90. Slipyj to Angelo Dell'Acqua, 27.ix.1963, *Arch.Pat.* 19:179.
91. "Permanent Synod of the Ukrainian Catholic Particular Church," 4.vi.1972, *Arch.Pat.* 73:204.
92. Muzyčka (1983) 25.
93. Polons'ka-Vasylenko (1964).
94. See chapter 3, pp. 43-44 above.

In a letter to Archduke Wilhelm, dated at L'viv 13 June 1918, Šeptyc'kyj wrote:

> I understand that a part of the General Synod of the Ukrainian Church that is to be assembled on the twenty-first of this month is thinking of offering me the dignity of Ukrainian patriarch. In part this step is the affirmation in a concrete manner of the autocephaly of the Ukrainian Church.... But I cannot accept any-thing except an election that is absolutely free, coming from a great majority, and one that gets a canonical validity in accord-ance with the principles of the Eastern Church. It goes without saying that such an election would be tantamount to an accep-tance of the Union. For the moment, the powers that I have received from Pope Pius X can suffice.[95]

Metropolitan Slipyj must certainly have been struck by yet another parallel with his mentor's career when, sometime after his arrest in 1945, he was presented with a document to sign "in which I would renounce the Pope, and for that they would make me [Russian Or-thodox] metropolitan of Kiev"—an offer that was confirmed in 1961 by one of his later judges.[96] Repeatedly in his captivity he was "urged to apostasize" from the Catholic Church, but each time he made it clear that for him, as for Šeptyc'kyj, the Union was not a negotiable item.

Slipyj was to learn during his years of trial and imprisonment just how much of an impression the paradoxes manifested in Šeptyc'kyj's political maneuvering had made on his enemies. For it appeared to Slipyj that one of the principal grounds for the suspicions directed against him by the Soviet authorities was his connection with Met-ropolitan Andrej and with what were called in the summer of 1946 "the alleged 'crimes' of Metropolitan Andrej Šeptyc'kyj."[97] One scholar has summarized the Soviet portrayal of Metropolitan Andrej as follows:

> Sheptyts'kyi is portrayed in the worst possible light: as an Austrian spy, as a fascist, a plunderer of Ukrainian cultural relics, and as committed to Polonization and Germanization of the Ukraine, and as "probably" one of those responsible for the arrest of Lenin at Poronino.[98]

95. As reprinted in Korolevskij (1964) 156; the purported transcript must be read in the light of the extremely curious history of the document as such, described by Korolevskij (1964) 422 n. 26.
96. Slipyj, *Spomyny* 112.
97. Slipyj, *Spomyny* 123-24.
98. Farmer (1980) 202.

Slipyj reported that his Bolshevik accusers took "a very hostile position toward the late Metropolitan Andrej" as an alleged spy against the Czarist régime already during the First World War[99]—the very same Czarist régime that they themselves had overthrown, indeed the same Czarist régime that had arrested Šeptyc′kyj[100]—and that they charged Slipyj with having supported Šeptyc′kyj in his subsequent "counter-revolutionary" activity against the Bolsheviks.[101] Yet the KGB later spread the slander that Slipyj had poisoned Metropolitan Andrej. Šeptyc′kyj′s brother took several physicians to a notary to swear out an affidavit that the metropolitan had died a natural death, but the notary was afraid to do it.[102] At one point Slipyj was told by his captors, under threat of being forced to stand in water or of having his bones broken, that he had to sign a document declaring that "Metropolitan Šeptyc′kyj has committed crimes against the Soviet Union."[103] One of them even told Slipyj that in fact he was being held in prison as a replacement for Šeptyc′kyj, "since he is dead and we cannot punish him."[104]

For Šeptyc′kyj and then for Slipyj, however, the Union of Brest-Litovsk with Rome was not only the countervailing force by which to oppose amalgamation with the Russian Orthodox Church; it was as well the guarantee of universality. To the metropolitan of L′viv-Halyč, that universality meant a responsibility for Ukrainian Catholic faithful everywhere. As Slipyj said of Šeptyc′kyj on the thirtieth anniversary of his death, "not only the Church in Ukraine and in Russia troubled his soul. He looked far more broadly, beyond the European cordon. He was concerned about the fate of our faithful in America" and throughout the world;[105] that included Canada and South America.[106] When Slipyj wrote those words about Šeptyc′kyj in 1974, he himself was engaged in a long-standing campaign to vindicate the authority of the metropolitan of L′viv-Halyč, even in exile, over the Ukrainian diaspora, even over Ukrainians who were living within Roman Catholic dioceses.[107] It was a campaign that went back to the days when Šeptyc′kyj had been metropolitan, and that had some of its origins in

99. Slipyj, *Spomyny* 172.
100. Slipyj, *Spomyny* 54.
101. Slipyj, *Spomyny* 125.
102. Slipyj, *Spomyny* 115.
103. Slipyj, *Spomyny* 117-18.
104. Slipyj, *Spomyny* 115-16.
105. Slipyj, *Tvory* 9:220.
106. Slipyj, *Tvory* 13:298.
107. See chapter 9, pp. 174-81 below.

the predicament of the Ukrainian Church in the Western Hemisphere.[108] The apostolic letter of Pope Pius X, *Ea semper* of 14 June 1907, establishing the ordinariate of Philadelphia for the Ukrainian Rite in North America, had specified that the Ukrainian bishop was required to obtain jurisdiction from all the territorial Latin Rite bishops within whose diocesan borders Ukrainian Catholics lived. This would have subordinated the authority of the Ukrainian Rite everywhere to that of the several local episcopal ordinaries, and therefore would have made the international rôle of the metropolitan of L'viv-Halyč primarily an honorific one.[109] But in the decree *Cum episcopo* of 17 August 1914, issued three days before his death, Pius X undid the damage of *Ea semper* by confirming the authority of the Ukrainian Rite exarch, and the responsibility of the Ukrainian Rite hierarchy was seen as one that transcended diocesan lines. Šeptyc'kyj expressed that responsibility (and authority) by his travels and correspondence with the worldwide Ukrainian community.[110] In his "anxiety for all the churches" before his captivity and especially in his "frequent journeys" after his liberation,[111] Josyf Slipyj affirmed that tradition of Šeptyc'kyj.

Slipyj was to express his filial devotion to "my great predecessor, the Servant of God Metropolitan Andrej,"[112] and to his memory in many ways, including messages to the faithful on the anniversaries of his death. The first opportunity Slipyj ever had to do that came on 1 November 1963, at Saint Peter's in Rome a few months after liberation.[113] His tribute in 1967, when he himself was seventy-five, contained an amusing anecdote about Šeptyc'kyj's great age, when someone asked him, "Do you mean to say that you are still alive?"[114] On 1 November 1969 he once more paid tribute to Metropolitan Andrej,[115] and the following year he spoke of 1 November as a special day on the Ukrainian calendar because of its various associations, but especially because it was the anniversary of Šeptyc'kyj's death.[116] There were tributes again in 1972 and in 1973.[117] Because 22 December 1973 was the thirty-fifth anniversary of Slipyj's consecration as bishop by

108. Mudryj (1973) 109-13.
109. See Heuser (1907).
110. Korovleskij (1964) 85-122.
111. See chapter 11, p. 216 below.
112. Slipyj, *Tvory* 14:195.
113. Slipyj, *Tvory* 12:99-102.
114. Slipyj, *Tvory* 12:255-56.
115. Slipyj, *Tvory* 13:39.
116. Slipyj, *Tvory* 13:72.
117. Slipyj, *Tvory* 13:183; 232.

Šeptyc'kyj, it was a fitting occasion for yet another memoir.[118] But the thirtieth anniversary of Šeptyc'kyj's death in 1974 became the occasion both for an oral presentation in a sermon[119] and for an encyclical letter to Ukrainians everywhere.[120] The following year there was yet another homage to the memory of Metropolitan Andrej.[121] Others followed in later years.[122]

Even during Šeptyc'kyj's lifetime, moreover, Slipyj had erected a monument to him on the grounds of the theological seminary in L'viv, but that was destroyed by the invading Soviet army in 1939.[123] He made up for it by placing the figure of Šeptyc'kyj in the apse of the Church of Saint Sophia in Rome, right between Saints Cyril and Methodius.[124] For Slipyj at any rate, the most important such monument, however, was his participation in the campaign for Šeptyc'kyj's beatification, which he supported with full documentation.[125] The documents of his life, Slipyj wrote, served as "proof of his untiring industry [*joho nevsypuščoji robotjaščosty*] and of his love for his Ukrainian Catholic Church" and should therefore qualify him for beatification and eventual canonization.[126] Beatification has been defined as "the act by which the church *permits* that at certain fixed places . . . a servant of God who has died 'in the odor of sanctity' be honored in public worship with the title 'Blessed.'"[127] The campaign for Šeptyc'kyj's beatification and eventual canonization had been going on already during Slipyj's imprisonment. Thus at the second conference of Ukrainian Catholic Bishops, held at Philadelphia on 2-3 November 1958, while Slipyj was still in the Soviet camps, the Holy See was urged to move toward the beatification "in consideration of the heroic virtues and of all the writings of the Servant of God Andrej Šeptyc'kyj."[128] The motion was repeated at subsequent bishops' conferences, including the one that was held at Winnipeg, Manitoba, the year before Slipyj's liberation.[129]

118. Slipyj, *Tvory* 13:253.
119. Slipyj, *Tvory* 13:296-99.
120. Slipyj, *Tvory* 9:218-22.
121. Slipyj, *Tvory* 13:337.
122. Slipyj, *Tvory* 14:187.
123. Slipyj, *Spomyny* 66, 84.
124. Slipyj, *Tvory* 13:229.
125. Slipyj, *Tvory* 14:125-27.
126. Slipyj, *Tvory* 10/11:147 (148).
127. *LTK* 2-I:493-97 (T. Ortolan, s.v.: Béatification).
128. "Conference of the Ukrainian Catholic Bishops," 2.-3.xi.1958, resolution 21, *Arch.Pat.* 73:8.
129. "Episcopal Conference of the Catholic Bishops of the Byzantine-Ukrainian Rite," 2.-3.vii.1962, *Arch.Pat.* 73:19.

As soon as he was liberated, Slipyj took charge of the proceedings. On 2 March 1963 he wrote a lengthy epistle to the Secretary General of the Holy Office, Alfredo Cardinal Ottaviani, to express his "great sorrow" that the beatification of Šeptyc'kyj had seemed "inopportune," and to send an impassioned plea for it to proceed, on the basis of how much this step would mean "to all my faithful in the Soviet Union."[130] Ten days later he voiced the same sentiments to another cardinal of the church, Arcadio Larraona,[131] and three and a half years later he was still writing to Cardinal Larraona about the matter.[132] Other Vatican officials, too, were importuned, including representatives of the Sacred Congregation of Rites.[133] Ukrainian synods and bishops' conferences continued to agitate for Šeptyc'kyj's beatification as well.[134] In 1971, after the synod of Ukrainian bishops in October had once more urged beatification,[135] Slipyj appointed Stephan Harvanko to succeed Bishop Michael Hrynchyshyn as the "postulator" whose task it would be to press the legal case for beatification.[136] The sequence of volumes in the somewhat desultory work of producing a critical scholarly edition of the writings of Šeptyc'kyj seems at least in part to have been determined by the legal demands of the beatification process.[137] Slipyj did not live to see this process of beatification consummated; but when it is, it will stand as yet another of his memorials to Andrej Šeptyc'kyj, whose "far-seeing plans and gigantic works" and "great genius"[138] had been so decisive in his personal and priestly formation.

130. Slipyj to Alfredo Ottaviani, 2.iv.1963, Arch.Pat. 29:202-10.
131. Slipyj to Arcadio Larraona, 12.iv.1963, Arch.Pat. 28:225.
132. Slipyj to Arcadio Larraona, 29.ix.1966, Arch.Pat. 35:280.
133. Slipyj to Pietro Amato Frutaz, 11.x.1965, Arch.Pat. 33:169.
134. "Archiepiscopal Synod under the Direction of Major Archbishop and Cardinal Kyr Josyf," 1969, resolution 16, Arch.Pat. 73:90.
135. Slipyj, Tvory 13:129.
136. Slipyj to Stephan Harvanko, 27.xi.1971, Arch.Pat. 40:386.
137. Slipyj, Tvory 10/11:147 (148); 14:222.
138. Slipyj, Tvory 13:297.

Part Two

The Vocations of Josyf Slipyj

Profile of a Confessor

The ecclesiastical context of Josyf Slipyj's life, which has been the primary object of our investigation up to this point, is reasonably well documented—thanks in part to the assiduous fostering of scholarly editions and monographs from Ukrainian history that he himself had encouraged and sponsored throughout most of his life.[1] In that sense the history of the Ukrainian Church is somewhat exceptional, for the general situation of Ukrainian historiography is more accurately described in the opening sentence of a learned and perceptive essay by a leading scholar, who has surveyed the state of archival collections in various of the republics of the Soviet Union, and has charted in her earlier books the formidable difficulties encountered by historical scholars in other Soviet archives.[2] With that background, Patricia Kennedy Grimsted has recently expressed the judgment that "Ukrainian historians, or historians of Ukraine, have had a difficult time writing Ukrainian history because it is difficult and often impossible to gain access to the basic archival sources needed."[3] "One of the most difficult problems in trying to deal with archives in the area now constituting the Ukrainian SSR," she continues a little later, "is that the territories in question never constituted a single political entity before 1945, and more precisely, if one includes the Crimean oblast, before 1954." As a result, "the records of actual Ukrainian provenance themselves, or more broadly of Ukrainian pertinence, have been the result of, and are subject to, a wide variety of local archival traditions and divergent record-keeping practices in different regions."[4]

The ecclesiastical career of Josyf Cardinal Slipyj, as distinguished from his ecclesiastical context, is subject to all of the problems itemized by Patricia Kennedy Grimsted, as well as to the additional special problems created by the events of his own life, as a result of which "the archival legacy of Josyf Slipyj" presents an even more chaotic and lopsided picture than do the archives of Ukrainian history in general. On the one hand, the final two decades of Slipyj's life are the subject of an entire archive in Rome, which contains several hundred volumes and literally thousands of documents. Apparently he, or his archivists, saved all the requests for tickets to papal audiences he ever received from cler-

---

1. See chapter 7, pp. 141-42 below.
2. See Grimsted (1972) and Grimsted (1981).
3. Grimsted (1985) 1.
4. Grimsted (1985) 5.

gy and faithful during those two decades, every Christmas card as well as the saint's day cards he exchanged with others named Joseph, including József Cardinal Mindszenty of Budapest and Josef Cardinal Beran of Prague. Yet for the data of his personal biography, especially for those of his early life, as distinct from the data pertaining to his ecclesiastical career, we are largely—most of the time, indeed, exclusively—dependent on the scraps of information that appear as *obiter dicta* in his own later correspondence, and on the autobiographical memoirs that he himself prepared from time to time during those same later years, chiefly in Ukrainian but sometimes also in Italian or German; among the most interesting of these from the personal perspective are his rather extensive remarks on the occasion of his eightieth birthday, 17 February 1972,[5] and the somewhat briefer autobiographical reflections on the thirtieth anniversary of his accession as metropolitan, delivered on 2 November 1974,[6] and on his eighty-fifth birthday, 17 February 1977.[7]

In the longest of these memoirs he himself notes that he did "not have in my possession any documents at all" from his childhood.[8] For reasons to be considered in greater detail later,[9] that lacuna extends through most of the years of his life before his release from imprisonment and his arrival in Rome. The journals of his early travels were largely lost, as he put it, "through the ravages of time [*iniuria temporis*]."[10] Also for the years of Slipyj's imprisonment, the documentation—or, at any rate, the documentation to which a scholar can gain access at the time of this writing—is sparse.[11] At the request (or the command) of the authorities, Slipyj wrote an autobiography while he was in prison,[12] but that does not seem to have survived. The various official collections of charges against him, with whatever documentary support they may have had,[13] seem likewise to have disappeared from sight. What has recently been said about the biography of Slipyj's contemporary, Anthony Eden, applies *a fortiori* to his: "For the biographer, speculation on how matters might have been different is one of the most perilous of indulgences."[14]

5. Slipyj, *Tvory* 13:148-53.
6. Slipyj, *Tvory* 13:299-301.
7. Slipyj, *Tvory* 14:139-41.
8. Slipyj, *Spomyny* 9.
9. See chapter 8, pp. 146-48 below.
10. Slipyj, *Tvory* 13:50.
11. Slipyj, *Spomyny* 187.
12. Slipyj, *Spomyny* 161-62.
13. Slipyj to N. V. Podgorny, 17.ii.1961, *Arch.Pat.* 28:90 (125).
14. James (1987) 29.

Therefore also, what Slipyj had once said about Thomas Aquinas is, for rather different reasons, at least as true of him as well: "About the details of the life of Thomas we know precious little [*duže malo*]."[15] Although there is a considerable literature about Cardinal Slipyj, including a martyrological biography in Ukrainian entitled *The Invisible Stigmata*, consisting largely of excerpts from newspapers translated from various languages into Ukrainian,[16] a proper biography of Josyf Slipyj in the usual historiographical sense of that word is impossible. What is possible is a historical portrait—or rather a series of portraits—of several of the principal vocations of his lifetime as they appeared and then were reflected in the feverish activity of his final years; for the idea of his life as a vocation seems to have been strongly in his mind right after his liberation.[17] Those vocations took their rise at particular times, and in that sense they can be treated chronologically here; Slipyj himself suggested, on his eightieth birthday, that his life had been divided into three stages of roughly twenty-five years each: as a student, as a professor and rector, and as a prisoner.[18] But the continuities of vocation that Josyf Slipyj manifested amid the catastrophic discontinuities to which the vicissitudes of his life subjected him require that each of them be followed here from the time it took its rise to its final configuration. As he affirmed concerning himself in a letter to Pope John Paul II, the emphasis of this book must lie "not on my own person," but on these vocations.[19] It was an accent that he would continue, also in the battles over the patriarchate.[20] "Not about my own person, but about our church" was also how Slipyj described the content of his reflections while in prison, when he seems to have planned out, sometimes in great detail, much of the grand strategy he would follow in his divine vocation as its metropolitan if he were ever to be released.[21] As his editors have noted, that experience was the crucible of his later career.[22]

In characterizing him in the title of this book as "Confessor between East and West," we are following a precedent set already during Slipyj's lifetime by previous writers about him and by Slipyj himself.

15. Slipyj, *Tvory* 2:67.
16. Rudnyc'ka (1971).
17. Slipyj, *Tvory* 12:39.
18. Slipyj, *Tvory* 13:149.
19. Slipyj to John Paul II, 5.ix.1980, *Arch.Pat.* 118:165.
20. For example, Slipyj, *Tvory* 13:152-53; 283.
21. Slipyj, *Spomyny* 192.
22. Slipyj, *Tvory* 12:5-6 (11-12).

He was saluted as "confessor" on 19 October 1963, a few months after being set free,[23] and as "metropolitan confessor" the following year.[24] The Jesuit theologian Wilhelm DeVries wrote a brief biographical memoir about him in German, entitled "Cardinal and Major Archbishop Josyf Slipyj, a Confessor of the Catholic Faith."[25] Slipyj described the history of the Ukrainian Church, especially under the leadership of Metropolitan Andrej Šeptyc'kyj, as "the pilgrimage of a confessor [ispovidnycka put']",[26] and the Ukrainian Church as a church of confessors and martyrs.[27] In his Testament he thanked God "for having given me the grace of being a witness to and a confessor of Christ."[28] And a few days after the death of Josyf Slipyj, Pope John Paul II himself, in his memorial tribute, called the Cardinal (in Ukrainian) "ispovidnyk viry [Confessor of the Faith]."[29] "Confessor [ὁμολογητής]" was a quasi-technical term in patristic theology for one who had been "under persecution" or "under sentence of death . . . , suffering mutilations and forced labor," but who did not in fact die a martyr's death.[30] Although it has been applied to various figures from church history,[31] it acquired special significance by its association with Saint Maximus "the Confessor," who was, as it happens, "a member of that small and select group of saints of the church who belong almost equally to the Western and to the Eastern traditions of Christian spirituality"[32] and who therefore has a particular relevance to this investigation of conflict and concord between East and West as reflected in the life and thought of Josyf Slipyj. Slipyj recalled that Maximus had "spent a long time in the West and learned to know the Latin explanation of the Trinity" and of other doctrines—as, of course, would Slipyj himself.[33] Although Maximus was ignorantly blamed by some medieval theologians for various heresies, including that of Abélard,[34] it was in fact, Slipyj noted elsewhere, Maximus the Confessor who had "purified the works of Pseudo-Dionysius the Areopagite of their

23. Slipyj, Tvory 12:102.
24. Slipyj, Tvory 12:149-50.
25. Reprinted in Slipyj, Tvory 10/11:9-13.
26. Slipyj, Tvory 13:323.
27. Slipyj, Tvory 14:117.
28. Slipyj, Tvory 14:474.
29. See the epigraph to this volume, pp. ix-x above.
30. Lampe (1961) 957.
31. NCE 4:141-42 (Edward Byron Day, s.v. Confessor).
32. Pelikan (1985) 1.
33. Slipyj, Tvory 1:139.
34. Slipyj, Tvory 1:254 n. 1.

Neoplatonism"[35] and who had thus rescued later thinkers from heresy.[36] Maximus had died in the regions of the Black Sea now identified as Ukrainian.[37] With the title, *"Maksim Ispovidnyk,"* therefore, Maximus also appears in a mosaic at Slipyj's church, Saint Sophia in Rome. Significantly, the standard Ukrainian manual of patrology—a book that Slipyj sponsored[38]—declares of him: "Maximus the Confessor belongs to the very greatest thinkers of the Eastern Church."[39]

"Sluha Božij [Servant of God]" was, and is, the title used by Slipyj and his faithful for Andrej Šeptyc'kyj, in anticipation of his beatification;[40] but *"ispovidnyk viry* [Confessor of the Faith]" would seem to be the most appropriate title for Slipyj himself, as he called himself (in Italian) in an address to Pope Paul VI[41]—or, as he put it in 1973 while describing a colleague, "a confessor for Christ, for the church, for unity, and for the Apostolic See."[42]

35. Slipyj, *Tvory* 1:404.
36. Slipyj, *Tvory* 2:117.
37. Slipyj, *Tvory* 13:328 (329-30).
38. See chapter 7, pp. 139-40 below.
39. Laba (1974) 430.
40. See chapter 5, pp. 91-93 above.
41. Slipyj, *Tvory* 14:125.
42. Slipyj, *Tvory* 13:226.

6

Svjatyj Toma z Akvinu: Thomism with a Slavic Accent

Throughout his life, and especially during his later years and at the Second Vatican Council, Josyf Slipyj was known everywhere as a passionate spokesman for the distinctive traditions of Eastern Christianity. Therefore it may seem surprising to discover that when Slipyj identified the historical sources of Slavic theology as "Holy Scripture, the liturgy, the works of Saint Gregory Nazianzus, and other works of the Eastern tradition,"[1] he was not giving an account primarily of his own theological education and intellectual formation. For his own roots were more complex: within that triad of sources he would have had to substitute the name of Saint Thomas Aquinas for the name of Saint Gregory Nazianzus; on the other hand, more than most other Thomists of his time he would have needed to cite the liturgy (meaning thereby the Eastern liturgy, as recited in Old Church Slavonic) as a determining force in his thought; and yet his own scholarly work on Scripture, in his doctoral dissertation of 1918 at Innsbruck, was almost completely devoid of Eastern emphases, including the Eastern emphasis on the liturgy as a hermeneutical principle.

The tension represented by that complex interrelation between Thomism and the East was an undercurrent throughout his years as a student, and it was to recur throughout his career as a theologian and

---

1. Slipyj, *Tvory* 5:90.

churchman. It is even given iconographic expression in the mosaics of the Church of Saint Sophia, which Slipyj would build in Rome; many decades after his formal study of Thomas Aquinas, that church was to contain an Eastern-style mosaic of Thomas as well as of Augustine, along with the customary Eastern representations of "Saint Gregory Nazianzus and other [spokesmen] of the Eastern tradition." Some of his Ukrainian critics, whom he accused of collaboration not only with Russian Orthodoxy but with Russian Communism, attacked him for his adherence to scholasticism, which they regarded as a betrayal of the Eastern and Slavic tradition.[2] Even at the end of his life, his young seminarians used to refer to Josyf Slipyj affectionately as "a Thomist in a *klobuk*," a reference to the distinctive headgear of a Ukrainian clergyman that he would often wear. He was an Eastern Slavic disciple of the theologian he called—in the title of a monograph published in 1925, but apparently written for the commemoration at L'viv, the year before, of the 650th anniversary of the death of Thomas Aquinas[3]—"Svjatyj Toma z Akvinu."[4]

The dichotomy between East and West, symbolized by those seemingly incongruous combinations, runs through the entire history of Slipyj's life. Unlike the Polish-born Roman Catholic Roman Andrej Šeptyc'kyj, in whose thought the tension between East and West also appears but in a different configuration,[5] Slipyj was born directly into the tradition of Eastern spirituality, although there had been Roman Catholics as well as Greek Catholics in his family.[6] The record of the Greek Catholic parish in Zazdrist', where he was born on 17 February 1892, apparently contained an erroneous notice of his real name. In 1944 Volodymyr Tarnopil'skyj, then the parish priest in Zazdrist', wrote to Slipyj that "it can in fact be asserted with moral certainty that your real surname is Kobernyckyj." Father Tarnopil'skyj had learned this from a certain Nykola Dyčkovskyj, who had died in 1930 at the age of eighty. According to Dyčkovskyj, "your grandfather and great-grandfather" had acquired the name "Slipyj" (which means "blind" in Ukrainian), because of a history of severe eye trouble which ran in the family; and so the name "Slipyj" had passed into the records. The people of the parish had nevertheless continued to call Josyf's father and brothers "Kobernyckyj." When his father was orphaned, he had been adopted

2. Slipyj, *Spomyny* 81.
3. Slipyj, *Spomyny* 62.
4. Slipyj, *Tvory* 2:29-100.
5. See chapter 5, pp. 85-87 above.
6. Slipyj, *Spomyny* 5.

by Roman Dyčkovskyj, so that the entire family carried that name as well; it was likewise the maiden name of Josyf's mother.[7]

"Zazdrist'," Slipyj would later recall, "lies on a high plain between Seret and Zbruč, near the town of Strusiv in the Terebovel'skyj district. From there it is very easy to see the Terebovel'skyj and Strusivs'kyj hills, covered with forests."[8] (At the end of the First World War, Slipyj returned to Zazdrist', to find it in ruins.[9]) He recalled as well that in his parental home there had been "numerous icons of the saints" and that as a small child he had "learned to make the sign of the cross" (presumably from right to left, according to the Eastern fashion) and to recite the daily prayers.[10] His mother had a special devotion to the Mother of God and to the Immaculate Conception. That was why he selected the Feast of the Immaculate Conception for his consecration as bishop in 1939.[11] He also maintained a deep personal attachment to the dogma of 1854 by which the doctrine of the Immaculate Conception had become official.[12]

"Not having in my possession any documents at all," Slipyj wrote in 1963, "I estimate that I began going to school most likely in the year 1898/1899."[13] At the age of nine or ten he was sent away to continue his schooling in Vyšnivčyk, because the school there had four grades; the fourth grade was in German, but the school still preserved a Ukrainian identity and had a Ukrainian principal, whereas the school closer to home "had a Polish character." From the very beginning of his elementary education, then, Josyf Slipyj was to learn the lesson of linguistic minorities everywhere, that for him as an Eastern Slav to get along in the world it would be necessary to acquire one or more Western languages: after his native Ukrainian came Polish, then German, then the rudiments of Latin. As a further step of his induction, already during his childhood years, into the problem of East-West relations, he also remembered seeing a Byzantine-style church and monastery in Strusiv, which, during "the Latinizing period" under the Austrian Emperor Joseph II, had been transformed into a Latin church—a case of architectural and liturgical "hybridism" that seems even then to have made an impression on him.[14]

7. Volodymyr Tarnopil'skyj to Slipyj, 15.xi.1944, *Arch.Pat.* 28:18-19.
8. Slipyj, *Spomyny* 1.
9. Slipyj, *Spomyny* 55.
10. Slipyj, "Breve note autobiografiche," *Arch.Pat.* 32:161.
11. Slipyj, *Spomyny* 86.
12. Slipyj, *Tvory* 13:252-54; 345-47.
13. Slipyj, *Spomyny* 9.
14. Slipyj, *Spomyny* 22, 29.

The linguistic preparation begun in elementary school and continued between 1903 and 1911 in the *Gymnasium* at Ternopil'—where he improved his Latin, added French, and then went on to Greek as well—stood him in good stead in his later university studies. The German was necessary at Innsbruck, and after that he made use of the Latin at the Gregorian University in Rome. Already in the *Gymnasium* he had a sense of being caught between his desire to become a priest and his equally keen interest in scholarship: "I cherished the idea [*Ja lelijav dumku*] that I could be not only a priest, but also a professor" and have it both ways, he later acknowledged;[15] the one thing he was quite sure he did not want to be was a parish pastor.[16] Although, when he applied for admission to theological study at L'viv, most of the seminarians were intent on the pastoral ministry (and on marriage) and did not share Slipyj's interest in scholarship, that interest did receive further support and cultivation also in his seminary years, for it was at L'viv that he was first introduced to scholastic philosophy and theology, which was to prove so decisive for his intellectual and scholarly development.

Recognizing the true vocation and scholarly potential of the young seminarian, Metropolitan Andrej Šeptyc'kyj directed him to continue his studies at Innsbruck. As Slipyj put it (in words already quoted earlier),

> Already in the *Gymnasium* and after that in the University I dreamt of becoming a university professor, except that I thought that this could be an impediment to my priestly vocation. But when my predecessor, the Servant of God Metropolitan Andrej Šeptyc'kyj, to whom I disclosed the intimate secrets of my soul, sent me to pursue higher studies in Innsbruck, that decided the destiny of my life as a priest. For this I am grateful to him from the depths of my heart, as much as I am to my own parents.[17]

Although Slipyj had already been attending some university lectures while a seminarian at L'viv, it was in Innsbruck that for the first time he came to know by personal experience what a real university and real university-quality research could be.[18] It was a standard that was to remain with him for the rest of his life. Innsbruck was one of the first

15. Slipyj, *Spomyny* 46.
16. Slipyj, *Tvory* 13:151.
17. Slipyj, "Brevi note autobiografiche," *Arch.Pat.* 32:162.
18. Slipyj, *Spomyny* 53-54.

places to which Slipyj was invited after his release from prison.[19] Similarly, he would always cherish the memory of his graduate study at the Gregorian University, an Alma Mater "so great, so famous, and so dear to my heart," deriving comfort during his imprisonment from the recollection of his professors and schoolmates there.[20] He spoke with special admiration and fondness of the "supremely profound"[21] scholarship of the Belgian Jesuit Alphonse Delattre.[22] During his later years, as for example upon his receiving the red hat as cardinal in 1965, that bond with the *Gregorianum* was preserved.[23]

Two of the three major scholarly works that came out of these years of university study at Innsbruck and Rome dealt with the East-West dichotomy, but the first of the three did not. For his doctorate, which he received at Innsbruck in 1918, Slipyj wrote a dissertation on the concept of "life" in the Gospel and First Epistle of John.[24] Some years later, he voiced his regret "that Eastern scholars did not give more diligent attention to biblical studies, since because of their knowledge of the languages they could have carried it out without much effort."[25] The latter half of that statement was, of course, a reference not to Slavs, but specifically to Greek scholars for the New Testament and to at least some Near Eastern scholars for the Old Testament; but the first half was, unfortunately, an accurate description of all Eastern Christian scholarship. In such a statement Josyf Slipyj was no doubt reflecting the experience of his own research as a doctoral candidate. Indeed, it was not only the lack of Eastern (not to say Eastern Catholic) scholarship that he had to lament:

> As far as the [scholarly] literature is concerned, we are, regretfully, unable to mention any Catholic work on this specific topic, for in fact there has not appeared a book or even an article dealing with it. Our theme has received more attention from Protestants, and their investigations have been considered here. The principal source for our own investigation is to be found in the Catholic commentaries.[26]

19. Slipyj to Angelo Dell' Acqua, 21.x.1963, *Arch.Pat.* 29:250; see also Slipyj, *Tvory* 12:103-4.

20. Slipyj to Paolo Muñoz Vega, 19.iii.1963, *Arch.Pat.* 117:15a.

21. Slipyj, *Spomyny* 57.

22. See *DTC*, "Tables générales," 3:919, for a brief bio-bibliography of Delattre.

23. Paolo Muñoz Vega to Slipyj, 25.i.1965, *Arch.Pat.* 117:57; Slipyj to Paolo Muñoz Vega, 29.i.1965, *Arch.Pat.* 117:58.

24. Slipyj, *Tvory* 1:29-90.

25. Slipyj, *Tvory* 1:405.

26. Slipyj, *Tvory* 1:32.

In the light of the state of Roman Catholic biblical scholarship throughout the church in the period before the First World War, or perhaps even until the issuance of the encyclical *Divino afflante Spiritu* by Pope Pius XII in 1943,[27] that lament is understandable.

Less clear, however, especially by contrast with Slipyj's (and Šeptyc'kyj's) emphasis on the patristic sources of Christian theology, whether Eastern or Western, including the patristic sources of such Western exegetical classics as the *Catena aurea* of Thomas Aquinas,[28] is the almost total absence of any reliance on the church fathers, whether Greek or Latin, in Slipyj's own exegetical monograph. Some years later, discussing the problematical exegetical foundation for the Western doctrine of the *Filioque*, he was to criticize the Italian Roman Catholic scholar Vincenzi for "paying little attention to the tradition" in his "exegesis of 'ὁ παρὰ πατρὸς ἐκπορεύεται' (John 15:26)."[29] But in his own exegesis of key passages in which the Gospel of John and the First Epistle of John spoke about "life," Slipyj paid considerably less attention to the patristic exegetical tradition than Vincenzi had. For example, in the light of the effect that Augustine's interpretations of the eucharistic references to "the bread of life" in the sixth chapter of the Gospel of John have had throughout Western theological history,[30] some consideration of these Augustinian interpretations would appear to have been germane to the theme of Slipyj's monograph on the concept of "life." Slipyj did interpret that chapter as a reference to the Eucharist, but without a discussion of the contradictions in Augustine.[31] Later on, in his first teaching assignment as a professor at L'viv,[32] which consisted of lectures in dogmatics dealing with the doctrine of the sacraments, he would concern himself specifically with the most disturbing among the Augustinian statements about the Eucharist,[33] and he did of course continue to apply that chapter to the Eucharist.[34] Here in his dissertation on Saint John he did cite Augustine's exegesis of John 1:4 and of John 2:19-21, and (by way of a secondary source) of John 5:26.[35]

Of the Greek fathers, Clement of Alexandria and Irenaeus ap-

27. *AAS* 35 (1943):297-325.
28. Slipyj, *Tvory* 2:76.
29. Slipyj, *Tvory* 1:109 n. 78.
30. Pelikan (1971) 1:304-6; 3:218-19; 4:196-97.
31. Slipyj, *Tvory* 1:67-72.
32. Slipyj, *Spomyny* 60.
33. Slipyj, *Tvory* 6:223-24.
34. Slipyj, *Tvory* 14:148.
35. Slipyj, *Tvory* 1:46, 51, 62.

peared as authorities on Gnostic heresy.[36] Ignatius of Antioch appeared in a footnote;[37] and the *Commentary on the Gospel of Saint John,* written by Cyril of Alexandria sometime before 429,[38] seems to have been consulted only in connection with that troublesome sixth chapter.[39] Nor did Slipyj's exegesis reflect the differences of emphasis between the Greek and the Latin traditions in their interpretations of the saving power of the death of Christ, the centrality of the resurrection and of *Christus Victor* in Eastern pictures of redemption, as contrasted with the Latin emphasis on the death of Christ as vicarious satisfaction, as that emphasis had been systematized in the *Cur deus homo* of Anselm of Canterbury but anticipated by various of the Latin fathers.[40] Instead, he insisted, in opposition to several (Protestant) exegetes, that the Gospel of John did indeed teach the Anselmic idea of expiatory sacrifice.[41] Elsewhere he summarized the theological argument of *Cur deus homo* on the vicarious atonement without expressing any criticism of it at all, though he did criticize the "ontological argument" of Anselm for the existence of God; in that criticism of Anselm he was echoing the objections to it that had been raised by Thomas Aquinas.[42] In later years he seems to have gone beyond Anselm to a more characteristically Eastern view of the atonement, as when he asserted in 1977 that Christ had died in order to be resurrected.[43]

On at least one exegetical problem in the Gospel of John, however, Slipyj's monograph did consider, at least implicitly, the dogmatic differences between East and West. Twice in the dissertation he discussed the question of whether the Father or the Son was, in the language of the Fourth Gospel, the source of spiritual "life," concluding that "while the other apostles refer to the Father as the sole source from which everything flows, Saint John regards the Son as the fullness of life in which we all participate."[44] In the light of his later writings, that would seem to be an anticipation of his discussions of the differences between the Greek and the Latin fathers in their treatments of the *Filioque,* to which he turned in his *Habilitationsschrift* of 1923.[45] This dealt with the

36. Slipyj, *Tvory* 1:38.
37. Slipyj, *Tvory* 1:51 n. 36.
38. Quasten (1951) 3:123.
39. Slipyj, *Tvory* 1:71.
40. The classic interpretation of that difference is Aulén (1969).
41. Slipyj, *Tvory* 1:55-58.
42. Slipyj, *Tvory* 2:55.
43. Slipyj, *Tvory* 14:144.
44. Slipyj, *Tvory* 1:51, 61.
45. Slipyj, *Spomyny* 56.

trinitarian doctrine of the Byzantine patriarch Photius, the principal Eastern figure in the ninth-century schism over the *Filioque*.[46] For the degree of *Magister aggregatus* at the Gregorianum in 1924, furthermore, Slipyj turned to the question again.[47] In his dissertation there he analyzed the fundamental metaphysical and theological issue in the *Filioque*, the "spiration" of the Holy Spirit from the Son as well as from the Father—yet from only one *"principium"* or *"ἀρχή."*[48]

From Rome Slipyj returned to L'viv to begin his duties as a professor and to press on with his scholarly vocation, which, in keeping with his dual calling as churchman and as scholar, became as well "the reform of theological studies."[49] Especially as he began to take over more and more of the duties of Metropolitan Andrej, as he explained to Pope Paul VI in 1963, "I terminated work on my books in dogmatics, the volume on the history of medieval philosophy. . . . Thereafter I was completely dedicated to the affairs of the metropolitanate."[50] But the intellectual and theological foundations for his entire subsequent career, and for all of his subsequent vocations, had been laid here, in what Pope Paul, writing through his Secretary of State, called his "powerful contribution to theological scholarship."[51] Another Roman colleague was to refer to these theological works as "learned dissertations" and as "your profound studies as a young man."[52] And it was in these dissertations and studies, together with a group of shorter but important monographs and scholarly articles on related theological issues, that his "Thomism with a Slavic accent" was spelled out.

The Eastern component of Slipyj's theological thought is evident from his frequent use of the Greek church fathers. His most substantial mature work of dogmatic theology, a full-length treatment of the doctrine of the sacraments, came out of his first teaching assignment right after his appointment to the faculty at L'viv.[53] In it he made a point of urging more serious attention to the Eastern doctrine of the Eucharist, as set forth in the Liturgies of Saint James and Saint Basil and as expounded in the *Mystagogy* or *Catechetical Lectures* of the fourth-

46. Slipyj, *Tvory* 1:91-158.
47. Slipyj, *Spomyny* 57-59.
48. Slipyj, *Tvory* 1:211-331.
49. See chapter 7, pp. 123-24 below.
50. See chapter 9, pp. 172-73 below.
51. Jean Villot to Slipyj, 5.x.1974, *Tvory* 6:5.
52. Angelo Dell'Acqua to Slipyj, 4.iv.1968, *Arch.Pat.* 37:109. The letter was written on the occasion of the publication of the first volume of Slipyj's collected works *(Tvory)*, which, except for a few footnotes, all appeared in Western languages.
53. Slipyj, *Spomyny* 60.

century Greek church father, Saint Cyril of Jerusalem.[54] As he had observed already in his early work, it was a characteristic of Eastern theology, even more than of Western theology, to "move actively within the patristic circle of thought."[55] Even without resorting to an index of citations from the church fathers, it seems safe to estimate that he quoted from them far oftener than most of his Roman Catholic theological contemporaries were doing. He seems to have made it a point, moreover, usually to quote from them in the original Greek, and he lamented the ignorance of Greek among past and present Western theologians (as well as the corresponding ignorance of Latin among Eastern theologians).[56] Thus in probing the origins of the conflict over the *Filioque,* he reminded Western, Latin-speaking theologians of the richness and variety of theological terminology in Greek, precisely for such a controverted issue as the procession of the Holy Spirit: whereas Latin had basically only the one term *procedere,* Greek had, "in addition to ἐκπορεύεσθαι, other words besides, such as προϊέναι, προέρχεσθαι, χορηγεῖσθαι, προχεῖσθαι, ἐκλάμπειν, ἀναβλύζειν, etc."[57] For all his admiration of Augustine, Slipyj blamed the dominance of Augustinianism in Western theology for the inability (perhaps even the unwillingness) of Western theologians to understand the primary concerns of the Greek fathers.[58]

On the other hand, he could not help pointing out that most of the scientific contributions to the theological understanding of the Eastern tradition had in fact come from Western scholars.[59] That included Western scholars of Eastern liturgy and culture as well as of Eastern theology as such.[60] On the Roman Catholic side there had been the great editions of the Greek fathers, beginning already with Erasmus but climaxing in the work of the Maurists, whose editions of Basil the Great and John Chrysostom became standard and were incorporated into the Abbé Migne's *Patrologia Graeca.*[61] And although Slipyj was critical of the patristic scholarship of the liberal Protestant historical theologian Adolf von Harnack,[62] he found substantiation in Harnack's *His-*

54. Slipyj, *Tvory* 6:362.
55. Slipyj, *Tvory* 1:122.
56. Slipyj, *Tvory* 1:406-7.
57. Slipyj, *Tvory* 1:107-8.
58. Slipyj, *Tvory* 1:151.
59. Slipyj, *Tvory* 1:407.
60. Slipyj to Paul VI, 26.xii.1964, Slipyj, *Tvory* 12:165.
61. Knowles (1963) 33-62.
62. Slipyj, *Tvory* 1:136 n. 230.

tory of Dogma for the thesis that "all the scholarly developments of the West in the Middle Ages are merely a continuation of what the Greek Church had either experienced within itself or was still experiencing, howsoever weakly," which he quoted more than once.[63] And he could have found in Harnack substantiation as well for the preponderant role of Western scholars, including Protestant scholars, in the editing and interpreting of Greek patristic texts.[64]

Although in his expositions of the Greek fathers Slipyj was intent on pointing out the inadequacies of a Western theology that remained ignorant of the East, no less explicit a polemical purpose was his effort to drive a wedge between the Greek patristic tradition and the Eastern theology that had later developed in antithesis to the Latin West, as that theology had been articulated by Photius in the ninth century—and, not incidentally, as it was still being articulated by Greek and especially by Russian Orthodox theologians in the nineteenth and twentieth centuries. The Greek fathers had exerted a "fateful" influence on the trinitarian theology of Photius.[65] There was nevertheless "all the difference in the world" between Photius and the Greek fathers. Photius had been guilty of an "audacious deviation from the tradition" of the Greek fathers.[66] Sometimes Slipyj could even blame the "great confusion that [Photius] introduced into the doctrine of the procession [of the Holy Spirit]" on Photius's neglect of the Greek fathers and an unconscious adaptation of the worst features of the trinitarianism of the Latin fathers.[67] He was willing to cite Eastern Orthodox theology, specifically the *Orthodox Confession* of the Ukrainian Orthodox Metropolitan of Kiev, Petro Mohyla, as evidence, over against the Western practice, for the reception also by laypeople of both elements in the Eucharist, as a matter of "divine and apostolic law."[68] Similarly, he gave credit to Russian Orthodox theologians for their adherence to a sound doctrine of the seven sacraments.[69] But at the same time he attacked the Orthodox for their ignorant criticism of Western scholasticism on this doctrine.[70] Such ignorant criticism was of a piece with the long-standing neglect of each other's languages by

63. Slipyj, *Tvory* 1:196 n. 6; 2:50 n. 3.
64. See chapter 1, p. 18 above.
65. Slipyj, *Tvory* 1:95.
66. Slipyj, *Tvory* 1:114.
67. Slipyj, *Tvory* 1:122, 147-48.
68. Slipyj, *Tvory* 6:329.
69. Slipyj, *Tvory* 1:372-73.
70. Slipyj, *Tvory* 1:378-79.

the theologians of both East and West.[71] Even papal legates to Constantinople in the Middle Ages often did not understand Greek; and Photius, who was "otherwise a most erudite theologian"[72] and in fact "the most gifted and learned man of his time in the East, did not take the trouble to learn Latin."[73]

Thus Slipyj, who recalled with pleasure and pride that as a student he himself had "had an enormous love for Greek,"[74] had to acknowledge that Augustine, as he admitted in the *Confessions*,[75] had suffered from a "distaste for Greek [*nechit' do hreky*]."[76] Nevertheless Augustine had been able, using the Latin translations of the Greek fathers, especially of the treatise *On the Holy Spirit* by Didymus the Blind, to acquire a "good acquaintance" with the Greek views on the doctrine of the Trinity.[77] Therefore, as Slipyj insisted, *pace* Photius and later Eastern thinkers, there was no basic doctrinal difference between the Greek fathers and Augustine on the absolute dogmatic imperative to assert that there was one, and only one, "*principium*" or "ἀρχή" in the Godhead.[78] For while "the dogmas of the faith are the same, the explanations and arguments for them can be many and varied."[79] Indeed, "on the basis of the principle, 'nothing is in the will unless it was first in the intellect [*nihil volitum nisi praecognitum*],' Augustine, who regarded the begetting [of the Son] and the spiration [of the Holy Spirit] as products, respectively, of the divine intellect and will," had "far surpassed" any of the Greek fathers in his interpretation of the eternal procession of the Son and of the Holy Spirit from the Father in the Trinity.[80] For there had "remained an obscurity in the Greek schema" of the relations between the three persons, an obscurity that Augustine and the subsequent Western development had clarified by formulating their doctrine of *Filioque*.[81]

Slipyj's standard epithets for the church fathers are quite indicative of their relative standing in his pantheon. To a Western audience he could speak of "Saints John Chrysostom, John of Damascus,

71. Slipyj, *Tvory* 1:406.
72. Slipyj, *Tvory* 13:267.
73. Slipyj, *Tvory* 1:150.
74. Slipyj, *Spomyny* 37.
75. Augustine *Confessions* I.xiv.23.
76. Slipyj, *Tvory* 2:247.
77. Slipyj, *Tvory* 1:138.
78. Slipyj, *Tvory* 1:238.
79. Slipyj, *Tvory* 1:405.
80. Slipyj, *Tvory* 1:148.
81. Slipyj, *Tvory* 1:243.

Theodore of Studion, and others" as "giants who grew up on Byzantine soil."[82] Elsewhere he added the names of Saint Athanasius and the Cappadocians to the list of Eastern "giants."[83] But as soon as he had done so, he went on to speak of Saint Augustine as the one whose "theological accomplishments were a source of inspiration and satisfaction for many centuries," combining theological insight and psychological intuition in unique measure.[84] "Augustine goes the right way";[85] although he was not without theological predecessors, he was a "genius."[86] The Greek fathers, even the Cappadocians, were "somewhat unclear" in their trinitarianism, but "the point is made much more accurately in Saint Augustine."[87] In a brief but trenchant essay, dealing especially with the *Confessions*, Slipyj used the fifteen-hundredth anniversary of the death of Augustine, which was being commemorated all over the Western Church during 1930, as the occasion for an essay on his towering significance.[88] In his later years, Slipyj's appreciation of the Cappadocians, especially of Saint Basil, seems to have deepened markedly.[89] Speaking in Rome, but to a Ukrainian audience, on 14 January 1974, he went so far as to declare: "If there was anyone writing after Christ who understood Christ, that one was certainly Saint Basil."[90] Basil was, he said in his message to a symposium in Toronto, a "church father among church fathers."[91] Nevertheless it seems safe to say that most of the time no Greek father could match Augustine in Slipyj's estimation.

Yet it seems no less safe to say that Slipyj tended to look at Augustine—and at the Greek fathers—through Thomistic glasses. "The achievement of the Greek theological mind," he wrote, "was taken over by the medieval scholastics. To be sure, the primary church father in the Middle Ages was always Saint Augustine, but there is no doubt that the Greek fathers, too, gave a powerful impulse to scholastic theology."[92] Conversely, scholastic theology was the avenue to the true understanding and evaluation both of the Greek fathers and of Augus-

82. Slipyj, *Tvory* 2:112.
83. Slipyj, *Tvory* 2:49.
84. Slipyj, *Tvory* 2:52.
85. Slipyj, *Tvory* 1:114.
86. Slipyj, *Tvory* 1:133.
87. Slipyj, *Tvory* 1:146-47.
88. Slipyj, *Tvory* 2:247-54.
89. Slipyj, *Tvory* 13:212.
90. Slipyj, *Tvory* 13:261-62.
91. Slipyj, *Tvory* 14:367; see also Slipyj, *Tvory* 14:190-92.
92. Slipyj, *Tvory* 2:49.

Cardinal Josyf Slipyj

Andrej Šeptyc'kyj

Slipyj as professor

Slipyj as theological rector

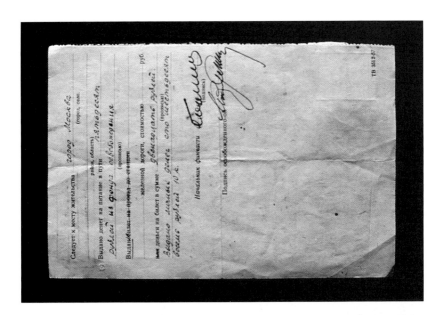

Official Soviet Liberation Document

Detail of liberation document

Slipyj in a borrowed cassoc with John XXIII

Slipyj with the Ukrainian hierarchy and Paul VI at the Ukrainian Catholic University

Slipyj with John Paul I after the pope's election

Slipyj with John Paul II

*John Paul II
kissing the hand
of Slipyj, who is
lying in state*

tine. Thomas may not have been as original a thinker as Plato or Aristotle or Augustine, but as a systematician he outdid them all[93]—even Duns Scotus, who was superior to him in acuity and genius.[94] Therefore when "medieval Augustinianism began to decline," it was Thomas Aquinas, "the wisest and altogether the most excellent of minds," who had the courage to oppose it;[95] elsewhere, too, Slipyj used the same words, "the wisest and altogether the most excellent of minds," to describe Thomas.[96] The authentic and Catholic Augustine, consequently, was the one whom Thomas had discovered and followed.[97] Indeed, as Étienne Gilson was pointing out at the very time when Slipyj was working on the relation between Augustine and the East, Thomas had rescued Augustine from himself by clarifying his metaphysics without jeopardizing his dogmatics.[98]

It was in this sense that, according to Slipyj, Thomistic scholasticism "provides a support for patristic theology" by harmonizing and clarifying what the fathers had said, more or less clearly.[99] Thomas had done so even on questions where his answer did not become the official one. Thus Slipyj—who had inherited from his parental home a special devotion to the doctrine of the Immaculate Conception of the Blessed Virgin Mary,[100] and who strove to interpret this teaching from an Eastern perspective even though it was not in fact part of the Eastern tradition[101]—could declare that "in the dogma of the Immaculate Conception Thomas did not give a solution, but there are present in him all the elements of the later Scotist argumentation."[102] In the light of the conflict over the Immaculate Conception throughout the fourteenth and fifteenth centuries between the Dominican pupils of Thomas and the Franciscan disciples of Duns Scotus, with the Franciscans asserting the doctrine that was eventually to be promulgated by Pope Pius IX in 1854 and many of the Thomists resisting it,[103] Slipyj's interpretation of Thomas's position does seem to err a little on the side of generosity.

What Slipyj said about the Thomistic interpretation of Augustine

93. Slipyj, *Tvory* 2:83.
94. Slipyj, *Tvory* 13:70-71.
95. Slipyj, *Tvory* 1:270.
96. Slipyj, *Tvory* 1:174.
97. Slipyj, *Tvory* 1:133.
98. Gilson (1926).
99. Slipyj, *Tvory* 2:47.
100. Slipyj, *Spomyny* 86.
101. Slipyj, *Tvory* 13:252-54; 345-47.
102. Slipyj, *Tvory* 2:96; see also Slipyj, *Tvory* 14:131.
103. Pelikan (1971) 4:38-50; 5:208-9, 278-79.

applied *a fortiori* to the understanding of the Greek theological tradition, whether patristic or Byzantine. One of Slipyj's favorite Greek quotations, which he also translated into Ukrainian,[104] was the exclamation of George Scholarius, who as Gennadius II became patriarch of Constantinople after the Turkish conquest in 1453:

> Oh Thomas, if you had only been born in the East rather than in the West! What an Orthodox you would have been! For then you would have been as sound in your thought about the procession of the Holy Spirit as you are when you speak so well about all the other [doctrines].

> [Εἴθε, Θωμᾶ, μὴ ἦσθα γεγονὼς ἐν τῇ δύσει ἀλλ ἐν τῇ ἀνατολῇ, ἵνα ἦσθα ὀρθόδοξος καὶ ἵνα ἐφρόνεις καὶ περὶ τῆς ἐκπορεύσεως τοῦ ἁγίου πνεύματος ὄρθως, ὡς καὶ περὶ τῶν ἄλλων λέγεις.][105]

With this Byzantine admiration for Thomas, Slipyj contrasted the slanders against scholasticism among modern Eastern Orthodox theologians, whom he found to resemble "Protestants and freethinkers" in this respect.[106] So obvious was this conviction to Slipyj that he could sometimes quote Thomas as the authority on the questions in dispute between East and West without even having to identify him by name.[107] His entire discussion of "Saint Thomas and the Theology of the East" was an effort to find affinities.[108]

Nevertheless, Slipyj recognized also the negative significance of scholasticism for the problem of the relation between those churches of the East that adhered to the Holy See and those that did not. "The separated [Christians]," he once wrote, "have not been accustomed to the scholastic ways of presenting the truths [of the Christian faith], even though scholasticism itself has its beginnings in the East, in the Oriental Christian tradition. Here [in the West] it obviously leads to different formulations of the same truths. According to the separated [Christians of the East], the Platonic philosophy is more congenial . . . to the mentality of Eastern Christians";[109] this Eastern preference for Platonism was shared in the West by Saint Augustine.[110] Nevertheless, the scholastics had discovered that not the Platonic philosophy, but the Aris-

---

104. Slipyj, *Tvory* 1:203; 2:88-89.
105. Quoted both times from Rackl (1922) 52.
106. Slipyj, *Tvory* 2:39.
107. Slipyj, *Tvory* 1:142 n. 258.
108. Slipyj, *Tvory* 2:87-92.
109. Slipyj, *Tvory* 5:137.
110. Slipyj, *Tvory* 2:251.

totelian, was the most congenial to the apologetic task of defending the content of the Christian faith.[111] At the same time, it was important to remember that "Saint Thomas did not eliminate Plato completely."[112] All his life, therefore, Slipyj was convinced that "the more profoundly the theologians of the East have known the works of Saint Thomas, the more firmly they have adhered to the Union" of Lyons, Florence, and Brest.[113] And he sought to reassure his fellow Slavs not to be concerned about the alleged dire consequences of such a Thomism:

> There is now no need to fear that by falling into the clutches of the *Summa* of Aquinas the East will lose its distinctive character in the development of theology. The supreme achievement of scholasticism [*scholjastyčnyj archytvir*] contains within itself the quintessence of theological learning and, as such, constitutes the indispensable foundation for further work [Eastern no less than Western].[114]

On the other hand, the more vigorous his conflicts with "the Latin mentality" and with various elements in the Vatican became during the final decade of his life, the deeper grew Josyf Slipyj's conviction that the warning implied in that reassurance was needed at least as much by Western as by Eastern theology. The study of Thomas Aquinas had to be accompanied by the study of John of Damascus,[115] because the "distinctive character" of Eastern thought deserved to be respected—and needed to be preserved—in any Slavic version of the Thomistic theological synthesis. That emphasis was consistent with the curriculum established by Metropolitan Rutskyj.[116]

So it had been historically, in the Ukrainian Thomism of the early modern period at L'viv-Halyč.[117] "With the fall of Constantinople [in 1453], the center of Eastern Orthodox [*nezjedynenoji*] theology passed over to Kiev," where even among the Orthodox the study of Thomism exerted a major influence.[118] Indeed, in the introduction to his monograph on Thomas, Slipyj could assert that "Ukrainian theology was regenerated and grew from the studies of Thomas."[119] While point-

---

111. Slipyj, *Tvory* 2:47.
112. Slipyj, *Tvory* 10/11:33.
113. Slipyj, *Tvory* 1:210.
114. Slipyj, *Tvory* 2:92.
115. Slipyj, *Tvory* 2:37.
116. Holowackyj (1957) 102-3.
117. Slipyj, *Tvory* 14:388-89.
118. Slipyj, *Tvory* 2:89.
119. Slipyj, *Tvory* 2:37.

ing out the linguistic and methodological difficulties facing any scholar who undertook to study scholasticism, Slipyj urged special consideration of Ukrainian Thomism as one of the most neglected fields for further research.[120] As part of his own continuing campaign to reclaim Metropolitan Petro Mohyla from the Orthodox, he relied on Mohyla's *Orthodox Confession of Faith [Pravoslavne ispovidannja viry]* for proof that "transubstantiation [μετουσίωσις, *peresuščestvlennja*]" had, since the Council of Lyons in 1274, become part of the Eastern Orthodox theological vocabulary, although in fact most of the proof from "tradition [*peredannja*]" that he was able to offer for transubstantiation came from Western rather than from Eastern sources.[121] Nor was that the only accommodation to the Western, Thomistic conceptual framework that had characterized Kiev-Halyč in the period associated with Metropolitan Petro Mohyla. Except for the perennial questions of the *Filioque* and of papal primacy, the thought of the Orthodox theologians in Kiev during that period "stands closest to Catholic [doctrine]."[122] And it had done so without losing its "distinctive character" as Eastern and Slavic.

Josyf Slipyj was of course obliged to address both of those perennial questions in his polemics against the Orthodox. During the years of his captivity it was the second, papal primacy, that would become the existential issue for him. One of his first tormentors, Jaroslav Halan, was the author of an anticlerical and atheistic screed with the title *I Spit on the Pope.*[123] "After several days, when I had been tortured to the extreme with interrogations" following his arrest, Josyf Slipyj would report later, "they gave me [a document] to sign in which I would renounce the pope, and for that they would make me [Orthodox] metropolitan of Kiev."[124] Such opportunities for "apostasy" from papal primacy came to him repeatedly in prison.[125] It was also while he was in prison that Slipyj received further opportunity to deepen his study of medieval philosophy and of Thomism—indeed, of "Thomism with a Slavic accent," and quite literally so. For his notebooks from those years contain excerpts and comments on Polish translations of two of the works of Étienne Gilson, to which Slipyj gained access while in the camps.[126] Gilson's Gifford Lectures of

120. Slipyj, *Tvory* 2:45-46.
121. Slipyj, *Tvory* 6:244-57.
122. Slipyj, *Tvory* 2:90-91.
123. Slipyj, *Spomyny* 108-9; see chapter 8, p. 151 below.
124. Slipyj, *Spomyny* 112.
125. See, for example, Slipyj, *Spomyny* 114-15, 117-18, 125, 169-70, 185, 192.
126. These excerpts have been transcribed by the director of the *Archivum Patriarchale*, Rev. Prof. Ivan Choma, and come to 57 typewritten pages.

1931 at the University of Aberdeen, *The Spirit of Medieval Philosophy*, had been translated into Polish and published in 1958. (There had also been translations into English, Japanese, Arabic, German, Italian, and Spanish.)[127] Also in 1958 there had appeared a Polish translation of Gilson's *Christianity and Philosophy*.[128] Slipyj's fellow prisoners recalled that he had used this material to lecture to them on the history of philosophy.[129] Étienne Gilson, in turn, joined with colleagues in the Académie Française, including André Maurois and Gabriel Marcel, in addressing a petition under date of 6 July 1961, asking for the release of Josyf Slipyj on humanitarian grounds.[130]

Although the relation to the papacy and the Thomist tradition were therefore central to his mature interests, during his early years as a scholar in historical theology it had been the *Filioque* that most engaged his investigations. His German monograph on Photius[131] was summarized in a shorter Ukrainian article on the same subject, "Photius and the *Filioque*," published in 1923.[132] His Latin monograph of 1926 on "spiration in the Holy Trinity" was basically a defense of the Western doctrine of *Filioque*.[133] There were as well several shorter pieces on the subject. Of scholars able to write in Western languages, Josyf Slipyj was, during the years between World War I and World War II, perhaps the leading authority on the theology of the *Filioque*; his only rival to that title might be the French Assumptionist Martin Jugie, whose assessment of his book on Photius and the *Filioque* Slipyj was pleased to cite[134] and whom Slipyj was able to quote (transliterating his name in Ukrainian as *Žjuži*) to good advantage also on other questions of doctrine and practice dividing East and West.[135]

The problem of the *Filioque* had become a bête noire to the Greeks.[136] Not only was the *Filioque* afflicted with "subtle and dry metaphysics,"[137] but it had also proved to be the most intractable of all dogmatic problems. Thanks to the development of scholasticism, Latin had acquired a measure of theological and philosophical precision that

127. McGrath (1982) 6-7.
128. McGrath (1982) 2.
129. Shifrin (1973) 249-50.
130. Petition of the Académie Française, 6.vii.1961, *Arch.Pat.* 28:91-109.
131. Slipyj, *Tvory* 1:91-158.
132. Slipyj, *Tvory* 2:157-70.
133. Slipyj, *Tvory* 1:211-331.
134. Slipyj, *Tvory* 3/4:828.
135. Slipyj, *Tvory* 6:201.
136. Slipyj, *Tvory* 1:143.
137. Slipyj, *Tvory* 1:93.

rendered it the most suitable for expressing many subtle distinctions and for avoiding confusion.[138] At the Second Vatican Council, where Josyf Slipyj was to spend most of his time vindicating characteristically Eastern forms of language and thought, he nevertheless found time to defend traditional scholastic Latin against various trendy neologisms that were current among the Council fathers.[139] For despite his admiration for the sophistication of patristic Greek as a medium for specifying the meaning of the trinitarian dogma,[140] Josyf Slipyj saw the Greek of Photius, grounded in the fathers though it was, as falling "far short" of the Latin of Boethius in theological precision.[141] "Many of the conflicts between Easterners and Westerners, such as that over ὑπόστασις and *persona*, were settled peacefully, but this time the situation was hopeless," Slipyj had observed.[142] Indeed, he ventured the suggestion that "in the history of dogma it is not possible to find many examples where the opponents understood one another as little as they did in the battle over the *Filioque*."[143]

A principal explanation for this intractability was the mutual ignorance of languages.[144] But the difference was even more fundamental than that. It pertained to varying ways of safeguarding the doctrine of the unity of the Godhead, which was, together with the Incarnation, the supreme mystery of the Christian faith.[145] The three schemata of trinitarian unity could not only be described verbally but diagrammed "graphically": the Greek fathers strove to safeguard the unity by emphasizing the rôle of the Father as the "ἀρχή" of both the Son and the Holy Spirit; Photius had picked up this patristic emphasis, but had exaggerated it into an exclusionary principle; and the Latins, following Augustine's lead, had found in the Spirit the unifying bond of "love [*amor*]" between the Father and the Son.[146] Slipyj explicitly identified himself with the Thomistic version of the Augustinian definition of the Holy Spirit as *amor*, and he schematized this, too, in graphic form.[147] It

138. Slipyj, *Tvory* 1:405.
139. Slipyj, *Tvory* 12:207.
140. Slipyj, *Tvory* 1:107-8.
141. Slipyj, *Tvory* 1:95-99.
142. Slipyj, *Tvory* 1:150.
143. Slipyj, *Tvory* 1:158.
144. Slipyj, *Tvory* 1:406.
145. Slipyj, *Tvory* 9:99, 109; 13:59.
146. The Greek patristic schema is diagrammed in Slipyj, *Tvory* 1:101; the Photian version in Slipyj, *Tvory* 1:121; and the Augustinian in Slipyj, *Tvory* 1:137.
147. Slipyj, *Tvory* 1:188-90; the discussion of the Thomistic doctrine, pp. 174-77; the graphic diagram, p. 186.

was a definition that he would continue to employ, also in sermons, the rest of his life.[148] Yet at the same time he continued to insist that there could be differences in the "explanation" of doctrines that did not jeopardize the framework of dogmatic unity.[149]

As such discussions of the nature of theological difference within doctrinal unity suggest, Josyf Slipyj was—without any explicit reference to John Henry Newman (whose portrait does, however, appear in the edition of Slipyj's works[150])—operating with a concept of development of doctrine that bore many affinities to Newman's. He saw the *Sentences* of Peter Lombard as evidence from the history of Western scholastic theology for the recognition that even a traditionalism committed to the repetition and preservation of patristic doctrine could not refrain from developing that doctrine further.[151] For the East, that recognition posed a special set of problems. Byzantine theology was characterized by "an extreme traditionalism" and "a great dependence on the fathers."[152] This had led to the widespread impression in the West that "Eastern Christians are so stubborn and tenacious in their adherence to the *status quo* as to preclude any progress."[153] But that impression was mistaken, as a study of the history of Christian doctrine in the East would show.[154] Above all, of course, the history of the doctrine of the Trinity in both East and West, even apart from the problematics of the *Filioque,* was a documentation of the inevitability of doctrinal development.[155] In the lapidary formula of John Courtney Murray, "I do not think that the first ecumenical question is, what think ye of the Church? Or even, what think ye of Christ? The dialogue would rise out of the current confusion if the first question raised were, what think ye of the Nicene homoousion?"[156]

Slipyj's recognition of the need for development in doctrine and "progress" in theology did not, moreover, apply only to the East itself. It applied as well to the West in its understanding and appreciation of the East,[157] as well as to the theology of Thomas Aquinas. In defending the Western doctrine of *Filioque,* Thomas himself had suggested an in-

148. Slipyj, *Tvory* 14:101 (1976) and 137 (1977).
149. Slipyj, *Tvory* 1:405.
150. Slipyj, *Tvory* 5:328.
151. Slipyj, *Tvory* 1:247.
152. Slipyj, *Tvory* 2:115.
153. Slipyj, *Tvory* 1:400.
154. Slipyj, *Tvory* 1:406.
155. Slipyj, *Tvory* 9:111.
156. Murray (1964) 53.
157. Slipyj, *Tvory* 2:103.

choate theory of the development of doctrine as the movement from implicit to explicit teaching.[158] On that basis Slipyj pointed out that "in dogmatics Aquinas acknowledges a progress, but not in the discovery of new truths, only in the understanding of those that have already been revealed [*v piznannju objavlenych*]"; and he urged that the same acknowledgment must be applied in turn to Aquinas himself. Thomas was also "a child of his time," and "an uncritical appropriation of his teachings" was faithful neither to the nature of Christian truth nor, for that matter, to the best in Thomism itself.[159] Rather, there needed to be further "progress of theology" and "the continued deepening" of its insights beyond Thomas, too.[160] It seems clear, on the basis both of Slipyj's explicit statements and of the methodology implicit in his theological practice, that he saw the primary means for such Thomistic "progress" in a new exposure of Western theology, including Thomist theology, to the riches of the Eastern heritage, whose "highly original point of view" and unique Christian experience "also manifest now the universality of the church of Jesus Christ."[161] He had long recognized that "the scholastic frame of mind"[162] could be a barrier to East-West understanding. But it seems clear that whenever, in his final two decades, he would be confronted with a rigid Thomism that seemed to possess no antenna for the Eastern tradition at all, he came to realize just how Eastern he was, Thomist or not.

158. Pelikan (1969) 120-21.
159. Slipyj, *Tvory* 2:98-99.
160. Slipyj, *Tvory* 10/11:40.
161. Slipyj to Lucca Di Schiena, 24.viii.1963, *Arch.Pat.* 29:122.
162. Slipyj, *Tvory* 5:137.

7

The Reform of Theological Studies

In 1925, only a few years after Slipyj had joined the theological faculty at L'viv, Metropolitan Andrej Šeptyc'kyj, having discovered that it was harder to find a seminary rector than a bishop,[1] appointed him rector of the major seminary.[2] When it was suggested that someone else, perhaps Auxiliary Bishop Josyf Bocjan,[3] should have the title of rector as an honorary designation, Šeptyc'kyj smiled and replied: "That much I could do myself, but who is going to do all that work?"[4] So Slipyj had to accept, "under obedience [pid posluchom]";[5] and in one way or another, he would devote the rest of his life, over half a century, to "the very difficult task"[6] of doing "all that work" of theological education, first under Šeptyc'kyj's supervision and then eventually by his own authority.

During the next twenty years at L'viv Slipyj undertook a program of pedagogical and theological renewal that he himself was to call, in a tribute to the encyclical issued by Pope Pius XI on Pentecost, 24 May 1931, *Deus scientiarum Dominus*,[7] "the reform of theological studies."[8]

1. Slipyj, *Tvory* 13:117.
2. For a summary of his administrative work, see Fedunyk (1963).
3. See the tribute of 1927 to him in Slipyj, *Tvory* 2:221-36.
4. Slipyj, *Spomyny* 62.
5. Slipyj, *Tvory* 13:151.
6. Slipyj, *Tvory* 13:49-50.
7. *AAS* 23 (1931):241-62.
8. Slipyj, *Tvory* 3/4:71-74.

For "the necessary reform" of the church, Slipyj always believed, "must begin with education in the seminary."[9] *Deus scientiarum Dominus* was a major turning point in the administrative history of the church's system of higher education.[10] Josyf Slipyj would often return to that encyclical in subsequent years, as a charter specifically for Ukrainian Catholic scholarship.[11] When, after those twenty years, the program was cruelly cut off by his arrest and incarceration, he went on, even in prison and the camps, doing what he could for scholarship and education. And after his release, although he certainly wanted—and perhaps expected—to return to L'viv,[12] where he would have resumed his ecclesiastical and educational duties, he was obliged to accept a change of venue from L'viv-Halyč to Rome, where "the reform of theological studies" once more occupied him, with the founding of "the Ukrainian Catholic University of Pope Saint Clement [*Ukrajins'kyj Katolyc'kyj Universytet Im. Sv. Klymenta Papy*]"—widely referred to among Ukrainian Catholics, and therefore also here, by the acronym *UKU*—which became, as he would call it in his last will and testament, "a sign and an encouragement [*zrazkom i poštovchom*],"[13] the focus and successor of the several institutional structures through which he had begun the program when he was still a young priest and scholar in L'viv.

UKU was chronologically the fourth such institution that Slipyj would administer during his half-century long educational career, the first three (of which he became head as Šeptyc'kyj's appointee) being the Major Seminary at L'viv, the "Ukrainian Scientific[14] Theological Society [*Bohoslovs'ke Naukove Tovarystvo*]," and the "Greek Catholic Theological Academy [*Hreko-Katolyc'ka Bohoslovs'ka Akademija*]." Succinctly, if perhaps somewhat effusively, his editors have summarized the relations among those institutions in L'viv-Halyč, in connection with the founding of the last of the three, the Greek Catholic Theological Academy:

9. Slipyj, *Tvory* 13:119.
10. See Ghellinck (1931) for a contemporary assessment of its importance.
11. See, for example, Slipyj, *Tvory* 3/4:314, 375, 380.
12. Slipyj, *Spomyny* 200.
13. Slipyj, *Tvory* 14:477.
14. Here as elsewhere, the precise translation of the Ukrainian word *nauka* creates difficulties, and we have sometimes rendered it as "scholarship" or as "learning" and sometimes as "culture." But because the "Ukrainian Scientific Theological Society" was consciously designed to be a parallel to the "Ševčenko Scientific Society at L'viv [*Naukove Tovarystvo imeny Ševčenka v L'vovi*]" (see Slipyj, *Tvory* 3/4:280), which has retained the name "Scientific" in the English version of its name, it seemed best to make use of that name here as well, despite the difficulties created by the (relatively recent) narrowing of the word in English to the natural sciences.

Metropolitan Andrej founded the Academy in 1929. Professor Josyf Slipyj worked out the statutes for it, making use of the constitutions of various Catholic universities and Catholic schools of higher learning in all of Europe. On the basis of the statutes he was appointed by Metropolitan Andrej of Halyč as the first rector of the Academy.

With the creation of the Theological Academy, the final stone was laid in the foundations on which Ukrainian theological thought was to be reared and to grow. It was intended that thereby the cadres both of well-trained Ukrainian clergy and of highly-qualified scholars would increase. To this end, a third institution, the Theological Academy, was added to the Scholarly Theological Society and the Major Seminary.

From the statutes and the intellectual richness of these three institutions, which were the creation of Professor Josyf Slipyj, there arose in the organism of the Ukrainian Church three mighty pyramids, which gave witness to Ukrainian theological thought, its spiritual formation and the high level of its intellectual enlightenment. This triad of pyramids was closely intertwined, because of their firm constitutional foundations and their intellectual-spiritual contents, for the purpose of serving the Ukrainian Church and of contributing to the spiritual treasury of the entire church universal.[15]

After Slipyj was set free, all of that would be continued in the atmosphere of *UKU,* an atmosphere that was more straitened and yet at the same time more emancipated. Under widely varying outward circumstances, the theological goals and educational philosophy of Josyf Slipyj had manifested an impressive consistency throughout those five decades. A brief review of Slipyj's administration of each of these four institutions, therefore, may well precede a consideration of his theological goals and educational philosophy.

The "Greek Catholic Major Seminary at L'viv [*Hreko-Katolyc'ka Duchovna Seminarija u L'vovi*]," to which Josyf Slipyj returned as professor after his graduate studies at Innsbruck and Rome (where he had also had an opportunity to observe other seminaries)[16] and whose rectorship he assumed soon thereafter, had of course changed in the intervening years since he had completed his seminary studies. In many ways, nevertheless, the problems—spiritual, disciplinary, and academic—that he had encountered there as a student still plagued it.

---

15. Slipyj, *Tvory* 3/4:18-20 (21); the English translation is my own.
16. Slipyj, *Tvory* 13:50.

There was, Slipyj mused, something about "the Ukrainian spirit" that was not congenial to running a tight ship; it was an observation that was to come to his mind frequently in later years, and not only in reflection on academic institutions.[17] Commenting on the status of the seminary under his predecessor as rector, the Basilian biblical scholar Teodosij-Tyt Haluščyns'kyj,[18] Slipyj spoke of a "lackadaisical system of order [lahidnyj porjadok]," as a consequence of which the students grumbled when, under Father Rector Josyf Slipyj, that system was replaced by a stricter discipline.[19] Slipyj blamed the conditions in part on the personal attitude of Father Haluščyns'kyj, whom Slipyj regarded as, among other things, a "Polonophile"[20]—never a compliment in his vocabulary, as his violent objection many years later to the slander that "Greek Catholics were renegades and Polonophiles"[21] made clear, though it was not perhaps as much of an epithet as "Russophile."[22]

He also blamed it on Metropolitan Šeptyc'kyj's mistake of ever having entrusted the administration of the Seminary to the Basilian Order at all. From the beginning, Šeptyc'kyj had been favorably disposed toward the Basilians because of his own affiliation with the Basilian Order.[23] He was also swayed by their historic ecumenical rôle in the reunion of East and West, as this had been defined by Pope Leo XIII. In December 1920 Metropolitan Šeptyc'kyj came to Rome, where Slipyj was pursuing his studies at the Gregorianum.[24] During that visit Šeptyc'kyj informed Slipyj of his decision to turn over the direction of the Major Seminary at L'viv to the Basilians. Slipyj disagreed with this decision, in part because he feared that, as monks, the Basilians would not understand the situation of seminarians who planned to marry before ordination.[25] Many years later the Basilians were still being criticized for having engaged in a campaign of "Latinization" of the liturgy at the seminary, by contrast with the "Byzantinization" being pressed by Metropolitan Šeptyc'kyj.[26] Šeptyc'kyj, having meanwhile

17. Slipyj, Spomyny 67.
18. See the notice about him in Slipyj, Tvory 3/4:316-17 (315).
19. Slipyj, Spomyny 64.
20. Slipyj, Spomyny 76.
21. Slipyj to N. V. Podgorny, 17.ii.1961, Arch.Pat. 28:77-78 (112-13).
22. See also Slipyj, Tvory 14:140.
23. That was Slipyj's opinion, which he continued to hold many years later: Slipyj to Gustavo Testa, 29.xii.1966, Arch.Pat. 35:500.
24. On Šeptyc'kyj's journey to Rome and beyond between late 1921 and late 1923, see Korolevskij (1964) 176-77.
25. Slipyj, Spomyny 58.
26. Ivan Praško to Gustavo Testa, 23.vi.1967, Arch.Pat. 36:208-21.

moved toward "restoration of Eastern monastic life in its pure form" as practiced by the Studites rather than by the Basilians,[27] eventually came to recognize the validity of Slipyj's objections, terminating the arrangement after the initial five-year term.[28]

The way Šeptyc'kyj announced the appointment of Slipyj to his new post (and the termination of the Basilian custody over the seminary) was by identifying him, in a conversation with Father Evsevij Bačyns'kyj, as "the new father rector." Because of "the resentment of the Basilians" toward both him and Metropolitan Šeptyc'kyj, Slipyj faced what even after all the years of his imprisonment he would go on calling "one of the most unpleasant experiences of my life—and I have had many, many of them."[29] That did not, however, deter him from immediately taking firm charge; as he demonstrated repeatedly throughout his life, nothing much ever could. Before revamping the administrative structure of the seminary, the new father rector consulted various Ukrainian lawyers for their advice.[30] In earlier times "a special set of regulations . . . according to which the students of the Seminary of L'viv could live did not exist."[31] Nevertheless, such "rules" had gradually evolved, so that Slipyj could build upon that foundation, as this had been developed in the specific circumstances of "the education of candidates for the clerical estate in the eparchy of L'viv" and "the establishment of a general seminary in L'viv."[32] The outcome was a new set of "Regulations for Students of the Greek Catholic Major Seminary at L'viv [*Pravyla dlja pytomciv Hreko-Katolyc'koji Duchovnoji Semynariji u L'vovi*]."[33] He would not, he said, "tolerate anarchy in the seminary," adding the wry explanation, "I could see that the order in the seminary would not be harmed by some regulations."[34] With continuing revisions,[35] this document was to stand as the basic set of statutes for education, spiritual formation, and community life in the seminary at L'viv throughout Slipyj's tenure.

Believing as he did that "it is the task of the major seminary to educate clergy who not only are concerned about the salvation of their

27. Korolevskij (1964) 260-83.
28. Slipyj, *Spomyny* 62.
29. Slipyj, *Spomyny* 63.
30. Slipyj, *Spomyny* 66.
31. Blažejovskyj (1975) 139; 212-18.
32. Marusyn (1963) 68-77.
33. Slipyj, *Tvory* 3/4:47-70.
34. Slipyj, *Spomyny* 65-66.
35. Thus the version of 1929 that appears in the edition of Slipyj's works is identified as "the third edition, revised and supplemented," Slipyj, *Tvory* 3/4:49.

own souls, but who can become good and sincere workers in the vineyard of Christ,"[36] he strove in the community life of the major seminary to eschew both the extreme to which the church was vulnerable, that of an anti-intellectual pietism, and the extreme to which the university was prone, that of an anti-devotional intellectualism. Slipyj felt, as rector, that he could tell which seminarians had come from religious homes and which had not.[37] Therefore the third chapter of the regulations laid out in detail what was expected of the seminarians in their private and public "devotion [pobožnist']."[38] It was followed immediately by a fourth chapter on "studies [studiji]," which was shorter but no less explicit in its insistence that "especially at the present time a clergyman must have a thorough knowledge of theological scholarship."[39] The relation of "devotion [pobožnist']" to "scholarship [nauka]" remained his lifelong concern.[40] And the principle of *mens sana in corpore sano* implied that physical exercise should play an important part in the total health of the seminarian and in the discipline of the seminary.[41] At all levels of education, Slipyj was concerned for a comprehensive program of what he would later call "spiritual, scholarly, and pedagogical guidance."[42]

Yet when these regulations for the major seminary spoke about arousing in the seminarians "an enthusiasm for scholarship,"[43] that did not imply at all that the clergy were to become professional scholars. Slipyj remembered from his own student days that most of them had no such interest, and for that matter no such capacity.[44] It must also be noted that, in the seminary study leading up to ordination as a Greek Catholic priest, scholarship did not assume the same position of importance that it had, for example, in the professional preparation and activity of ministers in the Protestant churches on the Continent. It did imply, however, that their professors, by contrast, were obliged to become precisely that: professional scholars. Slipyj insisted—and Metropolitan Šeptyc'kyj agreed—that the scholarly standards for professors at the seminary were to be patterned after (though not, per-

36. Slipyj, *Tvory* 3/4:51.
37. Slipyj, *Tvory* 13:151.
38. Slipyj, *Tvory* 3/4:53-56.
39. Slipyj, *Tvory* 3/4:56-58.
40. Slipyj, *Tvory* 14:186.
41. Slipyj, *Tvory* 13:51-53.
42. Slipyj, *Tvory* 12:31.
43. Slipyj, *Tvory* 3/4:57.
44. Slipyj, *Spomyny* 51.

haps, strictly enforced at an equal level with) those at the European universities, where it was a prerequisite that a candidate have published not only a doctoral dissertation but a *Habilitationsschrift*. On that basis, there were only three incumbent professors currently on the faculty of the major seminary at L'viv who were qualified.[45] (Presumably, these three were, in addition to Slipyj himself in dogmatic theology, Vasyl' Laba in patristics, together with Professor Teodosij-Tyt Haluščyns'kyj, who was the former rector, as well as Professor Tyt Myškovs'kyj, who had been a university professor since 1908 and to whom Slipyj would refer in 1938 as "our senior"[46]—both of these men being in Scripture studies.[47]) But by 1934 Rector Slipyj was in a position to announce, with obvious gratification, that there had been "new habilitations" and an increase of "scholarly production."[48]

A significant factor in the improvement was Metropolitan Šeptyc'kyj's decision of 1929, in recognition of the need of the seminary and of the church for the training of a larger cohort of indigenous Ukrainian Catholic scholars in the several fields of theology, to found the Greek Catholic Theological Academy, as "a center on its own terrain" for higher studies in theology by Ukrainians.[49] For both Šeptyc'kyj and Slipyj believed firmly that "unless we create a scholarly center, one of our own, we shall never attain to a position of our own in philosophical and theological scholarship."[50] Although the academy was not yet, and for the present could not be, a full-scale university, it was to have two of the traditional four university faculties of theology, philosophy, law, and medicine—namely, theology and philosophy, the latter as the traditional *ancilla* of theology, but also as a faculty of liberal arts—"to which a faculty of law and others are to be added."[51] The expansion of the academy through the establishment of the philosophical section on 27 June 1932, therefore, was a significant step in the evolution of the academy from its position as an adjunct of the seminary to the more complete university-level institution that both Šeptyc'kyj and Slipyj aspired to establish.[52] The academy differed fundamentally from the conventional state-run European university also in its system of gover-

45. Slipyj, *Spomyny* 68.
46. Slipyj, *Tvory* 3/4:739.
47. Slipyj, *Tvory* 3/4:316-19 (315).
48. Slipyj, *Tvory* 3/4:372.
49. Slipyj, *Tvory* 3/4:91.
50. Slipyj, *Spomyny* 68.
51. Slipyj, *Tvory* 3/4:98.
52. Slipyj, *Tvory* 3/4:377.

nance, since its rector was appointed directly by the Metropolitan of L'viv-Halyč, who retained ultimate authority over the academy, as well as over its rector and its professors and students.[53] In his inaugural declaration of 22 February 1929, Šeptyc'kyj invoked the memories of Saint Vladimir, Jaroslav the Wise, and Metropolitan Ilarion to describe the rôle that the theological academy was to play in the life and thought of the Ukrainian Church and of the Ukrainian people, as well as the reciprocal rôle that the Ukrainian Church was to play in the activities of the theological academy.[54] And in his address for the fortieth anniversary of the academy in 1969, Slipyj was able to express his gratification at how it had lived up to that expectation.[55] The Academy had stood as proof of what could be done to carry out theological mediation between the Eastern and the Western traditions.[56]

It was, of course, the hope of Šeptyc'kyj and Slipyj that the Roman Congregation for the Oriental Church, which had been created on 1 May 1917 by Pope Benedict XV in the motu proprio *Dei providentis*,[57] would confer upon their theological academy the authority to award an earned doctorate. But negotiations with Eugène Cardinal Tisserant[58] and that congregation for such authority seemed to have been blocked by jurisdictional disputes among various Roman congregations, especially, it would seem, between the Oriental Congregation and the Congregation of Seminaries and Universities, which had been created, also by Benedict XV, on 4 November 1915.[59] In the long and often stormy history of relations between Slipyj and the Oriental Congregation, this was one of the earliest in a series of encounters, from which he became convinced that what he often called "the Roman mentality" would always treat the Ukrainian Catholic Church as a dependent colony rather than as a self-standing sister church. The unwillingness to grant the Greek Catholic Theological Academy the right to confer the doctoral decree came in spite of the evidence, according to Slipyj, that "our students, on the basis of their work . . . at the academy, had an easy time obtaining doctorates at Polish, Czech, German, and Russian universities."[60] This

53. Slipyj, *Tvory* 3/4:99-100.
54. Slipyj, *Tvory* 3/4:261-62.
55. Slipyj, *Tvory* 13:41-45.
56. Slipyj, *Tvory* 14:185.
57. *AAS* 9 (1917):529-33.
58. Slipyj was to pay moving tribute to Tisserant in a memorial address of 4 March 1972, Slipyj, *Tvory* 13:155-57.
59. See Markham (1957) for an analysis.
60. Slipyj, *Spomyny* 76.

had been preeminently true of Slipyj himself, as well as of the young Šeptyc'kyj before him, Šeptyc'kyj having studied at Munich and Slipyj at Innsbruck, but it applied as well also to at least some of his colleagues in the seminary and the academy.

Slipyj believed that the founding of the theological academy by Metropolitan Šeptyc'kyj, which would eventually turn out nearly a thousand graduates,[61] was "undoubtedly a historic event in the life of our church and of our people."[62] An impressive collection of congratulatory messages and telegrams from within and beyond Ukrainian territory hailed its founding.[63] Press notices called the attention of readers in many different countries to the academy.[64] A Jesuit colleague from Louvain, for example, spoke of "the first rector of the academy, Dr. Slipyj, well known for his works in dogmatics on controversial questions."[65] Noting that under Austrian rule there had been in L'viv "a single theological faculty for Poles and for Ukrainians," a professor at the University of Zagreb in Jugoslavia expressed the hope that the academy would carry out its stated purposes of "preparing Greek Catholic priestly candidates for life as priests and of fostering theological scholarship."[66] Its mission was intended, however, to be considerably more comprehensive than that. As Slipyj described it in his rectoral address of 7 October 1934, it would send out "into the paths of modern thought young people, both clergy and laity, with developed minds and with a broader outlook,"[67] and not simply professional theologians.

The third of the "mighty pyramids"[68] through which Slipyj, with the backing of Šeptyc'kyj, strove to carry out the reform of theological studies was the "Ukrainian Scientific Theological Society [*Bohoslovs'ke Naukove Tovarystvo*]," whose statutes were issued at L'viv in 1924.[69] "As rector [of the academy and of the major seminary]," Slipyj recalled, "I was also chosen to be the head of the scientific theological society," but he was grateful that he succeeded in keeping the society and the academy from "getting in each other's way, even though they both had scholarship as their goal."[70] The reason for the creation of the society

61. Slipyj, *Tvory* 13:179.
62. Slipyj, *Tvory* 3/4:260.
63. Reprinted in Slipyj, *Tvory* 3/4:272-85.
64. Reprinted in Slipyj, *Tvory* 3/4:285-310.
65. Slipyj, *Tvory* 3/4:297.
66. In Slipyj, *Tvory* 3/4:309-10.
67. Slipyj, *Tvory* 3/4:379.
68. Slipyj, *Tvory* 3/4:20 (21).
69. Slipyj, *Tvory* 3/4:35-46.
70. Slipyj, *Spomyny* 70.

was the recognition that Ukrainian theological scholarship "among us lies, in large measure, in an uncultivated state [ležyt' u nas u velykij časty oblohom]," because scholarship in general faced difficult conditions, and a fortiori scholarship in theology.[71] The difference between the Ukrainian Scientific Theological Society and the Greek Catholic Theological Academy was, in Slipyj's formulation, that "the academy is a school of higher theological study, while the society accepts both professors and nonprofessors, clergy and laity, and covers a broader scientific range [naukovyj obsjah]."[72] At least until the theological academy could grow into a full-fledged university, the theological society, with the traditional four divisions of a university (theology, philosophy, law, and medicine), could supply some of that missing broader context for theological scholarship.[73]

To the objection that the creation of such a society threatened to spread the already skimpy resources of the Ukrainian people too thinly, there being several other such "societies" in existence, including the National Museum and the well-known Ševčenko Scientific Society, Slipyj's answer was that these other societies, despite their various names, were not primarily scientific and scholarly in their purpose, in the sense that the Ukrainian Scientific Theological Society was to be. That answer was reinforced by the fact that the theological society counted among its founding members some of the members of the Ševčenko Society and of the National Museum.[74] Šeptyc'kyj was the founder both of the National Museum and of the Scientific Theological Society.[75] The theological society was intended to bring together all those from both laity and clergy who were concerned with "our churchly culture [naša cerkovna kul'tura]."[76] According to article 19 of the statutes, the "sections" of the society corresponded to those of the traditional theological faculty: Bible; philosophy and dogmatics; history and canon law; and practical theology.[77] But in his report on the work of the society in the years 1936/37, Slipyj had to acknowledge that the activity of these sections "has not increased in these last years," with only the third section, that dealing with history and canon law, forming a significant exception.[78]

71. Slipyj, Tvory 3/4:37.
72. Slipyj, Spomyny 70.
73. Slipyj, Tvory 13:31-35.
74. Slipyj, Tvory 3/4:37-38.
75. Slipyj, Tvory 13:297.
76. Slipyj, Tvory 3/4:738.
77. Slipyj, Tvory 3/4:43.
78. Slipyj, Tvory 3/4:740.

The fifth article of the 1924 printing of the statutes of the society specified that "the society will issue its publications in the Ukrainian language, which is the official language of the society"; but it added that as necessity arose, it would publish also in other languages.[79] Slipyj could not have foreseen in 1924 that one such "necessity" would be the need to go into exile—major seminary, theological academy, scientific theological society, and all—and to attempt to continue their programs of scientific research and scholarly publication through the Ukrainian diaspora in North and South America, at the Free Ukrainian University in Munich, and finally at UKU in Rome. It was also at Munich that the Ševčenko Scientific Society in exile was to be based after its renewal in 1947, two years following Metropolitan Slipyj's incarceration.[80] The Ševčenko Scientific Society in exile was even the subject of a private audience with Pope Paul VI.[81]

During the years of his captivity Slipyj was unable to do anything concrete about "the reform of theological studies," but his disposition toward scholarship could not be crushed even by imprisonment. While in prison, he managed to get hold of scholarly books, even of some in patristics and early church history.[82] As he reminded others (and himself) in his captivity, he was a scholar but not a politician, and those who had power over him were politicians but not scholars.[83] Thus to the question from his captors, during an interrogation in Moscow, whether there was any way he could be useful to them, he replied, perhaps a bit disingenuously, that he could work in a library and prepare scholarly editions.[84] The perjured testimony and false accusations against him came from men who were not only godless and immoral, but also "often uneducated."[85] Similarly, when he was compelled as a prisoner to attend indoctrination lectures in Marxist ideology, he certainly found the politics distasteful and the atheism repulsive; but his explicit comment about the lecturers was that they were "nonsensical and poorly educated idiots."[86]

As soon as he was freed, therefore, he set about implementing his

79. Slipyj, Tvory 3/4:41.

80. Volodymyr Janiw and Volodymyr Kubijovyč to Gustavo Testa, 16.iii.67, Arch.Pat. 36:84-86.

81. Minutes of papal audience, 17.iii.1967, Arch.Pat. 36:101.

82. Slipyj, Tvory 13:202.

83. Slipyj to N. V. Podgorny, 17.ii.1961, Arch.Pat. 28:89 (124).

84. Slipyj, Spomyny 165-66; see also Spomyny 192.

85. Slipyj, Spomyny 119.

86. Slipyj, Spomyny 197.

educational plans. At the conference with his fellow Ukrainian bishops, according to the minutes, when Metropolitan Slipyj "presented to all the bishops present his project for founding the Ukrainian Catholic University in Rome," at an anticipated cost of five hundred thousand American dollars, the project was approved, but only by a vote of nine to five.[87] The following year, at the fourth session of the next bishops' conference, on 1 October 1964, he put the idea on the agenda again;[88] and eventually, the Synod of Ukrainian Catholic Bishops became the "patron" of the university.[89] One first step in the direction of creating a "university" was to establish a "scientific institute" for Ukrainian scholarship in Rome.[90] A second step was the resuscitation of the scholarly theological journal *Bohoslovija*, which had been founded by Metropolitan Andrej Šeptyc'kyj in 1924 and was edited by Slipyj in L'viv, but had to be suspended during the crisis of 1943. Now Slipyj resumed its publication and proudly sent copies of the first issue to his Roman colleagues.[91] Yet another such step was to elevate the status of the Minor Seminary of Saint Josaphat to the position of a "pontifical" institution.[92] That elevation was granted almost immediately.[93] Slipyj took the occasion to celebrate the developing prospects of Ukrainian theological studies.[94] He thanked the Vatican officials, including the pope, for the honor[95]—and then he went right ahead with his plans for *UKU*. Such an institution, he was convinced, would carry with it the "possibility for a future rebirth" of the entire Eastern Church.[96] To Pope Paul VI, soon after his elevation, he wrote a reminder of the "supplication" for a Ukrainian Catholic university that he had addressed to Paul's predecessor, John XXIII, and to the Sacred Congregation for the Eastern Church;[97] a week later, on 10 October 1963,

87. "Conference of the Catholic Bishops of the Ukrainian Rite," 17.x.1963, *Arch.Pat.* 73:36.

88. "Conference [changed in Slipyj's handwriting to: Synod] of the Catholic Bishops of the Ukrainian Rite," 1.x.1964, *Arch.Pat.* 73:42.

89. Slipyj, *Tvory* 9:115.

90. Slipyj to Amleto Cicognani, 15.xi.1963, *Arch.Pat.* 29:302-3. Similar statements appear in other correspondence on or around the same date.

91. Slipyj to Alfredo Ottaviani, 7.ix.1964, *Arch.Pat.* 31:368; Slipyj to Gregorio Agagianian, 7.ix.1964, *Arch.Pat.* 31:369.

92. Slipyj to Gustavo Testa, 26.iii.1963, *Arch.Pat.* 28:193-95.

93. Gustavo Testa to Slipyj, 6.iv.1963, *Arch.Pat.* 28:219.

94. Slipyj, *Tvory* 12:91-94 (95-97); see also Slipyj, *Tvory* 14:362-64.

95. Slipyj to Gustavo Testa, 21.v.1963, *Arch.Pat.* 28:323; Slipyj to John XXIII, 22.v.1963, *Arch.Pat.* 28:326. See the facsimile of the official charter from Pope John XXIII, Slipyj, *Tvory* 12:93.

96. Slipyj to Gustavo Testa, 25.x.1963, *Arch.Pat.* 29:260-61.

97. Slipyj to Paul VI, 5.x.1963, *Arch.Pat.* 29:209.

in an address of welcome to Pope Paul at a meeting in Rome of Ukrainian émigrés, he described such a Ukrainian Catholic university as a combination of the Ševčenko Scientific Society, the Ukrainian Academy of Sciences, the Ukrainian Scientific Theological Society, and the Ukrainian University.[98] To the Prefect of the Sacred Congregation for Seminaries and Universities, Giuseppe Cardinal Pizzardo, he submitted the outline of what he had in mind for his Ukrainian Catholic university.[99]

While acknowledging that a university was "a very noble ideal," Pizzardo insisted that the name "Center for Higher Ukrainian Studies [Centro di Studi Superiori Ucraini]" still came closer to "the actual reality" and that this was therefore the proper nomenclature, to avoid "any possibility of equivocation."[100] Undeterred, Slipyj proceeded in the following year to announce the founding of the Ukrainian Catholic University. Thereupon Pizzardo wrote again, and at considerable length, to express his "admiration for Your Eminence's pastoral zeal," but to insist yet once more that Centro di Studi Superiori Ucraini remained the more appropriate name.[101] In a twelve-page letter dated 20 January 1966, Slipyj nevertheless set forth to Cardinal Pizzardo a detailed rationale for the Ukrainian University of Saint Clement. He put that rationale into the context of the total history of the educational system in the Ukrainian Church, urging that the creation of a complete Ukrainian university was a logical extension of the "spiritual academy at Kiev" founded by Metropolitan Petro Mohyla. It was being founded in Rome only because of the Soviet occupation of the homeland, and it would be transferred back to the metropolitanate of L'viv-Halyč as soon as political circumstances there permitted. Meanwhile it would be held in trust for the Ukrainian people.[102] This implied, on the one hand, that the university was being "founded in Rome not only for today and tomorrow, but for all time," yet on the other hand that if at some future time there should arise "the possibility of transferring the university itself to Ukraine, the scholarly seat would remain in Rome."[103]

Although the pressure from Vatican officialdom in favor of the designation "center" rather than "university" did not cease,[104] neither did Slipyj's persistence. Perhaps it was true when he said twenty years

98. Slipyj, Tvory 12:98.
99. Slipyj to Giuseppe Pizzardo, 15.ix.1964, Arch.Pat. 31:376-78.
100. Giuseppe Pizzardo to Slipyj, 29.ix.1964, Arch.Pat. 31:411-12.
101. Giuseppe Pizzardo to Slipyj, 28.xii.1965, Arch.Pat. 33:289-92.
102. Slipyj to Giuseppe Pizzardo, 20.i.1966, Arch.Pat. 34:39-50.
103. Slipyj to Angelo Dell'Acqua, 24.ii.1967, Arch.Pat. 36:73.
104. Thus, for example, Jean Villot to Slipyj, 17.ii.1971, Arch.Pat. 40:219.

later that "my hand trembled when I founded this holy institution," but it trembled with excitement rather than with hesitation;[105] the founding of the university may well have been the achievement of which he was the most proud.[106] Such a way of proceeding was not altogether unfamiliar. Describing "the American booster" as "simply speaking in the future tense, asserting what could not yet be disproved," Daniel J. Boorstin has spoken about the "booster college" on the American frontier and about the booster's propensity for such grandiloquent designations as "university."[107] That propensity was characteristic also of the church's educational institutions in America, as can be seen from the example of "the rather pretentious privilege" of "obtaining the title of university for the abbey school" of Saint John the Baptist operated by the Benedictines in Minnesota.[108] Drawing upon the American experience, Slipyj argued that Harvard University had begun with eight students, but that *UKU* already had twenty-five, three times as many, and thirty professors; it had, moreover, published sixty scholarly tomes—proof enough that it had the right to be called a university.[109] That name was not only "on paper, as some people in the Roman curia suppose and even say in writing, but a reality."[110]

As Slipyj conceived of it, *UKU* brought together—in Rome as its "temporary location [*tymčasovyj osidok*]," but *Deo volente* eventually back in L'viv-Halyč, or wherever it would be, for the benefit of Ukrainians all over the world[111]—all three of the institutions through which he had, as rector, been carrying out the reform of theological studies in the Ukrainian context; for in fact all three of them had needed a total university to be truly effective. There had been at L'viv, in connection with the major seminary, "a nominal faculty [as part of] 'the Secret Ukrainian University,'" but this was largely a dead letter; and when, as rector of the major seminary at L'viv, Slipyj had proposed a kind of consortium of seminaries as a step toward developing such a faculty, his colleagues in the other seminaries did not seem interested.[112] Similarly, the theological academy "had arisen as a part [*častyna*] of the Ukrainian Catholic University, as much of it as could be realized under

105. Slipyj, *Tvory* 14:237.
106. Slipyj, *Tvory* 14:141.
107. Boorstin (1967) 296, 152-61.
108. Barry (1956) 143-45.
109. Slipyj to Jean Villot, 17.vii.1971, *Arch.Pat.* 40:218.
110. Slipyj to Jean Villot, 25.i.1971, *Arch.Pat.* 40:7.
111. Slipyj, *Tvory* 8:364.
112. Slipyj, *Spomyny* 79.

the political conditions existing then."[113] Although the Ukrainian Scientific Theological Society had a different purpose, that purpose could only be enhanced by the establishment of *UKU*.[114] And now the mission of the new Ukrainian Catholic University was explicitly defined as that of carrying out the vision set forth by Metropolitan Andrej Šeptyc'kyj, at the founding of the Ukrainian Theological Academy in L'viv, for the religious and cultural renewal of Eastern Europe.[115] "The fact of the existence of *UKU*," it was said at one of its faculty meetings in 1971, also served to call attention to "the scientific-pedagogical institute that flourished at L'viv between the two World Wars—the theological academy,"[116] of which it was "the immediate continuation."[117] And Rome had, of course, the inestimable additional advantage of being the intellectual and scholarly as well as the religious capital of Christendom, with its hundreds of educational institutions, libraries, and research centers, with all of which *UKU* could form connections.[118]

The "political conditions existing then" in L'viv had made it necessary to confine the work of the academy to the faculties of theology and philosophy.[119] At *UKU*, however, it became possible to add other faculties, so that the report issued in 1973, after ten years of its activity, enumerated five faculties:

1. Faculty of Theology;
2. Faculty of Philosophy and Humanities;
3. Faculty of Mathematics and Natural Sciences;
4. Faculty of Law and Social Sciences;
5. Faculty of Medicine.[120]

Closer inspection reveals, however, that the last of these, the Faculty of Medicine, was described as only "in the process of organization."[121] *Pace* Slipyj's insistent and defensive explanations about *UKU*, therefore, this faculty did not in fact exist as a "reality," but only "on

---

113. Slipyj, *Tvory* 7:5.
114. Slipyj, *Tvory* 13:35.
115. Slipyj, *Tvory* 8:360.
116. Slipyj, *Tvory* 8:103.
117. Slipyj, *Tvory* 13:48; 13:179; 9:325.
118. Slipyj, *Tvory* 13:111; 170-71.
119. Slipyj, *Tvory* 3/4:98.
120. Slipyj, *Tvory* 8:60-98.
121. Slipyj, *Tvory* 8:98.

paper";[122] nor was the Faculty of Law in fact offering the full course in jurisprudence. Thus the original two faculties to which the theological academy had been confined while it was at L'viv-Halyč, the theological and the philosophical, continued to be the primary ones also at *UKU*. Slipyj's own rôle as a professor there was concentrated on courses in the fields of his earlier theological and scholarly work:[123] apologetics, especially the Thomistic proofs for the existence of God as they were related to the doctrine of the Trinity; and the doctrine of the sacraments.[124]

As "the symbol of an idea,"[125] the founding of the Ukrainian Catholic University of Pope Saint Clement in Rome, which was intended to be (in his own words) "our only Catholic scientific center and in great measure the bulwark of our faith,"[126] created what was, in Slipyj's eyes, an altogether unique institution. "In 1963," he noted sadly, "all the universities in Ukraine are atheistic"; only *UKU* was not.[127] Its students could have gone to any university, but they had come here.[128] A secular university developed the use of reason, but it did not build character; a Catholic university did both.[129] And on the other hand, *UKU* occupied a place all its own among Catholic universities.[130] That gave it great importance for the Ukrainian diaspora, and through it for the homeland.[131] In his Testament, therefore, Slipyj said to his followers:

> With God's help and thanks to the generosity of the people of God, especially the laity, I was able to establish the Ukrainian Catholic University—a center of learning. . . . Atheism is now the official doctrine in Ukraine and in all the countries of the communist world. Therefore save the Ukrainian Catholic University, for it is a workshop in which are educated new generations of priests and lay ministers: fighters for truth and learning![132]

The creation of the university provided Josyf Slipyj with the opportunity, really for the first time, to articulate, in theory if not immediate-

---

122. Slipyj to Jean Villot, 25.i.1971, *Arch.Pat.* 40:7.
123. See chapter 6, pp. 114-19 above.
124. Slipyj, *Tvory* 7:150-53.
125. Slipyj, *Tvory* 13:170.
126. Slipyj, *Tvory* 8:143.
127. Slipyj, *Tvory* 13:73; 344.
128. Slipyj, *Tvory* 13:171.
129. Slipyj, *Tvory* 13:204.
130. Slipyj, *Tvory* 13:179.
131. Slipyj, *Tvory* 13:286.
132. Slipyj, *Tvory* 14:477.

ly in practice, the full range of the ideas and institutions that he had been pondering at least since the issuance of the encyclical *Deus scientiarum Dominus* by Pope Pius XI on 24 May 1931[133] had given him the occasion, in L'viv-Halyč, to speak about "the reform of theological studies."[134] The rubrics under which—as father rector of the major seminary, as rector of the theological academy, as "head of the scientific theological society [*Holova Bohoslovs'koho Naukovoho Tovarystva*],"[135] and now as rector of *UKU*[136]—he reported on the activities of these four institutions, for fifty years and more, would seem to commend themselves as a way of reporting also on his own educational philosophy and educational administration.[137]

Slipyj's accounts of the various educational and scientific institutions he headed usually began with the *professors*. This was not only because of his own identity as a professor, which he retained as metropolitan and, for that matter, as a prisoner in the gulags,[138] but because of his deep-seated conviction, which Metropolitan Andrej Šeptyc'kyj appears to have shared, that in the educational system of the church no less than in secular institutions the scholars of the faculty were the central element, upon whose success or failure depended the intellectual—and spiritual—integrity of the entire enterprise. When he found, upon taking office as rector, that the scholarly level of the faculty of the seminary had fallen below an acceptable level, he determined to raise it.[139] In his annual reports as rector about the academy and then later about the university, more space was devoted to the detailed itemization of the scholarly work of the professors (himself included) than to any other single body of data. The *curriculum vitae* of each member of the faculty included his publications.[140] Every book review, be it ever so brief, merited a proper bibliographical entry.[141] For example, the first edition of the patrology of Vasyl' Laba had expressed its appreciation to "Father Doctor Josyf Slipyj, Rector of the Greek Catholic Theological Academy in L'viv" for his help in facilitating its publication.[142] When Josyf Dačkevyč

133. *AAS* 23 (1931):241-62.
134. Slipyj, *Tvory* 3/4:71-74.
135. As his title is listed in Slipyj, *Tvory* 3/4:738.
136. "The office of Rector rests in the hands of Metropolitan *Kyr* Josyf," the catalogue explained: Slipyj, *Tvory* 7:6.
137. Similar rubrics appear in Slipyj, *Tvory* 13:75-76; 141 (143).
138. Slipyj, *Spomyny* 128.
139. Slipyj, *Spomyny* 68; Slipyj, *Tvory* 3/4:372.
140. Slipyj, *Tvory* 3/4:316-26.
141. Slipyj, *Tvory* 7:16-17.
142. Laba (1974) 5.

undertook a revised edition of Laba's book "a long distance to the West of our fatherland [*daleko poza Bat'kivščynoju zachodom*]," it was once again thanks to "the labors and funding of Major Archbishop and Cardinal Josyf VII in the theological publishing house of the Ukrainian Catholic University of Pope Saint Clement in Rome" that it could appear.[143] At the same time, "our professors" had the obligation to take their teaching responsibilities seriously.[144] It is instructive to read, even in their public and printed version, the minutes of faculty meetings, each officially attested with the signature "Josyf, Major Archbishop." The importance he attached to the faculty of *UKU*, as well as his close administrative supervision of it, can be seen in the statistic that out of the eleven faculty meetings from 1969 to 1973, i.e., between his seventy-seventh and his eighty-first birthday, Slipyj, with a crushing schedule of international travel and with all his other duties as metropolitan, personally attended all but one (the final one recorded, on 4 July 1973)—with sometimes as few as two other professors in attendance.[145] Presumably they had been arranged with his schedule in mind.

Prefaced by the explanation that the academic year 1963/64 "was taken up with preparatory labors connected with the official establishment of the university,"[146] the accounts of *courses of instruction* at the Ukrainian Catholic University in Rome, like the accounts at the Theological Academy in L'viv preceding it, give concrete evidence of the curricular and pedagogical definition of the "reform of theological studies" that Slipyj advocated. Already at L'viv, the listing of the courses indicates that the boundary lines, artificial at best, between the subject matter of the theological faculty and that of the philosophical faculty were largely being ignored. First-year students at the theological academy in the academic year 1931/32 took logic, the history of ancient philosophy, and Church Slavonic grammar alongside biblical hermeneutics (from Professor Myškovs'kyj) and introductory liturgics.[147] Even in the third and fourth years of the theological curriculum, moreover, the courses in Church Slavonic grammar were still required.[148] If the language in which the title of the course is designated indicates as well the medium of instruction, both Ukrainian and Latin were being used, with Slipyj himself, for example, lecturing three hours

143. Laba (1974) 7.
144. Slipyj, *Tvory* 7:103.
145. Slipyj, *Tvory* 8:99-112.
146. Slipyj, *Tvory* 7:150.
147. Slipyj, *Tvory* 3/4:415-16.
148. Slipyj, *Tvory* 3/4:417-18.

a week in Latin to the third year and three hours a week in Latin to the fourth year on *Dogmatica specialis*.[149] The catalogue of *UKU*, on the other hand, listed each course title in both languages, with Slipyj offering a two-hour course in eucharistic theology under the double title: *"Presv. Evcharystija z apologetyčnoho stanovyšča: De SS. Eucharistia sub aspectu apologetico."*[150] The practice of combining the traditional subjects of the philosophical and theological faculties, evident at L'viv, took the form at Rome of a single listing with the superscription: "Philosophical-theological Courses at the Ukrainian Catholic University in Rome."[151]

Although there may not be a Ukrainian phrase that is quite the equivalent of the English "Publish or perish," Slipyj's unrelenting insistence on *scholarly publication* expressed the Teutonic educational philosophy that teaching and research were inseparable. In the words of the memorial tribute to Slipyj by Pope John Paul II, "because he cared about scholarship, he founded the University of Saint Clement and published many documents and other materials." That emphasis was a principal factor in Šeptyc'kyj's creation of the Ukrainian Scientific Theological Society, one of whose major functions, according to its statutes, was to be "the publication of scientific theological works."[152] Despite the lack of interest in scholarship that he encountered among his colleagues, Slipyj, with Šeptyc'kyj's encouragement, went ahead with the publication of a monograph series under the auspices of the society.[153] In his report on the society's activities during 1936/37, therefore, Slipyj affirmed: "The Scientific Theological Society carried on its scientific task during 1936 and 1937 in several directions, first of all by means both of strictly scientific and of popular publications."[154] It was a mistake to suppose that the society was to be exclusively an association of clergy;[155] but in the nature of the case most of the authors of most of these theological publications, whether the "strictly scientific" ones or the more "popular" ones, were clergy, although the intended readership was broader. During the nearly sixty years from his initial involvement in scholarly publication, with the appearance of his own dissertation, *Habilitationsschrift*, and other early monographs, until his death, Slipyj had a significant part in the ap-

149. Slipyj, *Tvory* 3/4:420-21.
150. Slipyj, *Tvory* 7:151.
151. Slipyj, *Tvory* 8:137.
152. Slipyj, *Tvory* 3/4:41.
153. Slipyj, *Spomyny* 61.
154. Slipyj, *Tvory* 3/4:739.
155. Slipyj, *Tvory* 3/4:38.

pearance of literally hundreds of monographs and editions of source material, and he never stopped making suggestions and proposals to scholars about needed projects.[156] Thus the statistical report on *UKU* after ten years listed students and courses, but emphasized above all the one hundred scholarly volumes that it had produced.[157] As he himself knew, these volumes were not of uniform scholarly quality; and in the light of the subsequent collaborationist political activities of Havrijil Kostel'nyk, Slipyj must have found it bitterly ironic and, as he himself said, "painful,"[158] upon the publication of his collected works, to find his name paired with that of Father Kostel'nyk in the 1924 account of the society's scholarly publications.[159]

Both in L'viv and in Rome, Slipyj as educator always laid great emphasis on *libraries and collections*. At one point even as a prisoner he assembled samples of exotic flora and sent them to the museum of the Ševčenko Scientific Society in L'viv.[160] Also as a prisoner, he was taken to Moscow in 1953 and one of his guards, a lieutenant colonel, suggested that he visit the Lenin Library. He replied "Very gladly [*Duže rado*]!" and went on, as a scholar who had himself worked in many places and who was something of a connoisseur of research libraries, to make the following observations, as recalled and written down some ten years later:

> They put together several Moscow libraries and created the single Lenin Library. . . . There is a large hall for reading, and another for scholarly workers. There are long corridors with the various divisions, and electrical carts delivered the books that were on reserve. The director bragged about the arrangement, and I said to him that it might be more practical [to use the system] in the British Museum, which has a circular system. He agreed and did not say anything further. In a scholarly institution the atmosphere is bound to be a bit more free, and therefore I was somewhat more depressed when I came out of the library [back into the atmosphere of Moscow as a prisoner].[161]

Once he had gained access to the Lenin Library and other collections, he worked on a four-volume (or five-volume) *History of the Universal*

156. Slipyj, *Tvory* 9:247-48; 116.
157. Slipyj, *Tvory* 13:203.
158. Slipyj, *Tvory* 13:44; see chapter 8, pp. 159-60 below.
159. Slipyj, *Tvory* 3/4:39.
160. Slipyj, *Spomyny* 180.
161. Slipyj, *Spomyny* 168.

Church in Ukraine, which was eventually confiscated by the KGB and, as far as can be determined, no longer exists.[162]

The status of the libraries was an intrinsic part of any scholarly institution, and in his responsibilities as head of several such institutions Slipyj had consistently made that status part of his agenda. This was true not only of the instructional institutions—seminary, theological academy, and *UKU*—but also of the theological society, which under his leadership could boast of having acquired a substantial library, including some rare books and manuscripts.[163] *UKU* had a special problem; for, being compelled to start from scratch, it was obliged, in its ambition to become a comprehensive university rather than merely a seminary, to create its own collections—"a museum of natural history, a library, and an archive"—while setting up cooperative arrangements with other Roman collections.[164] The university created its own special archive of materials from Ukrainian history.[165] As the years went on, Slipyj could point with special pride to the growth of *UKU*'s library. By 1973 it had forty thousand volumes, ".almost as many as the ancient Congregation for the Propagation of the Faith [*Sacra Congregatio de Propaganda Fide*]" in Rome;[166] the following year the collection had grown to almost fifty thousand.[167] When, in the heady populist atmosphere of "liberation theology" during the Second Vatican Council, it was being suggested in some radical quarters that the Vatican should break up its libraries and museum collections and sell them off for the benefit of the poor, Cardinal Slipyj, speaking as one who had "tried to found a great many museums," denounced the suggestion as "the gravest of crimes."[168] The museum was "the witness of our glorious tradition."[169] The precedent for this interest in collections had been established already by the theological academy, part of whose "cultural rôle" on behalf of the Ukrainian people, as the nucleus for a Ukrainian university, had been seen as the need to found "a museum of its own" in L'viv.[170]

The Ukrainian Catholic University in Rome had, of course, a spe-

---

162. The account of this project appears in scattered references in Slipyj, *Spomyny* 167-69, 171, 176, 179-80, 183-85.

163. Slipyj, *Tvory* 3/4:743.

164. Slipyj, *Tvory* 8:103.

165. See Slipyj's tribute to the Archive and to its director, Slipyj, *Tvory* 13:41.

166. Slipyj, *Tvory* 13:236.

167. Slipyj, *Tvory* 13:309 (310-11).

168. Slipyj, *Tvory* 13:120-21.

169. Slipyj, *Tvory* 13:234.

170. Slipyj, *Tvory* 3/4:377-78.

cial problem also in the recruitment and training of its *students*, as the published statistics of its tiny student body demonstrate.[171] For while the seminary and theological academy at L'viv had served the entire Ukrainian Catholic constituency, the constituency for *UKU* was simultaneously smaller and larger: smaller, in that the political realities made attendance by Ukrainian students from the homeland impossible, but larger in that the entire Ukrainian diaspora was seen both as having a stake in the University and as providing a source of students for it. There were, Slipyj admitted, "very [*zamalo*] few students."[172] If it were not for the unfortunate divisions within the worldwide Ukrainian community, he urged elsewhere, there could have been a great many more.[173] That special problem belongs to the particular situation of Josyf Slipyj as metropolitan-in-exile.[174] It belongs here as well, however, because an essential component of Slipyj's (and Šeptyc'kyj's) educational vision had been in L'viv, and became again in Rome, the creation by the Ukrainian Church of "a center on its own terrain."[175] In the words of Slipyj quoted earlier, "unless we create a scholarly center, one of our own, we shall never attain to a position of our own in philosophical and theological scholarship"[176]—at L'viv-Halyč if possible, at Rome if necessary. To make *UKU* such a center for Ukrainian students from the diaspora, an important element of Slipyj's strategy was instituting summer instruction, to which an international student body especially from Canada and the United States and an international faculty of Ukrainian émigré scholars from many countries came for courses.[177] The summer courses at *UKU* were both important and distinctive,[178] and Slipyj was obviously pleased to describe a measure of success for the summer program.[179]

Yet it would be a grave misreading of Slipyj's educational vision to cite as negative evidence the statistics of the student body in the theological faculty, which between 1968 and 1973 never exceeded twelve full-time members. For "the reform of theological studies" that he had launched upon becoming rector of the major seminary at L'viv did not

171. Slipyj, *Tvory* 8:181-82. Other statistics appear in Slipyj, *Tvory* 13:151; 203; 309.
172. Slipyj, *Tvory* 13:179-80.
173. Slipyj, *Tvory* 13:112.
174. See chapter 9, pp. 174-79 below.
175. Slipyj, *Tvory* 3/4:91.
176. Slipyj, *Spomyny* 68.
177. See the notice in German from *Der christliche Osten* in Slipyj, *Tvory* 8:180-81.
178. Slipyj, *Tvory* 13:110-11.
179. Slipyj, *Tvory* 13:286.

stand or fall with the size of the student body, but with the total spiritual and intellectual life of the church, from whose tradition it was derived and to whose future it contributed. As Šeptyc'kyj had demonstrated in peace and in war, the roots of that spiritual and intellectual life ran deep. Slipyj demonstrated this again also in peace and in war, in freedom and then especially in captivity.

8

Not an Ordinary Prisoner

At the death of Metropolitan Andrej Šeptyc′kyj on 1 November 1944—
just at the time when Soviet Premier Joseph Stalin was insisting upon
a Ukrainian-Crimean location on the Black Sea for his upcoming sum-
mit meeting with President Franklin Roosevelt and Prime Minister
Winston Churchill[1]—everyone recognized that the position of the
Ukrainian people and of the Ukrainian Church between East and West
had become an even more ominous one. It was also clear that most of
the burden of the Ukrainian Church in that position would now fall
upon Josyf Slipyj, whom Pope Pius XII had designated on 25 November 1939 as Šeptyc′kyj's coadjutor with the right of succession and
whom Šeptyc′kyj had thereupon consecrated as bishop (in secret)[2] on
22 December 1939. On Saturday, 4 November 1944, in a release that was
to be significant for the future because of its acknowledgment of the
legitimacy of Slipyj's claims to be the rightful incumbent, the Soviet
News Agency Tass announced:

> L′viv, 2 November. On 1 November of this year in the city of L′viv,
> Metropolitan Andrej Šeptyc′kyj, head of the Greek Catholic
> Church in the Soviet Union, died at the age of 79. The funeral
> will take place on 5 November in the Church of Saint George at
> L′viv.

1. Kimball (1984) 3:377-81.
2. Slipyj, *Tvory* 13:299.

146

Metropolitan Josyf Slipyj has assumed the administration of the Greek Catholic Church.[3]

At that funeral, the general commandant of L'viv exclaimed: "How many crosses are going to be laid upon this young metropolitan! And how will he ever be able to bear them all?"[4] Within scarcely four months after Šeptyc'kyj's death, Slipyj was arrested by order of the Soviet authorities, and from 11 April 1945 to 27 January 1963 he was held in various jails, prisons, concentration camps, and forced labor gulags.[5] He was to declare afterward that "in the story of my life the Soviet period begins a special page," and a sad one.[6]

Both from the treatment he received there and from the way (to quote again from the memorial tribute of Pope John Paul II) "he passed through the tortures and sufferings of the Cross, similar to those of Christ on Golgotha [during those] eighteen years of imprisonment and suffering . . . yet did not crack, but like a hero resisted with dignity," it was evident that, in ways far transcending anything his prison guard and "*stukač* [torturer]" could have intended when he said it, it was true of Slipyj that "You are not an ordinary prisoner [*Vy ne obyčnyj zaključonnyj*]."[7] What has been pointed out earlier about the status of Ukrainian archives and of source material for the life of Josyf Slipyj applies *a fortiori* to this "page" in the story of his life. A "prudent silence" was enjoined on him after his release from prison: he was "not to talk about Soviet Russia, not to talk about his imprisonment"; for it was an important consideration of Vatican diplomacy—and was as well a condition of his release[8]—"not to transform 'the Slipyj affair' into a political question."[9] While urging in response that this was not simply a Ukrainian issue, but one involving many other peoples, including the American, French, and German peoples, and that "the death of 50 million human beings is not a trivial matter," Slipyj accepted the condition of "prudent silence"[10] and, unfortunately for later historians, felt him-

3. There is a copy of this news release in the library of Harvard University.

4. Slipyj to N. V. Podgorny, i.1961, *Arch.Pat.* 28:27 (62).

5. The chronology was painstakingly reconstructed on the first anniversary of Slipyj's death by Ivan Choma (1985).

6. Slipyj, "Brevi note autobiografiche" (1965), *Arch.Pat.* 32:162.

7. Slipyj, *Spomyny* 162.

8. See Choma (1984) 345-47.

9. Unsigned memorandum (presumably by Amleto Cicognani) dated 8.iv.1963, *Arch.Pat.* 28:220.

10. Slipyj to Amleto Cicognani, 18.iv.1963, *Arch.Pat.* 28:236-40.

self bound by it, at least to some degree, also in the years that were to follow. Nevertheless, the private memoirs that he prepared, and then reviewed and edited, but did not publish, in 1963/64 do contain a large amount of information about his years of captivity, as do his recollections upon the twenty-fifth and the thirtieth anniversaries of his arrest[11] and other *obiter dicta* by Slipyj himself and by others.

To the historian, unfortunately, all of these memoirs and recollections are at least as tantalizing and frustrating as they are informative, for repeatedly they refer beyond themselves to a documentation that is out of reach, perhaps forever. "During the Hitlerite occupation," Slipyj's narrative states, "there were brought to me, unearthed somewhere in a Soviet archive, denunciations against me by the Bolsheviks,"[12] but these seem to be lost. He later speaks about "the official reports of the public prosecutors [*protokoly slidčych*]," who had sought out information about him for the Soviet courts,[13] but these, too, are gone. There seem to have been "tens of volumes of my public prosecutions [*mojich desjatky tomiv slidstva*],"[14] and elsewhere he speaks of "twenty-some volumes of my protocols."[15] He refers by name to some of those who testified against him,[16] but does not provide details. His jailers had a "dossier [*delo* in Russian],"[17] which seems to have traveled with him from one concentration camp commandant to another, but no such *delo* seems to be in the available files. Even when he was ordered by Soviet officials, apparently in 1953, to prepare an autobiography, he explains, "I wrote it, but in very abridged form, giving the main dates but not going into detail about the torture and the persecution."[18] The exercise of composing that autobiography may have helped him ten years later when, after his liberation, he did write the memoirs we have, in which, at least to some extent, he did "go into detail about the torture and the persecution," but the earlier version does not seem to have survived.

The "prudent silence" has, then, in considerable measure been preserved, but there remains enough documentary evidence to add this portrait of Slipyj as "not an ordinary prisoner" to the other portraits of

11. Slipyj, *Tvory* 13:65-67; 322-24.
12. Slipyj, *Spomyny* 94.
13. Slipyj, *Spomyny* 119, 120-21.
14. Slipyj to N. V. Podgorny, 17.ii.1961, *Arch.Pat.* 28:90 (125).
15. Slipyj, *Spomyny* 187.
16. Slipyj, *Spomyny* 101, 106.
17. Slipyj, *Spomyny* 129-30.
18. Slipyj, *Spomyny* 161-62.

him that we have been examining in the preceding chapters. In fact, it is possible to trace some of the lines and characteristics of each of those other portraits also in this one. For it was as the disciple of Metropolitan Andrej Šeptyc'kyj that Slipyj was arrested and imprisoned, and at least to some extent they were getting at Šeptyc'kyj through Slipyj. Slipyj the Thomist was active in prison, too, lecturing on the history of medieval philosophy, with the help of Polish translations of the works of the French Thomist, Étienne Gilson. And Slipyj the scholar and educator took every opportunity, even when it came from his Soviet captors, to do research and to visit research libraries; he also wrote a multi-volume *History of the Universal Church in Ukraine and in the Soviet Union as a Whole.*

Being deprived of the "official reports of the public prosecutors [*protokoly slidčych*]" and the "dossier [*delo*]" just referred to, we cannot reconstruct with any great specificity the full slate of the official charges against Metropolitan Slipyj at the time of his arrest and at his several subsequent trials. Such an absence of official and legal documentation could be fatal to any attempt at a political biography of Josyf Slipyj. But for the purposes of the present "portrait" of him and of his vocations, it is far more important to learn what Slipyj himself took to be the basis of his indictment, conviction, and imprisonment than it is to ask what the Stalinist secret police and the Soviet kangaroo courts claimed he had done; for that matter, this interpretation may even prove to be more accurate as well, when and if the official documents should ever surface. In addition to the aforementioned memoirs and other postliberation sources, new documents do turn up from time to time, such as the letters from prison for Christmas and Lent 1954 that his editors have included in the ninth volume of his collected works.[19] The Patriarchal Archive of Saint Sophia in Rome also contains copies of two substantial documents of more than five thousand words each, bearing the heading "complaint [*žaloba*]" and addressed by Slipyj the prisoner in January and February of 1961 to Nikolaj Viktorovič Podgorny (Pidhornyj in Ukrainian), then the First Secretary of the Ukrainian Communist Party and, from 1965 to 1977, Chairman of the Presidium of the Supreme Soviet of the Union of Soviet Socialist Republics.[20]

These two highly revealing documents exhibit the courage and candor of Josyf Slipyj as he addressed a man who had, quite literally, the power of life and death over him. "We are not in an academy of sci-

19. Slipyj, *Tvory* 9:342-52.
20. Because each *žaloba* is framed in the form of a lengthy letter, I shall cite them as I am citing other correspondence from the *Archivum Patriarchale Sanctae Sophiae.*

ences, on an equal footing," Slipyj could write, "for in every respect we are incomparably different in size. You are a minister of state, and I am a prisoner without any rights whatever. I am a scholar, not a politician, and I am the metropolitan. You are not a scholar, but a political leader, and you are the one who has all the physical power in his hands."[21] But they bespeak as well the almost eschatological detachment of someone who had everything to lose and therefore nothing to lose. "Some of you are waiting until all we Greek Catholics die out," Slipyj stated, "but that is a vain expectation!" For the Greek Catholic Church abroad had become, remarkably, stronger than ever. "Here at home," he continued, "we ourselves shall die off, and all of you will die off too. But the Greek Catholic Church will endure in the catacombs."[22] When used to supplement Slipyj's later memoirs and in conjunction with the allusions to his imprisonment in his later correspondence, his letters of *žaloba* to Podgorny help to make possible a reconstructed account of his interpretation of what had happened to him.

Such an account must begin with the status of the Ukrainian Greek Catholic Church in the eyes of the Soviet government at the time of the death of Metropolitan Šeptyc'kyj on 1 November 1944. In an official letter to Pope Paul VI, sent a few months after his release and scarcely a week after the pope's election on 21 June 1963—the same letter had already been sent at the end of April (thus while John XXIII was still pope but lay near death) to Monsignor Angelo Dell'Acqua and to others in Rome[23]—Metropolitan Slipyj reported:

It was in the autumn of 1944, that is, some months after the second occupation of Western Ukraine by the Soviets. The representative of the Soviet government in L'viv insistently suggested to me that I seek for an official legalization of the existence of our church in the USSR, saying that this was what the members of other religious denominations had. After having consulted with expert persons in whom I had confidence, I sent a delegation to Moscow to obtain from the Soviet government the legalization of our church. In Moscow this delegation was accorded a very good reception: Stalin recognized our church, with my person as its primate. This official recognition was published in a notice on the pages of the journal *Pravda* [*Izvestija*] in December 1944.[24]

21. Slipyj to N. V. Podgorny, 17.ii.1961, *Arch.Pat.* 28:89 (124).
22. Slipyj to N. V. Podgorny, 17.ii.1961, *Arch.Pat.* 28:87 (122).
23. Slipyj to Angelo Dell'Acqua, 30.iv.1963, *Arch.Pat.* 28:175-79.
24. Slipyj to Paul VI, 30.vi.1963, *Arch.Pat.* 28:450.

For a brief time, the prospects for the church and its "young metropolitan" began to look up. Yet it was only a matter of time until the attacks on the church would resume.[25]

A membership of seven million Greek Catholic faithful out of a total Ukrainian population of forty-four million—thus roughly one-sixth—was, Slipyj felt able to say, in a phrase that he would repeat to the Communist First Secretary and to the Pope of Rome, *une quantité pas négligeable*,[26] as Stalin had also acknowledged when he granted the official recognition in 1944. But then, right after granting the recognition, "the Party and the Government changed their previous stand and withdrew recognition from the Greek Catholic Church."[27] There were "signs of great unrest and suspicion."[28] From what could be characterized as "a moderate attitude [*povzderžlyve stanovyšče*]" toward the Greek Catholic Church in L'viv, the Party there, early in 1945, was shifting once more to a stance of open hostility and undertook a campaign of harassment, as well as of increasing provocation. "Probably," Slipyj later surmised, "Jaroslav Halan, early in 1945, was preparing a plan to destroy the church." Halan was the author of *With the Cross or with the Knife?* [*Z chrestom či z nožem?*] and of *I Spit on the Pope* [*Pluju na Papu*].[29] Years later, while on a semi-furlough from his imprisonment, Slipyj would have the opportunity to study the official Soviet publications between 1940 and 1953, which he had not seen before; he discovered from those publications that no new laws had been promulgated out-lawing the Greek Catholic Church, only an administrative prohibition by the NKVD.[30]

It was only a matter of time before the campaign of harassment against the church in general would focus on its most important target, the new metropolitan of L'viv-Halyč. The blow fell on Wednesday, 11 April 1945—a date that would be observed in the Ukrainian diaspora, for example in Madrid, as "the anniversary of the incarceration of the hierarchy of the Ukrainian Church,"[31] as well as by Slipyj himself after he had regained his freedom.[32] At about seven o'clock in

25. Slipyj, *Tvory* 13:300.
26. Slipyj to N. V. Podgorny, 17.ii.1961, *Arch.Pat.* 28:79 (114); Slipyj to Paul VI, 6.ix.1963, *Arch.Pat.* 29:135.
27. Slipyj to N. V. Podgorny, i.1961, *Arch.Pat.* 28:23 (58).
28. Slipyj, *Tvory* 13:323.
29. Slipyj, *Spomyny* 108-9.
30. Slipyj, *Spomyny* 167-68.
31. "Misa solemne en rito bizantino," celebrated in Madrid by Hildebrando Antoniutti, papal nuncio in Spain, *Arch.Pat.* 119:12.
32. Slipyj, *Tvory* 9:128; 13:65-67, 322-24.

the evening, Slipyj had stepped out on the balcony of the metropolitan's palace to observe the planet Mars, which was very close to the earth at the time.[33] Soon the plaza before the Cathedral of Saint George was filled with guards. There was a great coming and going of automobiles, and a large number of police. The Soviet colonel in charge brought a warrant for Slipyj's arrest, and even many years later Slipyj could still recall his feeling of offense and violation at being seized and led away as though he were some kind of brigand.[34] He could also recall the clandestine atmosphere in which the whole operation had been carried out, for fear of the populace:

> You know very well [he would write to Podgorny more than fif-
> teen years later] that they arrested me under cover of night, took
> me under cover of night to Kiev, without anyone knowing where
> I had disappeared to. The [Greek Catholic] faithful were ready to
> pledge a collection of a million rubles for my liberation. I was
> judged in secret and by night, behind locked doors, and . . .
> without my having a lawyer or a defender.[35]

The only persons allowed to be present at the hearings were "the judges, the KGB, and the guards."[36] Slipyj was shocked but not really surprised by his arrest, for he seems to have been expecting something like this ever since Šeptyc'kyj's death. And now the punishment for what the authorities regarded as "the alleged 'crimes' of Metropolitan Andrej Šeptyc'kyj"[37] would fall on his successor: "they arrested me, all the bishops, and a large number of clergy and faithful."[38]

Yet the precise nature of those "crimes," whether allegedly committed by Andrej Šeptyc'kyj or by Josyf Slipyj, is not altogether clear. One of the first issues raised by Slipyj's captors was his alleged association with the Ukrainian nationalists who were battling against the Soviets under Roman Šuchevyč, commander-in-chief of the "Ukrainian Insurgent Army [Ukrajinska povstanska armija, UPA]."[39] This nationalistic and military activity had received the endorsement of Metropolitan Šeptyc'kyj.[40] Understandably, the Soviet leaders seem to have believed

33. Slipyj, Tvory 13:323.
34. This account is a paraphrase of the vivid paragraph in which Slipyj himself describes the arrest: Slipyj, Spomyny 110.
35. Slipyj to N. V. Podgorny, 17.ii.1961, Arch.Pat. 28:86 (121).
36. Slipyj, Spomyny 124.
37. Slipyj, Spomyny 123-24.
38. Slipyj, Tvory 13.300.
39. On Šuchevyč and the UPA, see Boshyk (1986) 63, 71-72.
40. See Armstrong (1963) 80-81.

that Šeptyc'kyj and then Slipyj could exert influence on Šuchevyč. "Your church has great influence," they said. "Couldn't your metropolitan put pressure on Šuchevyč to stop fighting against us?"[41] As one of its purposes, then, the arrest of Slipyj was apparently intended to provide them with leverage against Šuchevyč and the *UPA*.[42] A Colonel Chomjak was said to have told Slipyj's colleague, Father Kotiv, that "if I [Metropolitan Slipyj] did not proceed within two weeks to the liquidation of the *UPA*, I would be arrested and our church destroyed."[43]

But Šuchevyč was also seen as a collaborator with the German occupation forces, who had helped to create the *UPA* in opposition to Moscow. Therefore part of the accusation against the Ukrainian clergy and against Slipyj as their metropolitan was "collaboration with Germans and nationalists."[44] Just how little it took to set off such charges during this period is evident from the experience of a young opera singer in the Soviet Union, who in 1952 "mentioned on his questionnaire that as a fourteen-year-old boy he had lived in the German-occupied Ukraine. As a result, he was not cleared for almost two years, and joined the Bolshoi only after Stalin's death."[45] Thus at the end of 1943 and the beginning of 1944, Slipyj had been sent by Metropolitan Šeptyc'kyj as his representative to the funeral of a Ukrainian émigré in Nazi-occupied Prague, and en route he had also stopped in Vienna and Berlin.[46] After his arrest, the judge told him: "You went to Prague, and that had to be with a passport from the Gestapo!" Slipyj replied: "The passport was brought to me in my office, because I myself did not arrange the trip, but went at the behest of the metropolitan."[47] When they accused him of collaboration with the Nazis, he replied that it was not he who had collaborated with the Nazis, but Foreign Minister Vyacheslav Molotov, by signing the German-Soviet Treaty of Nonaggression on 23 August 1939 with the Foreign Minister of the German Reich, Joachim von Ribbentrop, and with Adolf Hitler.[48] Because the Ukrainians, at the end of the Nazi period, had not participated in the revenge against the German armies by the Poles and Russians, Slipyj explained many years

41. Slipyj to N. V. Podgorny, 17.ii.1961, *Arch.Pat.* 82-83 (117).
42. Slipyj to N. V. Podgorny, i.1961, *Arch.Pat.* 28:24 (59).
43. Slipyj, *Spomyny* 110.
44. Slipyj to N. V. Podgorny, i.1961, *Arch.Pat.* 28:39 (73).
45. Vishnevskaya (1984) 81.
46. Slipyj, *Spomyny* 96-97.
47. Slipyj, *Spomyny* 125.
48. Slipyj, *Spomyny* 187.

later, "this was leveled as an accusation against the Ukrainians by the Soviet régime, and on the basis of this slander even I was baselessly charged with 'Hitlerism.' "[49]

But such accusations, Slipyj insisted, would not hold. He was concerned not only for the Ukrainian victims of Communist persecution, but for such victims of Nazi atrocities as Tito Brandsma, whom he joined in nominating for beatification.[50] He had vigorously counseled all along against identifying the Ukrainian Church with "Hitlerite arrangements."[51] At times, of course, circumstances had made it true of Slipyj, as well as of Šeptyc'kyj, that (as the historian Bruce Catton once said about Horatio Seymour, governor of New York during the American Civil War) "he was an honorable extremist, driven by the cruel logic of events into speaking for forces which he would not ordinarily uphold, and behind him were men whom he himself would not endorse."[52] But even at that, Slipyj had refused, on the grounds of his being the metropolitan, to accept the chairmanship of the Ukrainian National Council (which Šeptyc'kyj had, however, been willing to serve as honorary chairman).[53] Slipyj saw himself obliged, in his ecclesiastical and pastoral capacity as metropolitan, to mediate between the extremists on both sides, instead of taking overtly political positions, whether in one direction or the other.[54]

And that, in his judgment, was the blindness at the root of both fundamental misconceptions among his accusers about him and about his church: first, they could not see that "the affairs of the church are not settled in political meetings [*mitingach* in Russian], but in churches"; second, they failed to recognize "that I am not an agitator and that agitation does not interest me."[55] Already much earlier, in his complex relations with the Polish régime during the 1920s and 1930s, while he was rector of the seminary at L'viv, he had been able to get by, precisely because he had insisted upon being "politically unengaged."[56] That insistence became all the more important when he was obliged to deal with the Nazi and the Communist régimes. In his

---

49. Slipyj to the Bishops' Conference of the German Federal Republic, 18.iii.1971, *Arch.Pat.* 40:53.
50. Slipyj to Paul VI, 5.viii.1963, *Arch.Pat.* 29:102-3.
51. Slipyj, *Spomyny* 97.
52. Catton (1984) 303.
53. Slipyj, *Spomyny* 96.
54. Slipyj, *Spomyny* 93.
55. Slipyj to N. V. Podgorny, 17.ii.1961, *Arch.Pat.* 28:86 (121).
56. Slipyj, *Spomyny* 67.

secret trial he was able to plead before Judge Krykun that he had not taken part in nationalistic activity.[57] He made the same plea when, in the camps, he was approached by some anti-Communist "revisionists" on a hunger strike: "I am no politician."[58] He did not intend thereby to minimize or to conceal his national consciousness as a Ukrainian: "Here in Ukraine and in its heart, Kiev," he wrote at the conclusion of his second *žaloba* to Podgorny, it was fitting for him to appeal to "national consciousness"—his own, but also Podgorny's, "since, no matter what you may say to yourself, you are Ukrainian and I am Ukrainian."[59] But it did mean that, as a Ukrainian "between East and West," he had had to endure pressure and persecution from Poles and from Russians, from the KGB and from the Gestapo,[60] as had the institutions he headed in L'viv.[61]

Some of the Soviet officials had acknowledged as much; for when they came to Slipyj in the prison camp, they did not treat him as (in the words of his accusation) "an enemy of the people [*voroh narodu*]," but as "the victim of political coincidence [*žertva polityčnoji konsteljaciji*]."[62] Slipyj could assert that even if there had been any such Ukrainian "collaboration with Germans and nationalists"—and he knew that there had—it had not taken place on his watch as metropolitan.[63] He knew that there had been "national chauvinism" in Ukrainian history, but the historic function of the Catholic Church had been to mitigate its effects, not to exacerbate them.[64] But because "Communist atheists cannot understand a religious issue,"[65] they had to reduce everything to a political-economic issue. Everything had to be considered "in a political forum" or not at all.[66] Thus it had taken Slipyj a while to understand "why in Moscow the leadership of the Ministry was so interested in having my *History of the Universal Church in Ukraine and in the Soviet Union as a Whole*, and how this had provided the occasion for my renewed arrest and condemnation to seven years in prison and the labor camps."[67] By the same irony that had prompted Soviet authorities

57. Slipyj, *Spomyny* 118.
58. Slipyj, *Spomyny* 191.
59. Slipyj to N. V. Podgorny, 17.ii.1961, *Arch.Pat.* 28:91 (126).
60. Slipyj to N. V. Podgorny, 17.ii.1961, *Arch.Pat.* 28:89 (123).
61. Slipyj, *Spomyny* 70, 100.
62. Slipyj to N. V. Podgorny, 17.ii.1961, *Arch.Pat.* 28:83 (118).
63. Slipyj to N. V. Podgorny, i.1961, *Arch.Pat.* 28:39 (73).
64. Slipyj to N. V. Podgorny, 17.ii.1961, *Arch.Pat.* 28:82 (117).
65. Slipyj to N. V. Podgorny, i.1961, *Arch.Pat.* 28:39 (74).
66. Slipyj to N. V. Podgorny, 17.ii.1961, *Arch.Pat.* 28:81 (116).
67. Slipyj to N. V. Podgorny, 17.ii.1961, *Arch.Pat.* 28:88 (123).

to attack Metropolitan Andrej Šeptyc'kyj for alleged disloyalty to a Czarist régime which they themselves had overthrown in the Bolshevik Revolution, Slipyj's *History*, which documented the contribution of the Greek Catholic Church to the maintenance of Ukrainian nationality and therefore to Ukrainian resistance against deracination and assimilation during the periods of Austrian and Polish (and hence Roman Catholic) dominance over Galicia, a dominance ended by Soviet political and military action, could become the basis for action against him now.[68] For the *History* seemed to indicate—and correctly—that the same Ukrainian national spirit would resist a Soviet-Russian-Orthodox campaign of deracination no less fiercely than it had the Austrian and Polish campaigns that had gone before.

In that sense, then, Slipyj could be attacked as, of all things, "an enemy of the people."[69] One of his interrogators asked him, "Have you ever been in Rome?" And when Slipyj admitted that he had (having, after all, received the degree of *Magister aggregatus* from the Gregorian University in 1924), the officer shook his head and exclaimed, "Rome, Rome!" All of that, Slipyj concluded, served to confirm his deepening impression "that my Catholic faith is the reason for my being persecuted in the concentration camps"; for they were shunting him around from one labor camp to another, and always further and further from L'viv and Halyč.[70] When he spoke to Podgorny of "eternal repetition and renewal of animosity [*vorožneča*] against the Greek Catholic Church and against me personally" on the part of his captors and interrogators,[71] therefore, that ordering of the objects of the animosity was significant: the Greek Catholic Church first, and only then Josyf Slipyj personally. That was what he had been told at the Ministry already in 1945: "If you were not the metropolitan, you would not be sitting here."[72] He quoted those words also to Podgorny fifteen years later, adding the comment: "This means that I am sitting for the cause of the church, a cause for which you, Mr. Minister, seek to accuse me over and over."[73] Similarly, the "hostile position toward the late Metropolitan Andrej" that was expressed by Slipyj's captors[74] would seem to have been directed at least as much against the Greek Catholic

68. Slipyj to N. V. Podgorny, 17.ii.1961, *Arch.Pat.* 28:82 (117).
69. Slipyj to N. V. Podgorny, 17.ii.1961, *Arch.Pat.* 28:83 (118).
70. Slipyj, *Spomyny* 137.
71. Slipyj to N. V. Podgorny, 17.ii.1961, *Arch.Pat.* 28:84 (119).
72. Slipyj, *Spomyny* 194.
73. Slipyj to N. V. Podgorny, 17.ii.1961, *Arch.Pat.* 28:87 (122).
74. Slipyj, *Spomyny* 172.

Church and the metropolitanate of L'viv-Halyč as against the person of Andrej Šeptyc'kyj himself.

If the real reason for Slipyj's arrest and imprisonment was indeed his position as metropolitan rather than some specific crime that he himself was alleged to have committed personally as "an enemy of the people,"[75] the obverse of his arrest was, paradoxically, the proposition that he as metropolitan now place himself at the service of the régime. When the Ukrainian delegation dispatched by Metropolitan Josyf to Moscow in 1944 were received by the General Staff of the Red Army, they were told: "We know that your church has great influence in the nation."[76] Also in Moscow, but much later, after his arrest, Slipyj himself was told that he could be useful to the authorities.[77] "There is no one else but you," he was told, who could do something to improve diplomatic relations between the Soviet Union and the Vatican.[78] They suggested to him that, accompanied by the First Secretary of the Ukrainian Communist Party, N. V. Podgorny, he should travel around Western Ukraine on a propaganda trip.[79] But the campaign to corrupt and suborn him by making him "helpful to us"[80] went much further than that idea. He reported that after his arrest in 1945 his captors had proposed that if he would renounce the pope and the Catholic Church, he would be "restored to freedom as the metropolitan of the Orthodox Church in Kiev or elsewhere [abo deinde]."[81] In the Italian translation of the letter prepared in 1963, Slipyj added, in his own hand, as a translation of that last phrase: "or some higher [piu alto] post,"[82] and in a talk on 2 November 1974 Slipyj spoke of being offered "the very highest position [najvyšče stanovyšče] in 1953 or so."[83] The meaning of those cryptic statements becomes more explicit in the covering letter of 1963, accompanying the Italian translation of the žaloba to Podgorny, where Slipyj described a later version of the attempt to win him over, which took place after the death of Lavrentij Beria in December of 1953: "It was proposed to me that if I separated myself from the Holy Apostolic See, I would be offered the post of suffragan to the patriarch of Mos-

75. Slipyj to N. V. Podgorny, 17.ii.1961, Arch.Pat. 28:83 (118).
76. Slipyj, Spomyny 107.
77. Slipyj, Spomyny 165-66; see also Spomyny 192.
78. Slipyj, Tvory 13:301.
79. Slipyj to N. V. Podgorny, 17.ii.1961, Arch.Pat. 28:86 (121).
80. Slipyj, Spomyny 165.
81. Slipyj to N. V. Podgorny, i.1961, Arch.Pat. 28:24.
82. Slipyj to N. V. Podgorny, i.1961, Arch.Pat. 28:58.
83. Slipyj, Tvory 13:301.

cow. This proposition was presented to me as extremely confidential."
Slipyj added: "After my categorical refusal, I was condemned to a hard
exile in Siberia."[84] He confirmed that interpretation of events also in his
memoirs.[85]

Such negotiation over high ecclesiastical posts was seen, both by
Slipyj himself and by the Vatican, as part of a grand strategy of what
might be termed "ecumenism Soviet style." As the Vatican journal
L'Osservatore Romano put it, that strategy involved a two-point
program: first, a reunion of the Ukrainian Greek Catholic Church (to
be separated from Rome) with the Russian Orthodox Church, under
the patriarchate of Moscow; second, adoption by that reunited Ukrainian Church of a policy of collaboration with the Soviet régime.[86]
Ecumenism Soviet style was aimed at the formation of a solid bloc of
Eastern Orthodox Christians in opposition to Poles and Roman
Catholics, under the leadership of the patriarch of Moscow (the
patriarch of Constantinople being regarded as ineffectual, religiously
and above all politically).[87] That had created the anomaly that a self-
professed atheistic state, which ever since the Revolution had been persecuting Russian Orthodoxy as the bulwark of the Czarist *ancien régime*,
was now taking sides on behalf of *Pravoslavie* in the millennium-long
schism between the Eastern and the Western Churches.[88] Almost taunt-
ingly, Slipyj challenged Podgorny, as an "atheist [*bezbožnyk*]," to explain why he should now have become a patron of *Pravoslavie* against
Catholicism.[89] Why, he asked, should the Greek Catholic Church of the
Byzantine Rite be more frightening to the Soviet régime than either the
Orthodox Church or, for that matter, the Roman Catholic Church of the
Latin Rite?[90] The answer, it seemed clear to Slipyj, lay in the very genius
of the Greek Catholic Church: unlike the Roman Catholic Church of the
Latin Rite, it followed an Eastern liturgy and thus appealed to the
deepest Ukrainian (and Russian) religious traditions; but unlike Ukrai-
nian and Russian Orthodoxy, it had an authority and a point of leverage
beyond the political boundaries of the Union of Soviet Socialist
Republics, in the Holy See and the papacy. That made it, in the eyes of

84. Slipyj to Angelo Dell'Acqua, 30.iv.1963, *Arch.Pat.* 28:277; Slipyj to Paul VI,
30.vi.1963, *Arch.Pat.* 28:452.
85. Slipyj, *Spomyny* 172.
86. *Oss.Rom.* 17.ii.1962.
87. Slipyj to N. V. Podgorny, 17.ii.1961, *Arch.Pat.* 28:76 (111).
88. Slipyj to N. V. Podgorny, i.1961, *Arch.Pat.* 28:34 (68).
89. Slipyj to N. V. Podgorny, 17.ii.1961, *Arch.Pat.* 28:88 (122).
90. Slipyj to N. V. Podgorny, 17.ii.1961, *Arch.Pat.* 28:80 (114).

a Soviet *bezbožnyk* no less than in those of a believing *Pravoslavnyj*, an alien element in Ukrainian and Russian culture, brought in by the Jesuits.[91]

After Stalin's initial stratagem of according recognition to the Greek Catholic Church, with, as Slipyj said, "my person as its primate,"[92] had been replaced by a policy which declared, "We will liquidate your church,"[93] that alien element was seen as an obstacle, but one that could be neither "liquidated" nor removed in any other way so long as Josyf Slipyj continued to preside over it as its metropolitan. What Stalin's new policy, replacing recognition, had become at the beginning of 1945, with Slipyj's arrest and imprisonment, made itself evident in the convoking of the so-called Synod of L'viv, which was held on 8-10 March 1946.[94] Three clergy of the Ukrainian Greek Catholic Church—Mychajil Mel'nyk, Antonin Pel'vec'kyj, and Slipyj's sometime associate Havrijil Kostel'nyk as the ringleader[95]—created a "Central Initiative Group," which had the ostensible purpose of working toward reunion between the Greek Catholic and the Orthodox Churches. To that end they brought together at the Cathedral of Saint George in L'viv (to quote the official statistics) 216 Greek Catholic clergy and 19 laymen.[96] In a historical-theological lecture Kostel'nyk drew a parallel between the time it had taken Christianity to develop from a Jewish sect into the Constantinian church and the similar length of time—precisely three hundred fifty years, from 1596 to 1946—during which the Ukrainian Catholic Church had been moving from the Synod of Brest toward its definitive form, reunion with Moscow; and he invoked the legacy of Saints Cyril and Methodius to call upon the delegates to exert all their strength for the return of the entire people of Halyč to the faith of their forefathers, the pure Christian faith of holy Eastern Orthodoxy.[97] In its four final resolutions, the meeting

1. annulled the decisions of the Synod of Brest of 1596, liquidated the Union, [and] broke with the Vatican . . . ;
2. affiliated with the Holy Eastern Orthodox Church of Russia . . .

---

91. Slipyj to N. V. Podgorny, i.1961, *Arch.Pat.* 28:35 (69).
92. Slipyj to Paul VI, 30.vi.1963, *Arch.Pat.* 28:450.
93. Slipyj to N. V. Podgorny, 17.ii.1961, *Arch.Pat.* 28:79-80 (114).
94. Its proceedings were officially published as *Dijannja Soboru Greko-Kat. Cerkvy u L'vovi 8.-10.III.1946* (1946).
95. The three are pictured in *Dijannja Soboru* (1946) 13.
96. Their names are listed in *Dijannja Soboru* (1946) 53-58.
97. The full text of the lecture is in *Dijannja Soboru* (1946) 63-75.

[and] His Holiness Aleksej, patriarch of Moscow and All Russia . . . ;

3. declared that in the efforts which all the freedom-loving nations of the entire world have put forth for their survival [isnuvannje], the Vatican stands completely on the side of criminal Fascism . . . ; and

4. sent official telegrams to the Ecumenical Patriarch of Constantinople [and others].

All four of these were unanimously approved.[98] Telegrams were also sent to Joseph Stalin (for the Soviet Union as a whole) and to Nikita Khrushchev (for the Ukrainian Soviet Socialist Republic).[99] And so, after a total of three days' deliberation, three and a half centuries of history were undone and the Greek Catholic Church was officially liquidated, while its primate, Josyf Slipyj, metropolitan of L'viv-Halyč, and his bishops languished in Soviet captivity. It was perhaps the supreme irony of all that the synod of 1946 opened its second day with the singing of a Church Slavonic requiem [Panachyda] for the late Metropolitan Andrej.[100] (Of the three members of the "Central Initiative Group," Mychajil Mel'nyk and Antonin Pel'vec'kyj had been made Orthodox bishops in February of that year, but Havrijil Kostel'nyk was a married man and therefore could not be.)

In addition to the official proceedings published in 1946, from which this material has been taken, there have been a few other attempts to treat the Synod of L'viv of 1946 as a legitimate church synod.[101] In doing so, the official Soviet party line has continued to describe Slipyj as nothing more than a "pretender" after the Synod of L'viv.[102] Most scholars and churchmen, however, deny the legitimacy of the synod on canonical as well as on theological grounds.[103] The Synod of L'viv was, in the words of one historian of Russian Orthodoxy, a "shotgun union,"[104] or, in the words of another historian, "a fake congress of the Church,"[105] or, in the words of a Polish cardinal, "in reality an extreme-

98. Dijannja Soboru (1946) 128.

99. Dijannja Soboru (1946) 141-44.

100. Dijannja Soboru (1946) 44.

101. So, for example, Prus (1985) 297-303.

102. Migovič (1985) 119.

103. Two representative accounts are Korolevskij (1964) 386-400 and Lužnyc'kyj (1954) 582-86.

104. Fireside (1971) 180.

105. Conquest (1986) 213.

ly sad event in the history of the Catholic Church in Ukraine," when Byzantine Rite Catholics "denied their religious rights."[106] Pope Pius XII repudiated it soon after it had happened.[107] Other popes did the same.[108] In the epilogue of a book published in the year of the Synod of L'viv, Robert Pierce Casey was warning that "the Vatican, the Soviet government, and the Russian Church are keeping a watchful eye on territories recently dominated by the U.S.S.R. . . . In this matter the Soviet government can be expected to act with the utmost firmness and caution."[109] And in the final chapter of his *History of Russia*, which was published in the year of Slipyj's liberation, Nicholas V. Riasanovsky, after lamenting that in 1945 the Orthodox Church of Russia had "declared complete loyalty to the regime, and supported, for example, its international peace campaign and its attempts to influence the Balkan Orthodox," went on to say: "More unfortunately, the two co-operated in bringing the two or three million Uniates of former eastern Poland into Orthodoxy."[110] Even before the Revolution, as the American historian of Orthodoxy, Donald W. Treadgold, suggests, "perhaps the most egregious, and even unnecessary, mistake of this sort [by the Russian Orthodox Church] was made in compelling the Uniats to break their organizational tie with Rome and affiliate with the Orthodox church. . . . It was ill-considered, hasty, and counterproductive."[111] But the Synod of L'viv in 1946 was all of that and more.

Slipyj's own interpretation of this joint action of the Soviet regime and the Orthodox patriarchate was, of course, unambiguous, as he would also explain in an official letter to Pope John Paul II.[112] The synod took its actions "under pressure from the police";[113] it had been carried out "under duress";[114] it possessed "no canonical validity."[115] He called it, quite simply, "the pseudo-synod of L'viv, organized by the KGB."[116] Or, as he specified in more detail to his colleagues:

106. Władysław Rubin to Slipyj, 23.xi.1981, *Arch.Pat.* 118:232.
107. Slipyj, *Tvory* 9:200.
108. Slipyj, *Tvory* 14:259.
109. Casey (1946) 194-95.
110. Riasanovsky (1963) 635.
111. Donald W. Treadgold in Nichols-Stavrou (1978) 35-36.
112. Slipyj to John Paul II, 29.vi.1981, *Arch.Pat.* 118:223.
113. Slipyj, *Tvory* 9:156.
114. Slipyj, *Spomyny* 152-53.
115. Slipyj, *Tvory* 9:67.
116. Slipyj to Jan Willebrands, 14.vii.1971, *Arch.Pat.* 40:216-17.

The KGB in its negotiations indicated that our church had been liquidated by the synod held at L'viv in 1946. But I explained to them, as I did the remainder of the facts in various memoranda to the government, that this was merely a rabble [accozzaglia] of about 120 persons, divided between timid priests and laymen. No Catholic bishop of ours participated in this synod. Therefore this synod did not have any legitimate authority to speak or make decisions in the name of our church. And in support of this proposition I quoted affirmations also from Eastern Orthodox authors, who say that a synod without its bishop is no synod.[117]

Only "an insignificant number of Ukrainian Catholic clergy" had been involved in its actions.[118] He found Father Havrijil Kostel'nyk beneath contempt, as (in words he quoted from Kost' Levyc'kyj, who was also a collaborator with the Communists) "the most stupid politician in Ukraine [najdurnišyj polityk na Ukrajini]."[119] Some years later, as a prisoner in Kiev, Slipyj was taken to the showing of a documentary film entitled The Synod of 1946 in L'viv—"the only film about the church ever made in the Soviet Union!" He watched Father Kostel'nyk declare his allegiance to the patriarchate of Moscow, and he dismissed the whole thing as a "farce."[120] And some years after that, as a free man in Rome, Slipyj took note of Kostel'nyk and his "renegade"[121] associates with the words: "May God have mercy on them!"[122]

That film and the repeated references by the KGB to the Synod of L'viv proved to him, however, what the real purpose of his arrest had been: to get him out of the way, so that the resolutions of the synod of 1946, or at any rate some such put-up legislation by some ecclesiastical agency, could successfully proceed to do what Soviet persecution had tried to do but had failed to do—to liquidate the Greek Catholic Church. The ideal of a reunion between the Ukrainian Greek Catholic Church and the Ukrainian Orthodox Church was one to which Metropolitan Šeptyc'kyj had been committed and to which, at any rate in principle, Metropolitan Slipyj remained committed. But it had to be a reunion that did not, by rupturing the existing unity as represented by the Union of Brest, exchange one schism for another; for, in

117. Slipyj to Angelo Dell'Acqua, 30.iv.1963, 28:278.
118. Slipyj, Tvory 9:171.
119. Slipyj, Spomyny 93.
120. Slipyj, Spomyny 194-95.
121. Slipyj, Tvory 9:276.
122. Address of 20 November 1969, for the fortieth anniversary of the Theological Academy, Slipyj, Tvory 13:44.

Šeptyc′kyj′s formula upon learning of the idea that he was being considered for the position of metropolitan of such a united Orthodox-Catholic Ukrainian Church, "it goes without saying that such an election would be tantamount to an acceptance of the Union."[123] But that was precisely what this action denied, and was explicitly intended to deny. The authority of Metropolitan Josyf, both his official ecclesiastical authority and the authority of his personal presence, was such that resolutions like those passed at L′viv in 1946 would have been unthinkable at any legitimate synod, viz., any synod over which he presided as bishop and metropolitan. Slipyj was confident enough of that to say to Podgorny in 1961: "There is no reasonable Communist today, not only in Ukraine but anywhere in the Soviet Union, who would confirm as legal the actions of 1945 and 1946,"[124] presumably referring to the Synod of L′viv as well as to other actions, including his arrest and imprisonment and the treatment he received in the jails and labor camps.

The "prudent silence" that Slipyj was told to keep after his release had applied specifically also to "his imprisonment."[125] And if one compares what, during his remaining years, he did say and write about it with the massive documentation about Soviet imprisonment that has become available from other sources in those same years, what stands out is the restraint of his language rather than the vividness of his accounts. Above all, it was the publication between 1973 and 1978 of *The Gulag Archipelago* by Aleksandr Solzhenitsyn, whom Josyf Slipyj saluted as his fellow "galley slave,"[126] that forced even Western apologists for the Soviet system to begin to come to terms with the reality of the *lager'*. For sheer literary power, Slipyj′s narrative cannot, of course, compete with Solzhenitsyn′s, nor is it intended to. But there is much in the three volumes of *The Gulag Archipelago*, as well as more generally in the work of Aleksandr Solzhenitsyn when seen as "a Christian writer,"[127] that is relevant to this portrait of Josyf Slipyj. Solzhenitsyn speaks of how "at war′s end and for many years after, there flowed uninterruptedly an abundant wave of Ukrainian nationalists" into Soviet prison camps, and he singles out "nationalists, especially the Ukrainians and the Lithuanians" (with "all West Ukrainian country people" in a special

123. Korolevskij (1964) 156.
124. Slipyj to N. V. Podgorny, 17.ii.1961, *Arch.Pat.* 28:88 (122).
125. Memorandum of 8.iv.1963, *Arch.Pat.* 28:220.
126. Slipyj, *Tvory* 14:159.
127. Schmemann (1973) 38-44; it should be noted that Father Schmemann developed this interpretation even before the publication of Solzhenitsyn′s later and more spiritual works.

category), as those "for whom a broad range of torture was automatically permitted"—especially, he adds, "in those cases where an underground organization existed (or was suspected)."[128] In addition to his particular comments about the persecution of religious believers, Orthodox and non-Orthodox,[129] Solzhenitsyn identifies "the so-called 'Eastern Catholics'—followers of Vladimir Solovyev" as those who "were arrested and destroyed in passing."[130] He could as well (or better) have called them "followers of Andrej Šeptyc'kyj and Josyf Slipyj," since Šeptyc'kyj was, in the apt phrase of Lubomyr Husar, "maybe the only individual who consistently, though critically, tried to turn [Soloviev's] theory into actuality."[131] And much of Solzhenitsyn's description of Ukrainians in the camps would apply to Slipyj and to those whom Slipyj describes in his own memoirs.

In the gulags, Slipyj observed wryly, "there were not a great many gentlemen [*džentel'meniv bulo nebahato*]."[132] To be sure, some of the conditions he describes are simply those that could be expected by anyone sentenced to hard labor anywhere; he was, for example, sent to work in a knitting mill, and later to dig potatoes.[133] In the hospital at Pečora— which had the reputation of being one of the worst of all the camps—a physician intervened to save him, considering his age and physical infirmities, from being assigned to a detail of prisoners who were chopping down trees.[134] Nevertheless, he was subjected to "torture with interrogations to the extreme," and to "brutalities so horrible that prisoners were dying off like flies" from sadistic guards who were "all psychopaths and bestial criminals."[135] Women prisoners had to endure sexual harassment from their guards as well as from male fellow prisoners.[136] He found the confinement immediately after having been sentenced the hardest of all to bear.[137] Things were even worse than he had imagined on the basis of what he had read;[138] indeed, they were worse than the Soviet officials themselves had realized.[139] And it seemed

128. Solzhenitsyn (1973) 1:86, 91, 99-100.
129. Solzhenitsyn (1973) 1:50-51.
130. Solzhenitsyn (1973) 1:37.
131. Husar (1972) 44.
132. Slipyj, *Spomyny* 148.
133. Slipyj, *Spomyny* 130, 147.
134. Slipyj, *Spomyny* 137, 140.
135. Slipyj, *Spomyny* 112, 163.
136. Slipyj, *Spomyny* 128.
137. Slipyj, *Spomyny* 126.
138. Slipyj, *Spomyny* 128.
139. Slipyj to N. V. Podgorny, 17.ii.1961, *Arch.Pat.* 28:90 (124).

that as one got further from Moscow the conditions deteriorated.[140] His tormentors threatened to break his bones, and in fact his hand was broken as a consequence of their abuse.[141] A guard brandished a gun "as though to make an end of me then and there," and Slipyj fully expected to be taken before a firing squad.[142] As he summarized the various stages of his imprisonment, "every stage was a terrible cross from God, and the very act of describing it is a great torment. Surrounded by bandits, in the midst of hunger and cold [sered holodu i cholodu], deprived of the possibility of taking care of my most fundamental needs, tortured by the guards, subjected to robbery, and the like."[143]

Through it all, however, in the words of Pope John Paul II, "he did not crack, but like a hero he resisted with dignity." Or, as Slipyj himself put it, "it was a great gift of God's love that I was able to endure all those torments . . . which were intended to crack me and bring me to the point of despair, but I patiently endured it all."[144] He sustained himself with his Christian and Catholic faith but also with his humanity, as expressed in the motto from Horace, *aequam in arduis servare mentem*.[145] A classic description of the moral and mental effect that such years of imprisonment can have is the epigrammatic sentence of Victor Hugo: "Jean Valjean entered the galleys sobbing and shuddering: he went out hardened; he entered in despair: he went out sullen."[146] Another and more detailed description appears in the account of the Roman galleys in *Ben Hur*:

> So, as the result of long service, the poor wretches became imbruted—patient, spiritless, obedient—creatures of vast muscle and exhausted intellects, who lived upon recollections generally few but dear, and at last lowered into the semi-conscious alchemic state wherein misery turns to habit, and the soul takes on incredible endurance.[147]

Slipyj's own "patience" and "incredible endurance" were of a quite different sort from all of that: he neither "entered in despair" nor "went out sullen." There were reports that he had prematurely aged in prison.[148] Yet in June 1953, when he was brought to Moscow, where he

140. Slipyj, *Spomyny* 163.
141. Slipyj, *Spomyny* 117, 135.
142. Slipyj, *Spomyny* 174-75, 114-15.
143. Slipyj, *Spomyny* 149.
144. Slipyj, *Spomyny* 115.
145. Slipyj, *Tvory* 13:108 (in Cyrillic characters); 155 (in Latin characters).
146. Hugo (1862) 74.
147. Wallace (1908) 142.
148. *Tiroler Nachrichten*, 2.iii.1963.

was interviewed by a General Zhukov (not to be confused with Marshal G. K. Zhukov, hero of the Red Army during World War II), Zhukov told him, as Slipyj reports: "You are a completely typical Slav: There is no way to tell from your behavior that you have been in a labor camp for eight years!"[149] One of Slipyj's more sadistic tormentors, after his attempts at the third degree had failed, "threw down his inkwell and screamed in his brutal fashion, 'What a set of nerves!' "[150] And one of his fellow prisoners wrote to him less than a year after his release: "In the camp . . . most men were a gray mass . . . but in my recollection you are sheer light."[151]

On the occasion of the metropolitan's ninetieth birthday in 1972 another fellow prisoner wrote to him: "We shall always remember your dignified behavior in the dreadful Soviet camps from where you were miraculously saved by the Lord's hand." To the other prisoners, and even to "the Soviet butchers," Slipyj had "personified calmness and human dignity," so that "by your kindness and sympathy, by the feeling of hope that emanated from you, you helped your camp-mates to withstand the suffering and not to fall into despair."[152] The writer of that moving tribute was Avraham Shifrin, who was, as he testified the following year before the Subcommittee on Internal Security of the United States Senate, "a proud Zionist."[153] In the light of what one recent history has described as "two solitudes"[154] and what another historian, Taras Hunczak, has recently called "an invisible wall separating the two communities, based on mutual suspicion, religious prejudice, ethnocentric beliefs and values, and popular myths, [which] prevented Ukrainians and Jews from reaching a genuine understanding,"[155] Slipyj's relations with his Jewish fellow prisoners deserve special comment. As Hunczak goes on to note, "the role of the Ukrainian Church and Metropolitan Andrei Sheptytsky constitutes a special chapter in the history of Ukrainian-Jewish relations. Sheptytsky's courageous stand against the persecution of Jews was probably unequalled in Europe."[156] In this respect, too, Slipyj proved to be a faithful follower of his mentor, Metropolitan Šeptyc'kyj.

149. Slipyj, *Spomyny* 165.
150. Slipyj, *Spomyny* 115.
151. Ferdinand Ceplichal to Slipyj, 26.i.1964, Choma (1985) 139.
152. Avraham Shifrin to Slipyj, 11.ii.1982, *Arch.Pat.* 111:190c.
153. Avraham Shifrin, "Testimony before Senate Subcommittee on Internal Security, Thursday, February 1, 1973," *Arch.Pat.* 111:174.
154. Aster and Potichnyj (1983).
155. Hunczak (1986) 39.
156. Hunczak (1986) 49.

Under the conditions of the camps, the "invisible wall" of which Taras Hunczak speaks came down rather quickly. One of the first fellow prisoners whom Slipyj met was a Jewish tailor who gave him good advice about how to get along.[157] Later he was imprisoned in Kiev with a Jewish poet named Buchbinder, with whom he had earnest conversations about literature and about religious faith. Slipyj especially remembered one of Buchbinder's poems about his Jewish religious traditions, and he noted with sorrow that Buchbinder was sentenced to prison for Zionism and "Jewish nationalism."[158] Another Jewish fellow prisoner said of Slipyj, as a friend of his wrote from Jerusalem, that "you 'act with love to people and respect to God.' You opened the world of God to him."[159] Also from Jerusalem, yet another wrote to him: "I am thinking today with special fondness of the minutes when I had the privilege of becoming acquainted with Your Excellency and of speaking with you. These moments will always remain unforgettable in my life."[160] Avraham Shifrin's reminiscences of his prison bunkmate are among the most detailed. To him, Slipyj was "a person who enjoyed an immense authority in the camps. By his sheer presence and with two or three words he knew how to get the attention not only of the prisoners who lived together with him, but of the officers." Even they had to recognize in him "a great and powerful personality, a man with a grand spirit." As a Jew and a Christian, Shifrin and Slipyj carried on extensive theological discussions, in which neither could accept the other's viewpoint but in which each developed a deep respect for the other.[161] Slipyj may have been thinking of these conversations, as well as of others like them, when he recalled making the point to some Jewish fellow prisoners that it was possible to be a Jew and a Christian at the same time—a point that they found puzzling.[162]

Other "invisible walls," too, came tumbling down. For not only was a Soviet camp a veritable League of Nations, with prisoners from all over Central and Eastern Europe, but believers from all the major religious traditions were thrown together: "Catholics, Eastern Orthodox, Protestants, various sectarians, Jehovah's Witnesses, Pentecostals, Seventh-Day Adventists, Muslims—and several dozen spies."[163]

---

157. Slipyj, *Spomyny* 131-32.
158. Slipyj, *Spomyny* 131-32, 149-50.
159. Rivka Alexandrovich to Slipyj, 2.xi.1971, *Arch.Pat.* 111:2.
160. Sigmund Mannheim to Slipyj, 21.xii.1966, *Arch.Pat.* 111:85.
161. Avraham Shifrin, Interview v.1973, *Arch.Pat.* 111:171-72.
162. Slipyj, *Spomyny* 190.
163. Slipyj, *Spomyny* 190.

And so Josyf Slipyj, who as an Eastern Christian knew and lamented the historical process by which "the Crescent was elevated over the Cross" through the conquests of Christian territory by Islam during the Middle Ages[164] and who regarded the fall of Constantinople to the Turks in 1453 as "a tragic event,"[165] shared his imprisonment with a mullah, and found him to be "a decent man . . . , content with his lot, God-fearing, who prayed often, bowed, and knelt down."[166] Even in prison, Metropolitan Slipyj knew himself and his church to be caught between East and West: he resented what he took to be collaboration by the Russian Orthodox hierarchy with the Bolsheviks and "the sad rôle in relation to our church [that] was played by the patriarch of Moscow,"[167] and at the same time he had experienced "a very unfriendly position toward our church" also from a Polish Roman Catholic bishop.[168] Yet when that bishop was arrested, Slipyj had sent a telegram of protest to Stalin; and in the camps he learned to know as brethren in the faith various Russian Orthodox and Ukrainian Orthodox clergy, who were subjected to humiliation, torture, and martyrdom, just as Greek Catholic clergy were.[169] Like others before and after him, Slipyj experienced an ecumenism of suffering.

As the conversations with Shifrin made clear, however, Slipyj's stance in that kind of ecumenism—and in any other kind as well—was consistently and unambiguously one of utter loyalty to his own vocation as priest and metropolitan. He may have seen Jehovah's Witnesses suffering for their version of the Christian faith, but that did not prevent him, in one of his first public appearances after being set free, from denouncing their denial of the immortality of the soul as a subversion of the Christian faith.[170] Above all, his loyalty had expressed itself liturgically. He recited the liturgy every day, usually from memory.[171] If he could, he would sing it with a congregation made up of believing fellow prisoners; but if he could not, he recited it alone in the dark[172] or "in a corner"[173] or in seclusion with other clergy.[174] When he was

164. Slipyj, *Tvory* 5:176.
165. Slipyj, *Tvory* 2:89; 12:187.
166. Slipyj, *Spomyny* 147.
167. Slipyj, *Spomyny* 121.
168. Slipyj, *Spomyny* 109.
169. See, for example, Slipyj, *Spomyny* 132-33, 135.
170. Slipyj, *Tvory* 12:35-36.
171. Slipyj, *Spomyny* 143, 158.
172. Slipyj, *Spomyny* 175, 127.
173. Slipyj, *Tvory* 13:152.
174. As recalled by Sigmund Mannheim to Slipyj, 21.xii.1966, *Arch. Pat.* 111:85.

thrown into solitary confinement, he took that as an opportunity to carry out an eight-day retreat.[175] The gift of some raisins from a well-wisher made it possible for him to extract juice to be used for wine in the Eucharist, but later he was able to obtain real wine for that purpose.[176] Even en route to Siberia he maintained his liturgical observance, and whenever his captors took him out of jail for a hearing or a trial, they had to caution him not to pray in public.[177] Repeatedly, fellow prisoners came to make their confessions to him, but he, as he says, "imposed only a tiny penance" under the circumstances;[178] he recognized, too, that some of those who came to confess were engaged in a campaign of entrapment.[179] Some medical students came to him wearing sacred medals hidden under their clothes.[180] He also exercised his pastoral ministry in rescuing a priest from suicide.[181] Occasionally he even carried out ordinations,[182] and at least once, just before his liberation, the secret consecration of a bishop.[183] This he reported to Pope John Paul II in a Ukrainian letter many years later.[184]

The liberation, when it came, seems to have been quite unexpected.[185] It was, moreover, not something done by Slipyj, but *for* him and *to* him, by the "improbable triumvirate"[186] of the President of the United States, the Pope of Rome, and the Premier of the Soviet Union. For that reason, the most relevant aspect of it for the purposes of this "portrait" is the insight it provides into Slipyj's "vocations." Above all, his liberation made it obvious that during the years of imprisonment Slipyj had never stopped "thinking about our church."[187] There is no other way to account for the detailed agenda with which he emerged at the time of his liberation and which he almost immediately set about implementing, from the full-blown schema for the Ukrainian Catholic

175. Slipyj, *Spomyny* 156.
176. Slipyj, *Spomyny* 123, 166-67.
177. Slipyj, *Spomyny* 174, 164.
178. Slipyj, *Spomyny* 123, 175-76, 156.
179. Slipyj, *Spomyny* 122.
180. Slipyj, *Tvory* 13:287-88.
181. Slipyj, *Spomyny* 141.
182. Slipyj, *Spomyny* 196, 197.
183. Slipyj, *Spomyny* 200.
184. Slipyj to John Paul II, 3.vi.1979, *Arch.Pat.* 118:99-100 (102-5).
185. It will be evident to those who have read the narrative of Choma (1984), which is based on all the available source material, that I am deeply indebted to it. It is readily available and therefore does not need to be reproduced here.
186. Under that title, Cousins (1972) has provided a firsthand account; see also Cousins (1967) for a briefer notice.
187. Slipyj, *Spomyny* 192.

University to the idea of the patriarchate, except to suggest that throughout his captivity he was planning and dreaming about the needs of his church. As his editors have put it, "these dreams and plans during imprisonment could be seen from the facts and deeds" of the rest of his life.[188] During the first year after his release, Josyf Slipyj managed to raise every major question that would occupy him—and sometimes obsess him—from then on. It was, he sometimes seemed to be saying, as though all of his previous life had been a preparation for these tasks, and, one senses, as though the nearly two decades he had spent as a prisoner were added to his normal lifespan so that he could carry out his vocation; that was, in fact, how the arithmetic of the years did work out.

The most interesting encounter Slipyj had during his entire imprisonment was probably that of June 1953 with General Zhukov, whom he found to be highly intelligent and genuinely cultured, with a fondness for literature, theater, and music, and who warned him not to do anything to compromise himself.[189] But the most important encounter for Slipyj's vocation was probably his negotiation with the KGB in Kiev during 1961. His own account of it is the most trenchant:

> In 1961 I was taken, in a first class railroad coach, from Mordovia to Kiev, where during lengthy negotiations the KGB presented me with two questions:
> 1. What would be my *maximum* requests from the Soviet Government? To this question I replied that my *maximum* request would be a return to the status that obtained before my arrest.
> 2. The second question was: What would be my *minimum* requests from the Soviet Government? To this I replied:
> a) To remove the prohibition regarding the Eastern Catholic Church in the U.S.S.R.
> b) To restore the Cathedral of Saint George and the metropolitan's palace, and to grant liberty to the clergy.[190]

In the event, Slipyj did not get his *maximum*, nor even his *minimum*, but was released from prison by the Supreme Soviet on the condition that he not return to L'viv, but go to Rome.[191] He had said from prison that he would not leave the Soviet Union unless he was compelled to do so

188. Slipyj, *Tvory* 12:12.
189. Slipyj, *Spomyny* 165-70.
190. Slipyj to Angelo Dell'Acqua, 30.iv.1963, *Arch. Pat.* 28:277-78; I have sought to reproduce the punctuation of the original.
191. See Choma (1984).

under escort.[192] But now, "under obedience [*pid posluchom*]" (the same phrase he used for his acceptance of the rectorship of the seminary in L'viv almost four decades earlier), he explained, "I had to come to Rome,"[193] where for the rest of his life he would be the Ukrainian metropolitan-in-exile.

192. Slipyj, *Tvory* 14:475.
193. Slipyj, *Tvory* 13:152.

9

Metropolitan-in-Exile

Josyf Slipyj's first question upon being informed that he was being set free from prison was: "Is the church free, too?"[1] And of course it was not. As for Slipyj himself, he was not free to return to L'viv;[2] but he was free in one sense to exercise his office as metropolitan, which, except for the few months between the death of Andrej Šeptyc'kyj and his arrest, he had been occupying *de jure* but not *de facto* since his accession in 1944.[3] That circumstance had placed, and would continue to place, ever greater value on his *de jure* status, as this had been communicated to him by Eugène Cardinal Tisserant.[4] "I am the metropolitan of the Greek Catholic Church in Ukraine" was how he opened his first *žaloba* to First Secretary N. V. Podgorny.[5] To General Zhukov he put the question, "Do you acknowledge me as metropolitan?" to which Zhukov replied, "We did not make you metropolitan, and we cannot depose you."[6]

And indeed, it was as "the heroic figure of the metropolitan of the Ukrainian Catholic Church, *Kyr* Josyf Slipyj" that he was addressed by his faithful in Rome immediately after his liberation.[7] But in fact he was

1. Slipyj, *Tvory* 13:152.
2. Slipyj, *Tvory* 14:475.
3. See his thirtieth-anniversary reflections of 2.xi.1974, Slipyj, *Tvory* 13:299-301.
4. Slipyj, *Tvory* 13:157.
5. Slipyj to N. V. Podgorny, i.1961, *Arch.Pat.* 28:23 (58).
6. Slipyj, *Spomyny* 165-66.
7. Address of welcome by seminarian Volodymyr Dac'ko, 10.iii.1963, Slipyj, *Tvory* 12:34.

in the anomalous position of being "the metropolitan of the Ukrainian Catholic Church"—but in Rome rather than in either Kiev or L'viv-Halyč. "These thirty years of being metropolitan," Slipyj would recall in 1974, "have consisted of writing secret letters, of penal servitude at hard labor, and of constantly moving around from one place to another."[8] In a "letter that had, for reasons of prudence, not been published in *L'Osservatore Romano*,"[9] he had, during his imprisonment, been greeted by Pope Pius XII on the fortieth anniversary of his priesthood "amid the bitterness of your exile."[10] Slipyj knew what it meant for scholars, intellectuals, and theologians to live in what has been called "the bitter air of exile," as a consequence of which "all work by living *émigré* writers is automatically unpublishable and often unmentionable in the Soviet Union."[11] Many years before, he had examined the situation of the Russian Orthodox Church in emigration immediately after the Revolution.[12] The example of great bishops who had gone into exile during previous centuries, such as Saint Athanasius and Saint John Chrysostom, proved to him that they had continued to exercise their functions as metropolitans and patriarchs even while they were compelled to live outside their provinces.[13] What he had not been fully prepared for was a situation as metropolitan-in-exile that would be "no easier than it had been in captivity."[14] The cancellation of the Union of Brest by the so-called Synod of L'viv was a heavier cross for Ukrainian fellow believers in the home country to bear than persecution and martyrdom.[15] But here in exile, here in the Rome for which he and his church had sacrificed so much, the Ukrainian metropolitan felt increasingly hemmed in by what he called, in one of the subtitles of a document submitted to the pope, the "negative attitude" he continued to encounter from "the sacred congregations of the Roman curia."[16] Sometimes, in his exasperation at that attitude, he would even resort to the hyperbole of declaring that he had never experienced such mistreatment from the atheists in the Soviet Union as he was experiencing now from fellow Catholics and fellow clergy in Rome.[17]

8. Slipyj, *Tvory* 13:300.
9. Quoted from a papal audience, 26.i.1962, *Arch.Pat.* 28:129.
10. Pius XII to Slipyj, 25.xii.1957, *Arch.Pat.* 28:16-17.
11. Karlinsky-Appel (1977) 9.
12. Slipyj, *Tvory* 5:370-73.
13. Slipyj to Gustavo Testa, 20.xii.1966, *Arch.Pat.* 35:499.
14. Slipyj, *Tvory* 13:152.
15. "Basilius Episcopus Luceoriensis" to Paul VI, 7.v.1967, *Arch.Pat.* 36:152.
16. Slipyj to John Paul II, 20.xi.1978, *Arch.Pat.* 118:60.
17. Slipyj to Paul Mailleux, 16.iv.1974, *Arch.Pat.* 117:235.

Above all, however, he felt obliged to define his position as metropolitan-in-exile in the fullest possible terms. As he saw it, that position laid upon him the primary responsibility for the Ukrainian Church, but it also thrust him, not entirely against his will, into the rôle of conscience of the Christian West and spokesman for the Christian East as a whole;[18] in fact, the very anomaly of being metropolitan only "in exile" helped in curious ways to confirm that rôle. He became, as he said, a close observer of church life everywhere,[19] to carry out that larger obligation.

Like Andrej Šeptyc'kyj before him,[20] Josyf Slipyj regarded himself, as the incumbent of the "peculiar"[21] position of metropolitan of L'viv-Halyč, as the archbishop and pastor of Ukrainian Catholics throughout the world. Not only did this help to create an ambivalent relation between the metropolitan and the Ukrainian bishops in the diaspora; it was also a major factor in the ongoing conflict between Slipyj and the Roman curia. To the extent that this special relation to Ukrainians everywhere was expressed in the drive for recognition of Slipyj as not only major archbishop (and cardinal), but as the patriarch of the Ukrainian Church, the status of the metropolitan-in-exile was an issue that would remain unresolved to the end of Slipyj's life, and even beyond. But even short of that drive for recognition as patriarch, the *de facto* basis of the metropolitan's position in exile, as distinct from the *de jure* basis provided by the Holy See, had to be his relation to the émigré communities scattered all over the Free World, to "the Voice of the Ukrainian Diaspora," as its weekly broadcast is called.[22] When he received a draft copy of the "Principles Underlying Proposed Revisions in the Canon Law [*Principia quae codicis iuris canonici recognitionem dirigant*]," therefore, he marked in his own handwriting the paragraph laying out the tension between a "clear and consistent territorial circumscription" of authority and the "exigencies of the modern apostolate" in various nations.[23]

It was, clearly, those exigencies that he believed must be the basis for defining his administration of authority as the Ukrainian metropolitan-in-exile. It corresponded to his own understanding of that situa-

18. Slipyj's view of that rôle will concern us in chapter 10.
19. Slipyj, *Tvory* 12:234 (230; 237).
20. Slipyj, *Tvory* 9:268.
21. Stasiw (1960) 193-94.
22. Leonid Rudnytzky to Werenfried van Straaten, 30.viii.1984, *Arch.Pat.* 66: 420-23.
23. *Arch.Pat.* 37:148.

THE VOCATIONS OF JOSYF SLIPYJ

tion when the Ukrainian Catholic archbishop of Winnipeg proposed
that the third paragraph of the projected "Constitution of the Church"
should read: "The Ukrainian Catholic Church embraces all the faithful
of the Ukrainian Rite in the lands of Ukraine and beyond its borders";
the words are underlined in red, apparently by Slipyj.[24] Referring
specifically to the archdiocese of Winnipeg, as well as to that of Philadelphia,[25] Slipyj explained: "They are daughters of the metropolitanate of
Kiev-Halyč, not sisters."[26] He had to have authority over "our priests"
wherever on the globe they happened to be, also because of "the possibility of a return to Ukraine," which might come "suddenly"; a system
of authority based on territoriality could cripple the response to such a
possibility.[27] As he was building his various projects in exile, especially
the Studion Monastery and the Ukrainian Catholic University, which by
their architectural solidity did seem to suggest a certain permanence, he
was obliged to explain that even if there were a return to Ukraine and
hence a transfer of the university to the homeland, a study center would
remain also in Rome.[28] On 3 March 1963, shortly after his release, therefore, he issued a call to Ukrainians everywhere to preserve "unity" at all
costs.[29] "Dispersed" though they were, all of them were united in the
Eucharist and in the Easter faith, expressed in the Slavonic cry "Chrys-
tos voskres!"[30] As he said to the Ukrainians of Canada on 17 June 1971,
they were to be held together by "one language, one faith of Christ, one
way of praying, one system of worship, one ritual, one national
Ukrainian consciousness, one great love for our legacy of princes and
warriors, for our culture, literature, and art, for our traditions and customs of statesmanship, strengthened by our history of many centuries."[31] It was necessary to "bear witness to the unity of the Ukrainian
nation in all lands" into which it had been dispersed.[32] And so when he
was criticized for never thinking about anything except the Ukrainian
question, his automatic reply could be: "Questo è giusto!"[33]

24. Maxim Hermaniuk to Slipyj, 27.x.1972, Arch.Pat. 73:n.p.
25. On this linkage, see also Slipyj, Tvory 9:96.
26. Slipyj to Amleto Cicognani, 8.i.1965, Arch.Pat. 32:14-15; see also Cicognani's response, 6.ii.1965, Arch.Pat. 32:140.
27. Slipyj to Gustavo Testa, 14.i.1967, Arch.Pat. 36:28.
28. Slipyj to Angelo Dell'Acqua, 24.ii.1967, Arch.Pat. 36:73.
29. Slipyj, Tvory 12:26.
30. Slipyj, Tvory 13:219, 96; 9:104.
31. Slipyj, Tvory 13:107; see also the similar formulation from Palm Sunday 1971,
Slipyj, Tvory 9:151.
32. Slipyj, Tvory 9:241.
33. Slipyj to Giovanni Battista Scapinelli, 5.xii.1963, Arch.Pat. 29:333.

That was, undeniably, the expression of an exile's nostalgia for "the beloved air of our native land,"[34] but it was more. It was also the recognition of an aggravated malaise and a profound crisis that threatened, and would continue to threaten, the very existence of the Ukrainian Catholic Church, not only in the "catacombs"[35] of the native land, but even more in the emigration. In an aide-mémoire from a papal audience of 1971, Archbishop Metropolitan Maxim Hermaniuk of Winnipeg trenchantly diagnosed the malaise and the crisis:

> The situation troubling the Ukrainian Catholic Church in the Free World is being aggravated every day and is becoming more and more dangerous, and that in the following ways:
> 1. the alienation of the spirits and hearts of the faithful in relation to the Holy See, as expressed in the Ukrainian press, radio, and television, and in certain public demonstrations;
> 2. the revolt of a party of the faithful against some of the bishops in the United States of America;
> 3. certain appeals that are being made for separation from the Catholic Church.[36]

Metropolitan Šeptyc'kyj had recognized the problem in his own generation and had striven to meet it.[37] But in Metropolitan Slipyj's generation the problem was infinitely more grave, above all because, for the foreseeable future, the metropolitan would have to be a metropolitan-in-exile, but also because the "exigencies of the modern apostolate"[38] now had to address a Ukrainian emigration of at least two million souls. On the positive side, what the Decree of the Second Vatican Council called "the instruments of social communication"[39] as developed in the period between Andrej Šeptyc'kyj and Josyf Slipyj made it possible, actually for the first time, for the Ukrainian metropolitan, even though in exile, to maintain lines of communication and of personal contact with his faithful throughout the world—except, of course, in Ukraine itself.

Metropolitan Slipyj took full advantage of all those instruments and of all the technology of radio, television, and especially jet aircraft. As Ol'ha Vitošyns'ka suggests, the sheer expenditure of energy and

---

34. Slipyj, *Tvory* 13:148.
35. Slipyj to N. V. Podgorny, 17.ii.1961, *Arch.Pat.* 28:87 (122).
36. Maxim Hermaniuk, "Pro-memoria" of audience with Paul VI, 16.vi.1971, *Arch.Pat.* 40:46.
37. See chapter 5, pp. 90-91 above.
38. *Arch.Pat.* 37:148.
39. Alberigo 843-49.

time in travels "between 1968 and 1970 to Canada, America, Colombia, Venezuela, Peru, Argentina, Paraguay, Brazil, Australia, New Zealand, Germany, Spain, Portugal, England, France, Austria, India, and Malta" by a man who had endured Soviet prisons for almost two decades and who was about to reach the age of eighty must fill any reader with admiration and awe[40]—and he went on doing it for another decade after that. More than seventy-five volumes of the Patriarchal Archive of Saint Sophia at the Ukrainian Catholic University in Rome contain "letters of the faithful [*Litterae Fidelium*]" and clergy from the United States;[41] and that does not include the many letters from America in other volumes. Two entire volumes contain the programs, announcements, handbills, tickets, and bills-of-fare for the divine services, receptions, banquets, rallies, and concerts throughout the Ukrainian diaspora all over the world at which the metropolitan was the guest of honor or celebrant (and usually the main speaker);[42] and these do not begin to exhaust the roster of such events to which he traveled. There being no other, he made himself personally the rallying point for the diaspora, as Vitošyns'ka's clippings from the world press demonstrate and as even a random sampling of a few of his contacts and communications in both the Southern and the Northern Hemispheres of the globe will illustrate.

When matrimonial cases raised problems of pastoral discipline in Argentina, they were referred to the metropolitan-in-exile.[43] There had been Ukrainians in Argentina since 1897.[44] But with the additional emigrations after the Second World War there were now roughly one hundred thousand Ukrainian Catholics in Argentina, enough, in Slipyj's judgment, to justify the creation of a Ukrainian eparchy there, though of course under the authority of the Ukrainian metropolitan.[45] He himself journeyed there several times, dedicating a statue of the Ukrainian poet Taras Ševčenko in Buenos Aires on 5 December 1971 and, by referring to Ševčenko's fondness for *The Imitation of Christ*, seeking to vindicate his Christian faith.[46] (The following year, on 18 June 1972, another such statue was dedicated on the campus of

---

40. Vitošyns'ka (1972) 7-10.
41. *Arch.Pat.* 195-257; 258-63; 373-74; 397-98.
42. *Arch.Pat.* 60-61, bearing the title *Jubilea*.
43. The documents are collected in *Arch.Pat.* 87:199-222.
44. Slipyj, *Tvory* 9:288-90.
45. Slipyj to Gustavo Testa, 1.xii.1963, *Arch.Pat.* 29:322-23; Slipyj to Antonio Caggiano, 1.xii.1963, *Arch.Pat.* 87:68-70.
46. Slipyj, *Tvory* 13:133-37.

UKU itself.[47]) From Perth, Australia, there came, on the occasion of the metropolitan's liberation, the message: "Wormest [sic] most sincere welcome *Confessor Fidei.* Best wishes. Prayers. *Mnohaja lita.*"[48] The Eucharistic Congress in Melbourne provided an opportunity for Slipyj to visit his own faithful there, as well as to deal with the Church as a whole.[49] Even the "Ukrainian Autocephalous Orthodox Church in Australia and New Zealand" joined in the communications with the Ukrainian Catholic metropolitan.[50]

In Germany the Ukrainian Catholic Church maintained an exarchate.[51] Speaking a language in which he, like Šeptyc'kyj, had long been fluent,[52] Metropolitan Slipyj thanked workers in the German Federal Republic for their hospitality to Ukrainian refugees.[53] Scarcely three months after his release he also turned his attention to the status of the Church of Saint Barbara in Vienna, which had historically been under the jurisdiction of the metropolitan of L'viv-Halyč, dating back to the time when Western Ukraine was Austrian territory, but which the government of the Austrian Republic would not consent to be administered by a foreign authority.[54] Because of his good relations with the Archbishop of Vienna, Franz Cardinal König,[55] he hoped to be able to rectify that situation. He was also grateful to Cardinal König for "the vigorous activity of Your Eminence on behalf of the Church of the East."[56] And in Canada Slipyj espoused not only the cause of the Ukrainian Catholics of Winnipeg and Toronto,[57] but also that of Eastern Rite Slovaks, who were entitled to their own auxiliary bishop.[58] The eparchy in Saskatoon had dealt with the waves of Ukrainian immigrants to Western Canada.[59] In Canada there was as well the special problem of the relations between the Ukrainian Catholic Church and the several

47. Slipyj, *Tvory* 13:164-70.
48. Ivan Ševciv to Slipyj, 11.ii.1963, *Arch.Pat.* 88:67.
49. Slipyj, *Tvory* 9:182.
50. Sylvester, Archbishop of Melbourne, Australia, and New Zealand, to Slipyj, 30.ii.1967, *Arch.Pat.* 88:57.
51. Slipyj, *Tvory* 9:120-22.
52. See chapter 5, p. 78 above.
53. Slipyj, *Tvory* 13:102.
54. Slipyj to Gustavo Testa, 1.vi.1963, *Arch.Pat.* 28:346-48.
55. Slipyj, *Tvory* 9:135-37.
56. Slipyj to Franz König, 15.xii.1966, *Arch.Pat.* 35:413.
57. For one example among many, see the account of June 1970 in Slipyj, *Tvory* 9:131-32.
58. Slipyj to Gustavo Testa, 21.ix.1964, *Arch.Pat.* 31:388; Gustavo Testa to Slipyj, 5.x.1964, *Arch.Pat.* 31:420 (with the *curriculum vitae* of Bishop Michal Rusnák, p. 421).
59. Slipyj, *Tvory* 9:186-87.

(at least five) Ukrainian Orthodox jurisdictions in North America.[60] As the Ukrainian Bishops' Synod under Slipyj's chairmanship put it, it was important to work for understanding with them.[61] But despite the "profusion" and "gratitude" with which the Orthodox received the Ukrainian Catholic Archbishop of Winnipeg,[62] relations remained strained.

As that resolution of the Ukrainian Bishops' Synod indicates, this body was the natural instrument for Slipyj as metropolitan, even as metropolitan-in-exile, to carry out his functions and exercise his authority throughout the Ukrainian diaspora.[63] While he had been in prison, the Conferences of Ukrainian Bishops, for example in 1958 and again in 1962, had been chaired by Metropolitan Maxim Hermaniuk of Winnipeg.[64] But at the conference of 28 March 1963, the first that Slipyj could attend, Hermaniuk and a colleague went out to escort him into the first session, and Hermaniuk "turned over to him the entire task of directing the conference."[65] Slipyj accepted the position, he explained, because it was appropriate to his office as the metropolitan of Kiev-Halyč.[66] He noted in a letter to his clergy of 1967/68 that in Ukraine it had been the metropolitan who had convoked the synod of bishops, as the precedent followed also by Metropolitan Šeptyc'kyj demonstrated.[67] Once that prerogative had been established, it was then possible for Slipyj, in 1969, to "ask [poprosyv]" Hermaniuk to take the chair, thus, in his judgment, appointing him to the post.[68] Meanwhile, the nature of the deliberative body itself was evolving. Not only are the minutes of the nine sessions of the conference in 1963 the first to be put down in Ukrainian, with Slipyj's name listed first,[69] but there was a change in nomenclature as well, and in more than nomenclature.

Earlier meetings, for example that of 1965, identified themselves as: "Conference of the Catholic Bishops of the Ukrainian Rite."[70] But

60. Jan Willebrands to Maxim Hermaniuk, 25.iv.1963, Arch.Pat. 28:260-61.
61. "Protokol" of Synod, 11.xii.1976, Arch.Pat. 73:278.
62. Maxim Hermaniuk to Jan Willebrands, 6.viii.1963, Arch.Pat. 28:262-63.
63. Stasiw (1960) 222-29.
64. Arch.Pat. 73:1; 73:15.
65. "Conference of the Catholic Bishops of the Ukrainian Rite," 28.iii.1963, Arch.Pat. 73:33.
66. Slipyj to Gustavo Testa, 23.xii.1966, Arch.Pat. 35:452-55.
67. Slipyj, Tvory 9:95.
68. "Synod of the Episcopate of the Ukrainian Catholic Church under the Direction of His Beatitude, Major Archbishop Kyr Josyf Slipyj," 19.ix.1969, Arch.Pat. 73:63.
69. "Conference of the Catholic Bishops of the Ukrainian Rite," Arch.Pat. 73:33.
70. Arch.Pat. 72:47.

the minutes for 1969 are headed: "Synod of Bishops of the Ukrainian Catholic Church, under the Direction of His Beatitude, Major Archbishop *Kyr* Josyf Slipyj,"[71] and in 1976 it was "The Episcopate of the Ukrainian Particular Church under the Direction of His Beatitude, Patriarch Josyf."[72] As late as 1981, Slipyj was complaining that in the official *Annuario Pontificio* it was still being listed as "Conference of the Ukrainian Catholic Hierarchy" rather than under that new designation.[73] When the nomenclature proposed for the *Annuario* listed it as a "synodical assembly" rather than as a "synod," he complained again that this terminology seemed to be an evasion.[74] Eventually he did get the designation "synod," though with an explanatory note that this was "a synod *extra territorium*."[75] The question of the metropolitan's prerogative in relation to the synod was to become a highly controversial one. One of Slipyj's fellow cardinals insisted that it had not been in Metropolitan Hermaniuk's power to renounce the chairmanship, nor in Metropolitan Slipyj's to appoint someone to it; for it was an elective office, with each bishop exercising a vote.[76] Another cardinal was even more peremptory in his rejection. "It was in no sense a canonical synod," he asserted, "because he [Cardinal Slipyj] does not have the authority to call one."[77] Yet another, the distinguished canonist Cardinal Felici, could speak of the authority of the metropolitan to give either "a personal response to questions" or "a common response jointly with the other bishops of the patriarchal [*sic*] synod or bishops' conference."[78] That distinction is often quite moot in the three documents bearing the title "Joint Pastoral Message [*Spil'ne Pastyrs'ke Poslannja*]" issued by the Ukrainian bishops during the Second Vatican Council:[79] the hands are the hands of the bishops, but the voice is the voice of the metropolitan, and anyone familiar with his letters and other writings will hear that voice throughout these so-called "common responses." The entire question of the status of the "Permanent Ukrainian Synod"[80] was to take yet another turn before Slipyj's death. For on his own papal authority, Pope John Paul II himself convoked a synod of Ukrainian

71. Under date of 19.ix.1969, *Arch.Pat.* 73:63.
72. *Arch.Pat.* 73:278.
73. Slipyj to Władysław Rubin, 22.ix.1981, *Arch.Pat.* 74:287.
74. Slipyj to Agostino Casaroli, 14.xi.1981, *Arch.Pat.* 74:290-91.
75. Agostino Casaroli to Slipyj, 7.xii.1981, *Arch.Pat.* 74:300.
76. Maximilian de Furstenberg to Slipyj, 3.vii.1972, *Arch.Pat. Patriarchat*:2.
77. John Krol, Interview of 15.xii.1971, *Arch.Pat.* 41:21-24.
78. Pericle Felici to Slipyj, 10.ii.1971, *Arch.Pat.* 40:24.
79. *Arch.Pat.* 9:11-19; 27-36; 39-58.
80. Maximilian de Furstenberg to Slipyj, 3.vii.1972, *Arch.Pat.* 41:181-82.

bishops, to meet on 24 March 1980.[81] To the end Slipyj went on arguing that since the synod was "the common expression of the unity of the episcopate of the Ukrainian Church," which was a "particular" Catholic Church with its own rights and prerogatives,[82] he, as metropolitan and major archbishop (and patriarch), should be the one to convoke it. In that argument he was reflecting the tension between "particular" and "Catholic" that had figured so prominently throughout Ukrainian history.[83]

Yet at least as important as these prerogatives of the Ukrainian metropolitan in relation to the synod, bishops, clergy, and faithful of his own church was the function Slipyj assumed on behalf of what came to be called by many "the church of silence."[84] Thus Mario Brini spoke about the *chiesa del silenzio*,[85] and Karol Wojtyła (soon to become Pope John Paul II) about the *kościół będący*.[86] It was especially the Premonstratensian priest Werenfried van Straaten who, through his program of ceaseless advocacy and fund-raising, made the *chiesa perseguitata*, or as his organization was eventually called, the *Kirche in Not*, a prominent part of the Catholic agenda in many portions of the world.[87] The organization received official papal approval on 25 March 1964.[88] But even before that, in fact shortly after his release from prison, the Ukrainian metropolitan was already in correspondence with Father van Straaten.[89] When five thousand copies of the Ukrainian *Children's Bible* were needed, it was van Straaten who came up with the resources for them.[90] Their correspondence would continue for over twenty years, until 21 August 1984, in one of the last letters written by Cardinal Slipyj before his death,[91] although van Straaten had announced to Slipyj earlier in a handwritten letter that on 16 November 1981 he had "entrusted to younger hands the direction of the work that I established

81. John Paul II to the Major Archbishop and Bishops of the Ukrainian Church, 1.iii.1980, *Arch.Pat.* 118:131.
82. Slipyj to John Paul II, 12.ii.1983, *Arch.Pat.* 118:281a.
83. See chapter 3, pp. 38-52 above.
84. See, for example, Amleto Cicognani to Slipyj, 2.vii.1964, *Arch.Pat.* 31:316.
85. Mario Brini to Domenico Chianella, 17.vi.67, *Arch.Pat.* 36:274.
86. Karol Wojtyła to Slipyj, 11.iv.1971, *Arch.Pat.* 118:20.
87. Volume 66 of the Patriarchal Archive of Saint Sophia, labeled "Kirche in Not," consists of correspondence and other materials, including notices of the transfer of moneys, involving the "Aiuto all chiesa che soffre" in its successive forms and names (including "Iron Curtain Church Relief").
88. Werenfried van Straaten to Slipyj, 10.xi.1964, *Arch.Pat.* 66:1.
89. Slipyj to Werenfried van Straaten, 28.iii.1963, *Arch.Pat.* 66:n.p.
90. Werenfried van Straaten to Slipyj, 25.viii.1981, *Arch.Pat.* 66:316.
91. Slipyj to Werenfried van Straaten, 21.viii.1984, *Arch.Pat.* 66:417-18.

34 years ago."[92] (His portrait now hangs, together with those of other friends and benefactors, on the wall of the principal lecture room of the Ukrainian Catholic University in Rome.) It was as advocate for "the church of silence" that Slipyj, in his comments of 8 September 1965 about the Decree on Religious Liberty of the Second Vatican Council, emphasized above all its implications for the freedom of the church from persecution by the state rather than the responsibility of the church to refrain from persecuting those who believe otherwise, which was the most novel feature of the Decree.[93]

He did so because he feared that Vatican *Ostpolitik* was in danger of jeopardizing the church in the East. Slipyj's extensive correspondence with the *Russicum* (or, to use its full official title, the *Pontificio Collegio Russo di Santa Teresa del Bambino Gesù*) warned continually of that danger.[94] The quest for rapprochement with the Russian Orthodox was a laudable goal, but the Ukrainian metropolitan was in a unique position to warn that "the pseudo-synod of L'viv, organized by the KGB" ought to serve as a cautionary tale.[95] Throughout the Soviet Union, it was extremely difficult to have a marriage ceremony performed in the presence of a priest and two witnesses, as church law specified.[96] Persecution of the church, especially of the Ukrainian Church, was meanwhile going on apace, as Slipyj told the pope.[97] There was, Slipyj told the entire papal Synod of Bishops in 1971, no greater injustice in all of history than what had happened to the Ukrainian people and church.[98] Even the Ukrainian Orthodox bishops, therefore, acknowledged the rôle being played by the Ukrainian Catholic Church and by its metropolitan in resisting Communist pressure.[99] Similarly, the Communist government acknowledged the importance of the church to the life of the nation.[100] When Pope John issued *Pacem in terris* on 11 April 1963 (which Slipyj carefully translated),[101] Slipyj, only recently released

92. Werenfried van Straaten to Slipyj, 6.xii.1981.

93. Slipyj, *Tvory* 12:202–4.

94. *Arch.Pat.* 117:193-240.

95. Slipyj to Jan Willebrands, 14.vii.1971, *Arch.Pat.* 40:216-17.

96. Slipyj to the Sacred Congregation for the Eastern Church, 18.vi.1963, *Arch.Pat.* 28:408-9.

97. Slipyj to Paul VI, 4.x.1963, *Arch.Pat.* 29:205-6; Slipyj to Angelo Dell'Acqua, 2.x.1963, *Arch.Pat.* 29:182-83.

98. Slipyj, *Tvory* 13:120, quoted again the following year, Slipyj, *Tvory* 13:163. See also his remarks of 3 October 1974, Slipyj, *Tvory* 13:287-89.

99. Slipyj to Giovanni Battista Scapinelli, 1.ii.1964, *Arch.Pat.* 30:59.

100. Slipyj to N. V. Podgorny, i.1961, *Arch.Pat.* 28:27 (62).

101. *AAS* 55 (1963):257-304.

from Soviet imprisonment, wrote within a week to congratulate him for going beyond the confrontation of the two superpowers, but also for refuting the Communists' claim of being the defenders of human dignity.[102] Just a month later, however, he wrote again to remind the pope that "the entire world is divided into two camps, with God and against God."[103] He pleaded with Pope John's successor, Pope Paul VI, to address "a special message to all his faithful Ukrainian children" who were suffering for their faith.[104] And he renewed the plea to Pope John Paul II, not to sacrifice the Ukrainian Church to the cause of détente with Moscow: *"nihil de nobis sine nobis!"*[105]

The Vatican's responses to these pleas were usually marked by courtesy mingled with caution.[106] Such responses, however, did not deter him from taking an active interest in the Ukrainian "church of silence" not only within the home country, but, in a phrase he sometimes employed, "behind the Iron Curtain" generally,[107] even if this were to bring him into conflict with fellow Catholic prelates. Thus he reminded Vatican officials that in predominantly Eastern Orthodox Romania there had been a Byzantine Rite Catholic Church, which at the time of its suppression by the Communist government on 1 December 1948 numbered one and one-half million faithful in five dioceses with six bishops, of whom four had died in prison and two others were still alive in prison.[108] His namesake and fellow exile, József Cardinal Mindszenty of Budapest (in Vienna by this time), took Slipyj's eightieth birthday as an opportunity to express solidarity with him.[109] Mindszenty was just six weeks younger than he, and the two together had become symbols of Christian resistance to Communism.[110] The Archbishop of Milan, Giovanni Battista Cardinal Montini, who on 21 June 1963 was to be elected pope as Paul VI, had written just two weeks before that election about an Eastern Rite priest who was the responsibility of Metropolitan Slipyj, as the successor of

---

102. Slipyj to John XXIII, 18.iv.1963, *Arch.Pat.* 28:242-44.
103. Slipyj to John XXIII, 28.v.1963, Slipyj, *Tvory* 12:69.
104. At a private audience with Paul VI, *Oss.Rom.* 13/14.xii.1976.
105. "Riservata personale per il Santo Padre," 29.vi.1981, *Arch.Pat.* 118:223-27; see also Slipyj, *Tvory* 14:257.
106. Amleto Cicognani to Slipyj, 24.iv.1963, *Arch.Pat.* 28:256; Jan Willebrands to Slipyj, 23.x.1971, *Arch.Pat.* 40:295.
107. Slipyj, *Tvory* 13:116.
108. Slipyj to Amleto Cicognani, 21.v.1963, *Arch.Pat.* 28:321-22.
109. József Mindszenty to Slipyj, 10.ii.1972, *Arch.Pat.* 41:97.
110. Eleanor Schlafly, executive secretary of the Cardinal Mindszenty Foundation in Saint Louis, to Slipyj, 21.iv.1969, *Arch.Pat.* 37:129.

Andrej Šeptyc'kyj, and Slipyj wrote to Montini acknowledging his interest.[111]

Nevertheless, those who, with the Ukrainians, could be seen as belonging to what Slipyj himself sometimes called not only "the East, but above all the Slavic East,"[112] including those in Jugoslavia and Czechoslovakia, had a special closeness to the Ukrainians; and, perhaps for the same reason, they could sometimes create special difficulties. In Jugoslavia and its predecessor states, the Ukrainian Catholic Church had long maintained an eparchy for its émigrés, which could observe its bicentennial in 1977.[113] There were also communities of religious related to the Ukrainian communities in Bosnia.[114] Slipyj was eager, despite the political situation, to cultivate fraternal relations with the Jugoslavs, particularly with the Croats, who shared the Catholic faith as well as other qualities with the Ukrainians.[115] In the course of exchanging Christmas greetings, the archbishop of Zagreb took the opportunity to express the hope of "a restoration of relations between the Holy See and our government."[116] The city of Prešov in northeastern Slovakia had been—and after World War II had remained—part of Czechoslovakia both politically and ecclesiastically, despite its Ukrainian population.[117] When Slipyj, who claimed authority and responsibility because of the Ukrainian element, attacked Basil Hopko, "the auxiliary bishop of Prešov," for his policies, Bishop Hopko responded in kind.[118] Vatican officials urged Slipyj to stay out of the matter;[119] and Slipyj, who after his liberation had apologized to the chief of Vatican protocol for lacking finesse and the Vatican style of writing,[120] now showed that he had learned it well by sending off a highly noncommittal reply.[121]

The status of the half million Ukrainian Catholics within the territory of Poland was one of the most vexing problems of all, as even the

111. Giovanni Battista Montini to Gustavo Testa, 6.vi.1963, *Arch.Pat.* 28:387; Slipyj to Giovanni Battista Montini, 12.vi.1963, *Arch.Pat.* 28:406-7.

112. Slipyj, *Tvory* 12:112 (111).

113. Slipyj, *Tvory* 9:288.

114. Venjamina Bodnarčyk to Slipyj, 18.xii.1967, *Arch.Pat.* 145:153.

115. Tadej ot Hrista Carja to Slipyj, 6.xii.1974, *Arch.Pat.* 145:16.

116. Slipyj to Franciscus Seper, 20.xii.1966, *Arch.Pat.* 35:437; Franciscus Seper to Slipyj, xii.1966, *Arch.Pat.* 35:438.

117. See chapter 4, p. 67 above.

118. Hopko's letter of 5.viii.1972 (in Italian translation), together with the article (in Slovak) from *Katolícke noviny* of Bratislava for 24.ix.1972, *Arch.Pat.* 41:246.

119. Maximilian de Furstenberg to Slipyj, 9.xi.1972, *Arch.Pat.* 41:245.

120. Slipyj to Igino Cardinale, 4.iii.1963, *Arch.Pat.* 28:143.

121. Slipyj to Maximilian de Furstenberg, 21.xi.1972, *Arch.Pat.* 41:244.

condition of their church buildings under a succession of Polish régimes made evident.[122] It was, of course, a problem that Slipyj had known firsthand from his own earlier days, when he had been a Polish subject. He also continued to be reminded of it through letters from his faithful there.[123] Sometimes he spoke of the persecution of Ukrainian Catholics as part of the general Communist campaign against the church.[124] But more often he charged that it was in fact worse in Poland than in the Soviet Union, for it was nationalistic as well as religious.[125] Its instigators, moreover, were not only the agents of the Polish Communist government but church people.[126] On 13 May 1963 Slipyj wrote to Pope John XXIII to plead for his church in Poland.[127] Then on 16 June he discussed with the primate of Poland, Stefan Cardinal Wyszynski, the possibility of appointing a Ukrainian bishop for the Eastern Rite faithful there, but found him "personally not in favor" of the idea, although "he puts the blame for the present status on the Polish government, which is in reality not the case."[128] Through third parties Wyszynski let it be known that he did recognize the Greek Catholics in Poland as a sizeable group that needed pastoral care, and he discussed the naming of a Ukrainian bishop for them.[129] He expressed the judgment that the idea of a bishop was "a legitimate desire," but that it was not possible now.[130] With Wyszynski himself Slipyj maintained a relation best described as correct but cool. On behalf of the faithful in Poland, Wyszynski wrote to Slipyj, congratulating him on his designation as cardinal, and Slipyj responded with a polite acknowledgment.[131] Yet just one day before writing that letter of acknowledgment, Slipyj was asserting that despite Wyszynski's claim to be defending the interests of Eastern Rite Catholics in Poland, "Cardinal Wyszynski has, frankly, done nothing to defend the affairs and interests of the Ukrainians, for the simple reason that he does not acknowledge their existence."[132] Nevertheless the correspondence continued;

122. Hordyns'kyj (1969).
123. For example, Christofora Malkovski to Slipyj, 10.vi.1984, Arch.Pat. 66:419.
124. Slipyj, Tvory 13:123.
125. Slipyj to Gustavo Testa, 11.iii.1965, Arch.Pat. 32:260-63.
126. Slipyj to Angelo Dell'Acqua, 2.i.1966, Arch.Pat. 34:4.
127. Slipyj to John XXIII, 13.v.1963, Arch.Pat. 28:311-12.
128. Slipyj to Paul VI, 1.vii.1963, Arch.Pat. 29:19-21.
129. M. Pryszlak to Agostino Casaroli, 14.xi.1967, Arch.Pat. 36:318.
130. Amleto Cicognani to Slipyj, 8.v.1964, Arch.Pat. 30:248-49.
131. Stefan Wyszynski to Slipyj, 2.iii.1965, Arch.Pat. 32:267; Slipyj to Stefan Wyszynski, 12.iii.1965, Arch.Pat. 32:266.
132. Slipyj to Gustavo Testa, 11.iii.1965, Arch.Pat. 32:260-63.

and in 1966, when Wyszynski's hopes to have the pope visit Cze-stochowa for the observance of the millennium of Polish Christianity failed to materialize, he used his Christmas greetings to write to Slipyj (among others) to express his disappointment.[133]

As metropolitan-in-exile, Slipyj also took it to be one of his primary responsibilities to the Ukrainian Church both in the homeland and in the diaspora to revitalize and strengthen the Ukrainian religious orders. "In olden times," he recalled, speaking about Ukraine, "every city, in fact every town, perhaps every larger village had a monastery, or at any rate a group of pilgrims. It would be a great blessing to our colonies if in every eparchy there could develop at least one monastery of the Studite Order."[134] To list the Ukrainian towns where they had worked was to catalogue their record of "noble activity [blahorodna dijal'nist']."[135] Yet he knew that religious orders East and West were facing a profound crisis. Speaking to a congress of nuns (and in English), he drew the contrast with that earlier flourishing state of the religious life. "In these past years," he told the sisters, "how many thousands of religious, who were told by Christ to rise above the world, left their convents and returned to the world! The houses of prayer have become deserts."[136] In a detailed report to the pope late in 1963, he enumerated the religious orders which had played a major part in the history of the Ukrainian Church, and he described their present status.[137] He did so again three years later. In that second report he spoke about the Redemptorists, the Salesians, the Franciscans, and the Verbites. The Redemptorists had been especially numerous, "having come from Belgium through the interest of Metropolitan Andrej Šeptyc'kyj at the time of the First World War . . . and working with great success in Western Ukraine."[138] Nevertheless, the two principal orders with whom Metropolitan Slipyj dealt were the Basilians and the Studites.

For the Basilian sisters and for the part they had played in Ukrainian history the metropolitan had high praise. After having commented the month before in great detail on their projected constitution,[139] he made the flat statement to a meeting of their chapter in

133. Stefan Wyszynski to Slipyj, 25.xii.1966, Arch.Pat. 35:489.
134. Slipyj, Tvory 9:313.
135. Slipyj, Tvory 9:23.
136. Slipyj, Tvory 13:271-74.
137. Slipyj to Paul VI, 6.xi.1963, Arch.Pat. 29:284-90.
138. Slipyj to Paul VI, 14.x.1966, Arch.Pat. 35:319-24.
139. Slipyj to the Sacred Congregation for the Eastern Church, 20.vii.1963, Arch.Pat. 29:55-75.

August 1963 that although their activity was useful wherever they worked, to the Ukrainian Catholic Church it was essential; and he pleaded with them not to commit the "sin" of surrendering the Eastern Rite.[140] Subsequent addresses to the Basilian sisters underscored their vital rôle in the spiritual and educational life of the Ukrainian Church.[141] It was, by reciprocity, his patronage of the Basilian sisters and of their chapter that, he was informed, "assures the Sacred Congregation [for the Eastern Church] of the good outcome of the chapter."[142] With the Basilian fathers, on the other hand, Slipyj's troubles went back to the time when he had, at Šeptyc'kyj's urging, taken over the direction of the major seminary in L'viv from its then rector, the Basilian Teodosij-Tyt Haluščyns'kyj. There had, moreover, always been tensions, paralleled in the history of many religious orders, between the authority of the metropolitan and the quasi-autonomous status of the Basilians.[143] Their exemption from the metropolitan's authority constituted a special problem.[144] When Slipyj spoke of the collision over the rectorate of the seminary as "one of the most unpleasant experiences of my life,"[145] therefore, he was clearly reflecting not only the tensions caused by his having replaced Haluščyns'kyj, but all the other tensions he had had over the intervening years with the *Ordo Sancti Basilii Magni*,[146] all of which made it very difficult for him to be either objective or fair about them.

To Cardinal Cicognani he poured out a nine-page catalogue of such tensions, which touched a great variety of questions, including the patriarchate, the question of his jurisdiction over the Ukrainian Church in Philadelphia, and problems of education and formation.[147] Two years later, in another letter to Cicognani, he asserted that "throughout the entire history of the Union [of Brest], and even more during the past 50 years, the Basilian congregation has been battling against our hierarchy, and especially against the metropolitan of

140. Slipyj, *Tvory* 12:71-72.

141. Slipyj, *Tvory* 13:61-64; 113-15.

142. Giovanni Battista Scapinelli to Slipyj, 29.vii.1963, *Arch.Pat.* 29:90a-90b. The authorization for him to preside at the meeting had also come from the Congregation for the Eastern Church: Giovanni Battista Scapinelli to Slipyj, 18.vi.1963, *Arch.Pat.* 28:407a; and Gustavo Testa to Slipyj, [18.vi.1963], *Arch.Pat.* 28:407b.

143. Wojnar (1949) 1:148-94.

144. Wiwarčuk (1963) 48-51.

145. Slipyj, *Spomyny* 63.

146. Wojnar (1949) provides a good orientation to their rise within Ukrainian church history.

147. Slipyj to Amleto Cicognani, 26.xii.1964, *Arch.Pat.* 31:513-21.

Halyč."[148] That entire history needed to be set straight.[149] Thus the Seminary of St. Josaphat was being administered as a Basilian institution, under the jurisdiction of the Sacred Congregation for the Eastern Church, but Slipyj asserted and defended the authority of the Ukrainian hierarchy over the seminary.[150] Slipyj came to the conclusion to which, he maintained, Metropolitan Šeptyc'kyj, although a Basilian himself, had been forced to come: "that the Basilian fathers, as partisans of Latinization, are not capable either of adapting to the exigencies of the separated Orthodox East or of satisfying the exigencies of Ukrainian Catholics"; and he had decided to put his support behind the Studites instead of the Basilians.[151] In so doing he was following the precedent established by Andrej Šeptyc'kyj himself, who, having begun as a Basilian, had laid the foundations for the renewal of the Studites and had built them a monastery near L'viv.[152]

Hardly a month after his arrival in Rome, therefore, Slipyj was writing to the Sacred Congregation for the Eastern Church to request, as "extremely useful and necessary," the establishment of a Studite monastery in Rome; he was doing so, he explained, at the behest of Klymentij Šeptyc'kyj, brother of the late metropolitan, who had been the second archimandrite of the Studites and had died in a Soviet prison.[153] He addressed his pleas for support on behalf of the project in many directions, including one to the pope himself.[154] He also wrote (in English) to Bishop Fulton J. Sheen, requesting his help "to re-establish the Studite Community of monks who follow the primitive rule of Oriental monasticism."[155] Originally Slipyj seems to have had the idea that the Redemptorists should build the Studite monastery, but that was vetoed as "inopportune and not very viable."[156] He was also concerned that there should be a central authority for the Studites, and he petitioned the Secretariat of the Sacred Congregation for the Eastern

148. Slipyj to Amleto Cicognani, 24.ix.1966, *Arch.Pat.* 35:278.
149. Slipyj to Gustavo Testa, 11.xii.1967, *Arch.Pat.* 36:330-31.
150. Gustavo Testa to Atanasio Welykyj, 21.xi.1966, *Arch.Pat.* 35:368-69a; Slipyj to Gustavo Testa, 12.i.1967, *Arch.Pat.* 36:19-21.
151. Slipyj to Gustavo Testa, 29.xii.1966, *Arch.Pat.* 35:500.
152. There is a convenient summary in Prokoptschuk (1967) 113-21.
153. Slipyj to the Sacred Congregation for the Eastern Church, 12.iii.1963, *Arch.Pat.* 28:162-63.
154. Slipyj to Paul VI, 2.vii.1963 [corrected by Ivan Choma from 2.vii.1964 on the manuscript], *Arch.Pat.* 29:22-23.
155. Slipyj to Fulton J. Sheen, 9.v.1963, *Arch.Pat.* 28:305-6.
156. Guglielmo Gaudreau to Gustavo Testa, 2.vii.1963, *Arch.Pat.* 29:26-27.

Church to establish that.[157] By the following year he was able to announce with joy that "finally" the monastery had been founded.[158] The official *Decretum* establishing it was dated 1 October 1965, and the Congregation for the Eastern Church promulgated its official approval, signed by Cardinal Testa, on 26 October.[159] "In Ukraine," Slipyj lamented, "Studite monasteries are closed, and the monks are driven out." Consequently, the opportunity to found this Studite monastery near Rome was for him a way of forging a link to the most glorious chapters in the history of the Eastern Church and to the great renewer of Eastern (and authentically Basilian) monasticism, Saint Theodore of Studios.[160] Therefore "the biography of Saint Theodore is, all by itself, a most beautiful possible sermon to elevate the spirit and a summons to work and sacrifice."[161]

The special needs of the Ukrainian Church in exile, including the need for renewal of the religious orders, also served to confirm Metropolitan Slipyj in his profound conviction, as he expressed it in February 1965, that "all the faithful, the clergy, and the great majority of the bishops, in the actual conditions of disunity within our church and our people, see their salvation in unification under the guidance of the major archbishop."[162] By that time, moreover, the metropolitan and major archbishop already bore the title of cardinal through the action of Pope Paul VI—and, albeit without the action of Pope Paul VI, the title of patriarch as well.

157. Slipyj to Gustavo Testa, 25.x.1963, *Arch.Pat.* 29:259.
158. Slipyj to Gustavo Testa, 25.viii.64, *Arch.Pat.* 31:358.
159. *Arch.Pat.* 33:150-51; 188.
160. Slipyj, *Tvory* 13:158.
161. Slipyj, *Tvory* 13:79.
162. Slipyj to Amleto Cicognani, 8.ii.1965, *Arch.Pat.* 32:145-48.

10

Cardinal (and Patriarch)

When Josyf Slipyj, as a prisoner, put the question to one Soviet official, "Do you acknowledge me as metropolitan?"[1] and to another made the declaration, "I am the metropolitan of the Greek Catholic Church in Ukraine,"[2] it was clear that this title of metropolitan was extremely important to him. Titles were always important to him, because for him they were always much more than titles. Slipyj had an intense interest—or, as many came to believe, an inordinate interest—in ecclesiastical titles, as well as in all the prerogatives, major or minor, that went with them. Corridor gossip during the Second Vatican Council was replete with anecdotes about his strenuous insistence on his rightful place in processions, on programs, in press notices; and his correspondence from those years is replete with no less strident declarations of insistence on his being addressed and listed in the proper way. Obviously, this was not without a touch of personal vanity. But it was much more than that. Coming as he did from a church tradition in which the liturgy was normative, he knew that "mere form" is never "mere." And living as he did in exile, he also knew that to an émigré community symbol and reality are inseparable, and that therefore a title could be all-important for an institution or for an individual prelate—be that title "synod" or "university," "metropolitan" or "patriarch." Once the title was established, the reality could, and often did, somehow follow.

1. Slipyj, *Spomyny* 165-66.
2. Slipyj to N. V. Podgorny, i.1961, *Arch.Pat.* 28:23 (58).

The converse, and the consequence, of this interest was that he was condemned to a lifetime of what he himself admitted to be "my great preoccupation and bitterness" over such questions.[3] He felt called upon repeatedly to compose enormous jeremiads and detailed apologias in response to various personal accusations, many of them having to do, directly or indirectly, with his titles and with the rights and privileges thereunto appertaining.[4] Beyond the title *Kyr* (apparently derived from the Greek κύριος), a general term in Ukrainian for a prelate, "metropolitan of L'viv-Halyč" or "metropolitan of Kiev-Halyč" was the basic designation. But the most common term of respect and endearment for Josyf Slipyj within the Ukrainian community was—and, for that matter, continues to be, even years after his death—"His (or Your) Beatitude [*Blažennišyj*]." Thus the minutes of the Conference of Ukrainian Bishops (soon to be called "Synod of Bishops of the Ukrainian Catholic Church") from the year 1965 contain the following notice: "On the basis of the custom and the legal right of the Eastern churches, the Bishops' Conference resolved that the Major Archbishop should bear the title 'His Beatitude [*Blažennišyj*]' "; there was one dissenting vote.[5] It is instructive in this connection to trace the development of nomenclature in the titles of the successive volumes of his *Tvory* or collected works, most of which were issued while he was still living. In volume 1, published in 1968, he is identified as "Cardinal Josyf, Major Archbishop"; beginning with volume 2 in the following year, it is "*Kyr* Josyf, Major Archbishop and Cardinal"; and from volume 7/8, which came out in 1976, to the volumes still appearing, his title has become "Josyf, Patriarch and Cardinal."

It is not merely instructive, but fascinating, to trace the sequence of titles in Slipyj's own biographical sketches of the two fifteenth-century churchmen whom we have identified in an earlier chapter as, along with Andrej Šeptyc'kyj in the twentieth century, Slipyj's rôle models in theology and ecumenical churchmanship: Isidore of Kiev and Bessarion of Constantinople.[6] In his sermon of 8 March 1964 to commemorate the five-hundredth anniversary of Isidore's death (which took place on 27 April 1463), Slipyj listed Isidore's titles as:

3. Slipyj to Mario Brini, 11.x.1966, *Arch.Pat.* 35:310.
4. To cite only one example among many, the twelve-page letter to Gustavo Testa, 29.xii.1966, *Arch.Pat.* 35:497-508.
5. "Conference of the Catholic Bishops of the Ukrainian Rite," 30.iii.1965, resolution 5, *Arch.Pat.* 73:50.
6. See chapter 4, pp. 64-65 above.

"metropolitan of Kiev, cardinal of the Holy Roman Church, dean of the college of cardinals, and patriarch of Constantinople."[7] Of these titles, Slipyj himself at the time held only the title "metropolitan," and was struggling to be recognized as metropolitan of Kiev, not only metropolitan of L'viv-Halyč; "cardinal" was to come only the following year, while "patriarch" was to be yet another matter. By 1972 he was a cardinal, but in speaking about Bessarion on 18 November of that year he recited a no less autobiographical variation on the sequence he had invoked earlier for Isidore: theologian, cardinal, patriarch.[8]

The remembrance of "the mighty enterprises of Cardinal Isidore, metropolitan of Kiev" sprang to Slipyj's mind again in 1965, when he was named cardinal by Pope Paul VI. In a capsule history of the Ukrainian Church, beginning with the apostle Andrew and Pope Clement I and continuing with Cyril and Methodius and then with Vladimir, Slipyj, expressing his appreciation that "our metropolitan is being numbered in the college of cardinals . . . as a symbol for all our suffering," pointed out that he was "the fourth cardinal in our history."[9] The notification had come to him from the pope *sub secreto*, under date of 10 January 1965.[10] Cardinal Cicognani sent his congratulations, and then on 22 February the official diploma of appointment.[11] Many other messages of congratulation followed, including one from the archbishop of New York, Francis Cardinal Spellman.[12] There was also a greeting from the Basilian sisters in Zagreb, Jugoslavia.[13] Eugène Cardinal Tisserant, who had presented Slipyj as the successor of Metropolitan Šeptyc'kyj in 1939,[14] now wrote to him about the proper garb for the new cardinal to wear.[15] (Tisserant was also to be the one to write to Slipyj about the changes in the cardinals' garb that had come out of the discussions at the Second Vatican Council.)[16] Slipyj in turn

7. Slipyj, *Tvory* 12:118 (123).
8. Slipyj, *Tvory* 13:187-88.
9. Slipyj, *Tvory* 12:178.
10. Paul VI to Slipyj, 10.i.1965, *Arch.Pat.* 32:17.
11. Amleto Cicognani to Slipyj, 13.i.1965, *Arch.Pat.* 32:19; 22.ii.1965, *Arch.Pat.* 32:181. The diploma and accompanying documents are reproduced as frontispieces to Dragan (1966).
12. Francis Spellman to Slipyj, 26.i.1965, *Arch.Pat.* 32:119.
13. Basilian Sisters to Slipyj, 15.iv.1965, *Arch.Pat.* 145:193; see also Dmytro Stefanjuk (Vukovar) to Slipyj, 17.iv.1965, *Arch.Pat.* 145:162B.
14. Slipyj, *Tvory* 13:157.
15. Eugène Tisserant to Slipyj, 2.ii.1965, *Arch.Pat.* 32:132.
16. Eugène Tisserant to Slipyj, 6.v.1967, *Arch.Pat.* 36:184-86.

wrote to the papal major domo requesting five hundred tickets to the public consistory for his Ukrainian clergy and faithful.[17]

The detailed, if somewhat breathless, account by one of those in attendance at the consistory and other ceremonies opens by identifying "the memorable week of February 21, 1965" as "truly historic Ukrainian Days," because of the "indelible impression that Ukraine and Ukrainians were in the center of attention, that for Ukraine and Ukrainians the events of these days have enormous value and significance."[18] The new Ukrainian cardinal was also deeply moved by these events, finding in them "the crowning point of all the benefits and blessings" he had received. His elevation was, indeed, a major event for him:

> In the life of every man, and especially in the life of a priest and of a bishop, there are certain particular moments that form a turning point, closing one period of his life and beginning a new one. Without doubt, elevation to the dignity of a cardinal belongs among such moments. . . . For me, being named a cardinal at the hands of the Holy Father, Pope Paul VI, does constitute such a moment.[19]

Among its many other honors and privileges, the status as a cardinal of the Roman Church helped to clarify the ambiguity of Slipyj's citizenship. The Pontifical Commission for the State of Vatican City sent him a formal document, designating him as a Vatican citizen.[20] Upon his release from imprisonment he had been issued a Soviet passport with his picture as a convict, dated 2 February 1963 and valid for one year.[21] His first Vatican passport carried the stipulation "with permission," and enabled him to make such trips as his return visit to Innsbruck. Then on 15 May 1968 he received a Vatican diplomatic passport, signed by Cardinal Cicognani, and a new one on 24 February 1976, signed by Cardinal Villot.[22]

"Crowning point" and "turning point" though it surely was both

17. Slipyj to Federico Callori de Vignala, 15.ii.1965, *Arch.Pat.* 32:166.

18. Dragan (1966) n.p.

19. Slipyj, "Brevi note autobiographice scritte dal Cardinale Jozyf Slipyj nel 1965," *Arch.Pat.* 32:161.

20. Pontifical Commission for the State of Vatican City to Slipyj, 1.vi.1966, *Arch.Pat.* 34:217.

21. See the photographs of this passport in the illustration section.

22. These passports, both the one from the Soviet Union and those from the Vatican, are in the Patriarchal Archive of Saint Sophia in Rome, where I have examined them.

for him personally and for his Ukrainian Church, the "elevation to the dignity of a cardinal" was just as surely not enough, either for him or for the church. For long before Pope Paul VI had conferred this dignity on him, Slipyj was agitating for other titles which, in the total scheme of things, mattered even more to him than the red hat. There was even some suspicion that the cardinalate was a way of deflecting that agitation and, not incidentally, of granting the Ukrainian archbishop a Western, Latin title in place of the more traditional Eastern ones to which he was laying claim. One of these was "metropolitan of Kiev-Halyč— primate," which the papal secretary of state had "canceled." Slipyj wrote to him less than half a year after his liberation, to urge that "this title does not signify some sort of juridical prerogative, but is purely a historical title," and one that was acknowledged by all the Ukrainian hierarchy. "I therefore humbly request," he concluded, "that this historic title be left intact."[23] Slipyj insisted that "with the renewal of the metropolitanate of Halyč, Pope Pius VII on 24 February 1807 transferred the rights and privileges of the metropolitanate of Kiev to the metropolitanate of Halyč."[24] He explained that "when the Soviet armies and government came into Western Ukraine," he had been urged by his clergy "to assume officially the title of metropolitan of Kiev and Halyč, as this has been recognized by ancient tradition." That title had been granted to Metropolitan Andrej Šeptyc'kyj, "and [de] jure to his successors," by Pope Pius X in a letter of 2 January 1921 written by Pietro Cardinal Gasparri, and Šeptyc'kyj had signed official documents as "metropolitan of Kiev."[25] The Vatican replied that according to its records that title had been conferred on Šeptyc'kyj with the explicit stipulation that it was being granted "to the metropolitan, but not to his successors by ordinary and proper right."[26] Slipyj was not convinced by this, "and my argument remains firm."[27] In support of the argument he cited precedents going back to metropolitans in the fifteenth century.[28]

The designation "major archbishop [archiepiscopus maior in Latin, or in Ukrainian verchovnyj archyjepiskop]" could be seen as in some sense an alternative title, if not perhaps quite as a substitute; it was as well an uncommon term, particularly in Western canon law.[29] Its

---

23. Slipyj to Amleto Cicognani, 3.vii.1963, Arch.Pat. 29:32-33.
24. Slipyj, Tvory 9:157.
25. Slipyj to Congregation for Eastern Churches, 26.vi.1963, Arch.Pat. 28:420-21.
26. Gustavo Testa to Slipyj, 1.x.1963, Arch.Pat. 29:184.
27. Slipyj to Gustavo Testa, 23.x.1963, Arch.Pat. 29:258.
28. Slipyj, Tvory 10/11:50.
29. Rizzi (1964) summarizes the canonical legislation.

meaning and requirements had been formulated in *Cleri sanctitati*, which Pope Pius XII had issued as a motu proprio on 2 June 1957.[30] On the basis of those requirements, the Sacred Congregation for the Eastern Church determined at the end of 1963 that "the metropolitan of L'viv of the Ukrainians is to be termed 'major archbishop' "; the action was approved by Pope Paul VI and dated at Rome on 23 December 1963.[31] The diploma of office, signed by Cardinal Cicognani and bearing that date, was transmitted to Slipyj.[32] Allowing only Christmas and New Year's Day (New Style) to intervene, Slipyj wrote back to Pope Paul: "This is not only a personal honor for my poor person, but a great distinction and elevation for our persecuted church." Then immediately he added: "This is a historic act and the first step toward the Ukrainian patriarchate, which will undoubtedly have great and salutary consequences for the development of our church in the future."[33] Grammatically it may be unclear whether the antecedent of that closing relative clause, "which will undoubtedly etc.," was meant to be "historic act" or "Ukrainian patriarchate," but there was nothing unclear about his meaning: he wanted to be acknowledged as patriarch, not only as major archbishop.[34] A few weeks later there came a public explanation from Vatican sources not only that "the figure of 'major archbishop,' like the figure of 'patriarch,' which it approximates [*a cui si avvicina*], is a figure characteristic of Eastern canon law," but that "it involves a faculty that is, considered in itself, superior to that of the patriarchs themselves."[35] Slipyj was not satisfied with that explanation, either historically or canonically, and was not put off by it.[36] Meanwhile he went on pressing the title of major archbishop for all that it was worth, urging that it was illogical to separate a major archbishop from the (other) patriarchs in the makeup of the Sacred Congregation for the Eastern Church.[37] He also claimed that as major archbishop he possessed the authority to convoke synods, which Vatican officials would not concede.[38]

Yet that did not imply that he would in any way be deterred from

30. *AAS* 49 (1957):433-600, canons 324-39 (pp. 530-35).

31. *AAS* 56 (1964):214.

32. *Arch.Pat.* 29:365.

33. Slipyj to Paul VI, 4.i.1964, *Arch.Pat.* 30:9.

34. Agenda of synod of 31.x.1971, Slipyj, *Tvory* 13:128.

35. "Servizio Informazioni Chiesa Orientale," 278:1-4 (31.i.1964).

36. Slipyj to Antonio Samore, 2.vi.1967, *Arch.Pat.* 36:141-44.

37. Slipyj to Amleto Cicognani, 30.viii.1967, *Arch.Pat.* 36:279- 81a.

38. Ihor Monzak, "Rezjume z privatnoj rozmovy" with Mario Brini, 23.xii.1966, *Arch.Pat.* 35:456-59.

his quest for the patriarchal title.[39] The title of patriarch was, or at any rate at Slipyj's hands it was becoming, what he called it in 1971: "the center of our present worldwide yearnings and strivings."[40] Thus the title of this tenth chapter of our portrait of Josyf Slipyj (except for the parentheses, which we have added) comes from Slipyj's own formulation of the titles for himself, as for example when he signed himself on 9/22 March 1979 as "patriarch and cardinal."[41] But the ideological presupposition underlying that signature, and therefore this chapter title, is expressed more adequately and fully in a statement that Slipyj made later in the same year, when he explained that in 1965 Pope Paul VI had "conferred the dignity of a cardinal on His Beatitude Patriarch Josyf [vidznačuvav hidnistju Kardynala Blažennišoho Patrijarcha Josyfa]."[42] "Beatitude" and "patriarch" were, therefore, to be identified as titles that had already belonged to him long before 1965, by virtue of his metropolitan office; "cardinal" was (in the phrase of the Sermon on the Mount) "added unto" these, and not vice versa. And, speaking on his eightieth birthday, he would not let himself be discouraged by those who said that his struggle for the patriarchate had been a failure.[43]

What made all of this so important to Josyf Slipyj—and, presumably, to the Ukrainian Catholic Church?[44] The patriarchal title ought to be seen in the broader context of the need of the Ukrainian Church to affirm its identity and distinctive character, especially as that need had been articulated during Slipyj's lifetime, first by Šeptyc'kyj and then by Slipyj himself. At the Congress on Church Union held in L'viv in 1936, to which Josyf Slipyj delivered a scholarly analysis of the liturgical variety of the churches and of the dogmatic differences between them, three of the resolutions passed by the assembly had read:

3. The Eastern character of Ukrainian Catholicism in what concerns its organization, rite, and ecclesiastical discipline should be based

39. The Patriarchal Archive of Saint Sophia contains an entire volume bearing the title *Patriarchat 1963-1978*, which is a collection of photocopies (often photocopies of carbon copies) of materials that are scattered throughout many of the other volumes of the archive. This volume is not itself numbered in the series, nor are its pages numbered; therefore we have not, except in a few cases, cited it directly. Nevertheless it has served as a guide to documents in the numbered volumes, despite the absence of explicit cross-references, except for the dating of letters, memoranda, and minutes.

40. Slipyj, *Tvory* 13:107; further comments, pp. 108-9.

41. Slipyj, *Tvory* 9:323.

42. Slipyj, *Tvory* 9:327.

43. Slipyj, *Tvory* 13:154.

44. Ivan Choma, "Pid uvahu," 4.iv.1966, *Arch.Pat.* 34:162, is a careful statement of the principal issues involved.

on the ancient Ukrainian ecclesiastical tradition going back to the times of Metropolitan Ruts′kyj;

4. All the ideas of Metropolitan Ruts′kyj, including the idea of a patriarchate in Kiev, are valid also at the present time for the growth of Ukrainian Catholicism, to guarantee that growth;

5. There is a necessity to defend the rights and privileges of the metropolitans of Halyč, successors to the glorious traditions of the metropolitans of Kiev-Halyč.[45]

For the rest of his life, until he died nearly fifty years later, Slipyj was doing battle on all three of those fronts: defending the Eastern character of his church in liturgy, in canon law, and even in doctrine; asserting the rights and privileges of the metropolitanate of Kiev-Halyč; and propagating "the idea of a patriarchate in Kiev," or, as it now had to be, at least temporarily, a patriarchate *of* Kiev though *in* Rome.

To his predominantly Western audience at the papal synod of bishops he felt obliged to explain that in the East the patriarchate was the "ordinary" polity of the church, which, while not instituted directly and immediately by Christ in the sense that the papacy and the episcopate had been, was nevertheless firmly grounded in the Eastern Christian tradition.[46] It was as well firmly grounded in the specifically Ukrainian tradition.[47] Slipyj was not unaware of the ambiguities of the patriarchal office, also in relation to the metropolitanate.[48] As a participant in the union congresses at Velehrad, he had as early as 1922 given attention to the divisive rôle that a patriarchal polity and the associated system of autocephaly had played in the ecclesiology of Eastern Orthodox theologians—or, as he termed them, "disunited theologians [*nezjedyneni bohoslovy*]"—and he reported on the presentation by the Russian Orthodox theologian Vytovtov about the Russian patriarchate.[49] The patriarchate did not, of course, interest Slipyj as such a symbol of resistance to Roman primacy. On the contrary, he found in the patriarchate as he defined it precisely that combination of particularity and Catholicity that he believed to have been the special characteristic of the Ukrainian Catholic Church.[50] For that reason, and for a host of other reasons as well, it was not to the patriarchate of Mos-

45. Slipyj, *Tvory* 5:142 (39).
46. Slipyj, *Tvory* 13:36.
47. Boreć′kyj (1970).
48. Milaš (1926) 315-19.
49. Slipyj, *Tvory* 5:73, 81.
50. See chapter 3, p. 38 above.

cow that he turned as a model, nor even to the patriarchates of Constantinople, Alexandria, Antioch, and Jerusalem, as these had been linked in the historic Eastern theories of "pentarchy." Rather, Slipyj took a special interest in those Eastern prelates who held that title now but who did so under the universal authority of the pope.

The presence of several such prelates at the Second Vatican Council was arousing the curiosity of Latin bishops who were also in attendance. Therefore there appeared in March 1963 a semiofficial bulletin explaining why it was that the Holy See honored such prelates with the patriarchal title (and, to be sure, making the point that it was the Holy See that was the source of the title). "These Eastern patriarchs," it specified on the basis of canon law, "are entitled to a particular honor. They enjoy, *sub auctoritate Romani Pontificis*, a plenipotentiary power over their entire patriarchate, the power of a jurisdiction of order and a personal one as well." The bulletin went on to make clear that at early councils such as the Council of Chalcedon in 451 the title had been reserved to the incumbents of the five patriarchal sees of Rome, Constantinople, Alexandria, Antioch, and Jerusalem, but that later it had been extended to, among others, the Catholicos of Armenia, the Coptic patriarch of Alexandria, the three (Syrian, Melchite, and Maronite) patriarchs of Antioch, the Armenian patriarch in Cilicia, and the Chaldean patriarch in Babylonia. In this entire catalogue, however, there was no reference at all to a Ukrainian patriarch.[51] That sort of explanation of the title "patriarch," and without any reference to Ukraine, was standard in Vatican publications.[52] As part of his campaign to correct that procedure, Slipyj entered into correspondence with the (other) Eastern patriarchs, cultivated their acquaintance, and sought their support.

Despite the pathetically tiny remnants of past ecclesiastical glory over which most of these patriarchs now presided, the tradition—and the title—remained.[53] In response to Slipyj's solicitations, several of them wrote in early 1966 to describe their church governance, to explain their canon law, and to provide Slipyj with the information he needed to press his own case for recognition as Ukrainian patriarch. These included the Chaldean patriarch, the Coptic patriarch in Cairo,

51. "Servizio Informazioni Chiesa Orientale," 267-68 (30.iii.1963).
52. So, for example, *Ann.Pont.* (1984) 1514-15.
53. See Pospishil (1960) 112-14 for a list of those holding the title according to Roman Catholic canon law.

the Armenian patriarch, and the Syrian patriarch of Antioch.[54] Again in August 1967 Slipyj corresponded with them about the possibility of bringing all the Eastern hierarchs together for a revision of the Oriental canon law that would take account of distinctively Eastern practice and legislation in a way that the Roman canon law was incapable of doing. There was an especially detailed response from the Melchite patriarch, Maximos V.[55] When he led the liturgy as guest celebrant in the Ukrainian cathedral at Melbourne, Australia, while attending a eucharistic congress there, Patriarch Maximos was likewise the source for a somewhat ironic judgment about the very idea of the patriarchate, one that Slipyj found particularly apt: "We have the title of patriarch, but we have neither a church nor an episcopate," Maximos asserted. By contrast, "you have bishops and clergy and faithful, and magnificent cathedrals. What you do not have is the title of patriarch, to which you are nevertheless fully entitled."[56]

In pressing for the patriarchate as he did, Slipyj believed that he stood firmly on the foundation of Ukrainian history, as the resolutions quoted earlier from the Congress on Church Union of 1936 already suggested when they spoke about "the idea of a patriarchate in Kiev" as one of the several "ideas of Metropolitan Ruts'kyj" that were "valid also at the present time for the growth of Ukrainian Catholicism."[57] He quoted Ruts'ky's statement of 1629 that the metropolitans of Kiev already "have patriarchal privileges and use them," so that "there is nothing lacking for the completeness of a patriarchal jurisdiction except the title 'patriarch' itself."[58] It was perhaps even more pertinent to Slipyj's overall strategy when he also quoted the celebrated Ukrainian Orthodox Metropolitan Petro Mohyla (whose *Orthodox Confession of Faith* [*Pravoslavne ispovidannja viry*] he had cited favorably in his lectures on the doctrine of the sacraments in support of the doctrine of the real presence and even of the doctrine of transubstantiation):[59] "If I could be patriarch, I would acknowledge the pope."[60] It was in keeping with

---

54. Chaldean patriarch to Slipyj, 23.iii.1966, *Arch.Pat.* 34:142a; Coptic patriarch to Slipyj, 24.iii.1966, *Arch.Pat.* 34:142b; Armenian patriarch to Slipyj, 29.iii.1966, *Arch.Pat.* 34:153a; Syrian patriarch of Antioch to Slipyj, 12.iv.1966, *Arch.Pat.* 34:109a.

55. *Arch.Pat.* 36:272-74.

56. Quoted "verbatim [*doslivno*]" in Slipyj, *Tvory* 9:253.

57. Slipyj, *Tvory* 5:142 (39).

58. Slipyj, *Tvory* 9:252 n. 1.

59. Slipyj, *Tvory* 6:252, 245.

60. Slipyj, *Tvory* 13:317.

that strategy when Slipyj reported to the pope that the Russian Orthodox observers at the Second Vatican Council had not only not opposed the idea of the patriarchate, but had regarded it as altogether natural.[61] On the other hand, he warned that if, as they were threatening to do, the Soviets were to establish an Orthodox patriarchate of Kiev first, the creation of a Greek Catholic patriarchate of Kiev-Halyč, and in exile at that, would look like "a pathetic imitation."[62] Therefore peremptory action by the pope or the council would be a preventive strike.

Ukrainian support for the idea of designating Slipyj patriarch had begun as soon as he was released from prison. "May the time come soon," came a message from a Ukrainian Basilian in Buenos Aires (who was to repeat this message thirteen years later in a Christmas greeting), "when Your Excellency will return to a free Ukraine and take your place on *the patriarchal see* in Kiev."[63] Later that year, on 10 October, the day before he was to make his impassioned appeal to the Second Vatican Council for a Ukrainian patriarchate,[64] Slipyj tried out his address on the assembled Conference of Ukrainian Bishops. "At the end," the minutes of the conference report, "he made the motion that the council should [be asked to] raise the metropolitanate of Kiev-Halyč to patriarchal dignity"; the motion was approved unanimously.[65] That motion was repeated, again with the unanimous approval of all the bishops who were present, at the next year's conference of bishops late in 1964, together with "the project of an official letter in support of the patriarchate."[66] 1964 was the year in which the Ukrainian movement for the patriarchate began moving toward a crescendo. Pope Paul VI was inundated with lengthy epistles from a great variety of sources, ranging from Hollywood artists to Redemptorist priests.[67] From Chicago there arrived a massive document, bearing eight pages of signatures and a lengthy documentation by Nicolaus Chubaty, former

61. Slipyj to Paul VI, 6.xi.1963, *Arch.Pat.* 29:282-83.

62. Slipyj to Gustavo Testa, 9.i.1964, *Arch.Pat.* 30:23.

63. Josyf Halabarda to Slipyj, 12.ii.1963, *Arch.Pat.* 87:76; our italics replace all caps in the original.

64. Slipyj, *Tvory* 12:89-90.

65. "Conference of the Catholic Bishops of the Ukrainian Rite," 10.x.1963, item 9, *Arch.Pat.* 73:35.

66. "Conference of the Catholic Bishops of the Ukrainian Rite," 17.ix.1964, item 2; and 23.x.1964, item 11, *Arch.Pat.* 73:40; 43.

67. Vassyl Yemetz to Paul VI, 2.viii.1964, *Arch.Pat.* 31:396-98; Michael Schudlo to Paul VI, 15.xii.1964, *Arch.Pat.* 31:490-508.

professor at L'viv and historian of the Ukrainian Church.[68] The Ukrainian participants at the Second Vatican Council transmitted another such petition.[69]

On the basis of these expressions of support, many of which had of course been inspired throughout 1964 from his own headquarters in Rome, Slipyj felt entitled to claim early in 1965 that this agitation for the Ukrainian patriarchate represented "a general movement" and was not, as its detractors claimed, confined to a few bishops and people.[70] The "general movement" was to continue throughout the remainder of that decade—in May 1967 there began appearing a periodical bearing the title *Za Patrijarchat* [For the patriarchate], which reprints documents, letters, petitions, and newspaper stories on the campaign—and throughout the next decades as well, as a brief sampling of the many documents will show. Thus in a homily on the Great Commission of Christ in the closing verses of the Gospel of Matthew, delivered to the synod of Ukrainian bishops in September 1969, Slipyj urged that "at the synod we must take a stand on what we as pastors and leaders ought to do . . . based on the principles of the patriarchal polity of our church."[71] In response the synod declared that the elevation to patriarchal dignity was a project "dear to the episcopate of our church."[72] The issue was on the agenda of the synod again in 1971.[73] In 1973, "the patriarchal constitution and the patriarchate" had been the first item on the agenda, but it was changed to the third item.[74] Two years later, Slipyj urged that pilgrimages to Rome for the 1975 Year of Jubilee be used as an occasion to lobby for the Ukrainian patriarchate.[75] In a "press communiqué" about the synod, dated 25 November 1980, the title "Father and Head of the Ukrainian Church, His Beatitude Cardinal Josyf Slipyj" was amended (apparently in Slipyj's own handwriting) to read "Patriarch and Cardinal."[76] And the Roman Catholic archbishop of Sydney promised the Ukrai-

68. Petition to Paul VI, 1.xi.1964, *Arch.Pat.* 31:445-58.
69. Ukrainian participants to Paul VI, 12.xi.1964, *Arch.Pat.* 31:460-64.
70. Slipyj to Amleto Cicognani, 5.iv.1965, *Arch.Pat.* 33:5.
71. Slipyj, Homily on Matt. 28:19, as reported in "Synod of the Episcopate of the Ukrainian Catholic Church, under the Direction of His Beatitude, Major Archbishop Josyf Slipyj," 29.ix.1969, *Arch.Pat.* 73:63.
72. Slipyj, *Tvory* 9:118.
73. Slipyj, *Tvory* 13:128.
74. "Sixth Synod," agenda for 18.xi.1973, *Arch.Pat.* 73:229.
75. Slipyj, *Tvory* 9:215.
76. "Presovyj komunikat" for 25.xi.1980, *Arch.Pat.* 74:190.

nian Catholic Council in Australia that he would "forward to the Holy Father your request that His Holiness . . . 'erect the Ukrainian Catholic Patriarchate . . . [and] nominate His Eminence Archbishop Major Joseph Slipyj as our first Patriarch.' "[77]

As the defensive tone of many of these statements suggests, the agitation among the Ukrainian bishops, clergy, and faithful for the establishment of the patriarchate was something less than the united front it usually claimed to be. For Slipyj's unfortunate habit of (in the words of Mario Brini) presenting his colleagues with "an accomplished fact"[78] and of not preparing the ground sufficiently beforehand had cost him the unanimity of support within his own constituency that he would have needed if there had been any chance of success for the patriarchal movement. The two chief areas of opposition were located within the Basilian Order and within the Ukrainian archdiocese of Philadelphia. It would be a mistake, and one that Slipyj's own polemical rhetoric sometimes seemed to abet, to assume that all the Ukrainian Basilians stood on the same side in the debate over the patriarchate. One of the most carefully documented statements of the case in favor of the patriarchate on the basis of canon law and conciliar decrees came from a Basilian historian.[79] Nevertheless, because the Basilians were regarded as devotees of "Latinization" in the liturgy[80] and as opponents of his policies in general, Slipyj saw them also, perhaps unfairly, as leading the charge against the patriarchate, as part of their resistance to his authority.[81] The Basilian congregation, he was convinced, was the persistent opponent of the Ukrainian hierarchy and of the metropolitan of Halyč.[82] For example, the Seminary of Saint Josaphat, as a Basilian institution, was claimed by the Sacred Congregation for the Eastern Church as belonging to its jurisdiction.[83] But Slipyj insisted that as an institution serving the needs of the Ukrainian Church in exile, the seminary came under the authority of the Ukrainian bishops, which really meant under his authority as metropolitan and patriarch.[84] The accusation of insubordination to the metropolitan was one that at least some Basilians

---

77. N. T. Gilroy to N. Karmazyn, 22.iv.1970, *Arch.Pat.* 88:100.

78. Ihor Mončak, "Rezjume z pryvatnoji rozmovy" with Mario Brini, 23.xii.1966, *Arch.Pat.* 35:456-59.

79. Wojnar (1970), which amounts to a legal brief.

80. Ivan Praško to Gustavo Testa, 23.vi.1976, *Arch.Pat.* 36:208-21.

81. Slipyj to Amleto Cicognani, 26.xii.1964, *Arch.Pat.* 31:513-21.

82. Slipyj to Amleto Cicognani, 24.ix.1966, *Arch.Pat.* 35:278.

83. Gustavo Testa to Atanasio Welykyj, 21.xi.1966, *Arch.Pat.* 35:368-69a.

84. Slipyj to Gustavo Testa, 12.i.1967, *Arch.Pat.* 36:19-21.

regarded as slanderous, as became clear in a letter from a Ukrainian-American priest to the Protoarchimandrite of the Basilians in Rome.[85] Slipyj forwarded the letter in an Italian translation to Cardinal Cicognani.[86] Yet, he lamented, in the atmosphere of the 1960s they were free to attack him, while he was being muzzled by the Vatican.[87] (For the sake of completeness, it should probably be added that toward the end of his life Slipyj addressed several conciliatory messages to the Basilians.)[88]

Meanwhile, already in 1963/1964 Archbishop Ambrosij Senyšyn (or, as he had Anglicized it, Ambrose Senyshyn), the metropolitan of Philadelphia, had become the principal spokesman within the Ukrainian hierarchy for the antipatriarchal position. When he requested of the supporters of the patriarchate that "all propagandizing and campaigning" for the cause should cease, citing as the grounds for his request the fact that Slipyj himself had "expressly dissociated himself from all such initiatives," Slipyj retorted that "this does not correspond with the truth."[89] Nor did it help to allay Slipyj's resentments and suspicions of Senyshyn as the standard-bearer of the opposition to the patriarchate when, shortly thereafter, a letter from Cardinal Cicognani containing the news that Senyshyn was to be designated an "assistant at the pontifical throne" also conveyed "the earnest wish of His Holiness" that this not become yet another occasion for a discussion of the patriarchate (perhaps also because all patriarchs were entitled to that designation *de jure*).[90] In this respect as in others, Slipyj was informed, "the wish of the Holy Father is tantamount to a command."[91] Late in 1966, "after an interruption and a silence of two years," Slipyj received what he called "a brutal letter" from Senyshyn on various such matters, which also transmitted a report on defamations of Slipyj that had been emanating from the Soviet embassy.[92] The alienation between the two hierarchs was clearly both personal and ecclesiastical, with Senyshyn becoming the spokesman for those bishops who feared that as "patriarch" Metropolitan Slipyj would encroach on their authority,

85. Pastor of Saint George's Ukrainian Catholic Church in New York to Atanasio Welykyj, 16.xi.1964, *Arch.Pat.* 31:469-73 (Italian translation of what was apparently a Ukrainian original).

86. Slipyj to Amleto Cicognani, 26.xii.1964, *Arch.Pat.* 31:520-21.

87. Slipyj to Angelo Dell'Acqua, 26.xi.1965, *Arch.Pat.* 33:225.

88. Slipyj, *Tvory* 14:212-13; 416-17.

89. Slipyj to Amleto Cicognani, 6.iv.1965, *Arch.Pat.* 33:8-10.

90. Amleto Cicognani to Slipyj, 22.iv.1965, *Arch.Pat.* 33:55.

91. Cited as from earlier correspondence in Gustavo Testa to Slipyj, 9.i.1967, *Arch.Pat.* 36:16.

92. Slipyj to Angelo Dell'Acqua, 14.xi.1966, *Arch.Pat.* 35:360.

both individual and collective, in an even more autocratic manner than he was already doing.

In addition to the Ukrainian diaspora, the other constituency that needed to be persuaded about the wisdom of establishing the patriarchate—and about the unanimity of the Ukrainian diaspora in support of it—was of course Rome. During these same years, therefore, Slipyj was also striving to present his case for being designated patriarch to various prelates, to the council, and to several popes in succession. In an audience with Angelo Cardinal Dell'Acqua on 26 August 1963, it was the first item on the agenda.[93] A week later Slipyj came back to Dell'Acqua, and once more *Patriarcato* was the first on his list.[94] Two weeks after that Slipyj had yet another audience with Dell'Acqua, where he returned to the topic yet again, though only at the very end.[95] Then in June of the following year, he presented his case to Cardinal Dell'Acqua one more time.[96] In the autumn of 1963 there were audiences with Igino Cardinale and with Amleto Cicognani, at both of which Slipyj lobbied for the patriarchate.[97] In a letter to Slipyj, Cardinal Cicognani acknowledged that the patriarchate was "certainly a grave and important matter, one that deserves profound study."[98] And in response to a letter from Slipyj dated 4 November 1963, Cardinal Testa assured him that the question of a Ukrainian patriarchate was receiving careful consideration.[99]

On 11 October 1963 Metropolitan Josyf Slipyj delivered his first address to the assembled fathers of the Second Vatican Council. Its concluding paragraph, whose key words he himself would go on quoting afterward (with the Latin transliterated in Cyrillic characters) also to his own constituency,[100] was both a request and a statement of hope:

> It is with confidence that all of us look to the council for relief and comfort, because, as has been said, the very fact of the coun-

93. "Udienza da S. E. Rev.ma Mons. Angelo Dell'Acqua 26 agosto 1963," *Arch.Pat.* 29:125.

94. "Udienza da S. E. Mons. Angelo Dell'Acqua, 2 settembre 1963," *Arch.Pat.* 29:127.

95. "Udienza," 15.ix.1963, *Arch.Pat.* 29:171.

96. "Udienza," 5.vi.1964, *Arch.Pat.* 30:289.

97. With Cardinale, 12.x.1963, *Arch.Pat.* 29:226; with Cicognani, 13.xi.1963, *Arch.Pat.* 29:296.

98. Amleto Cicognani to Slipyj, 25.xi.1963, *Arch.Pat.* 29:313.

99. Gustavo Testa to Slipyj, 13.xi.1963, *Arch.Pat.* 29:295.

100. For example, Slipyj, *Tvory* 9:94.

cil uplifts the Catholic Church throughout the world. Also in the East the council will undoubtedly make a great contribution to the improvement of the deplorable state of the church in various municipalities. Speaking in the name of our entire church, I earnestly request that, to manifest that beneficent influence, our principal metropolitan see of Kiev-Halyč may be accounted worthy of being raised to the status of a patriarchate and that thus the great efforts of Popes Urban VIII, Gregory XVI, Pius IX, and Leo XIII toward the creation of that patriarchate may finally be crowned with success. This will be a source of comfort for the Catholic Church in the East not only among the Catholics but also among the Orthodox. On that account the council will have earned the total devotion and the most sincere gratitude of Eastern Christians, and will have taken a giant step toward strengthening the Catholic faith in the East.[101]

The reason for presenting this appeal to the Council was that in the draft of the conciliar decree on the Eastern Churches (as well as in the text as it was definitively promulgated by Pope Paul VI on 21 November 1964) the authority to set up a patriarchate was said to be vested in either the pope or the ecumenical council (or the two in concert).[102]

Having addressed the ecumenical council, Slipyj could also appeal to the pope. In an audience with Pope Paul VI on 14 October 1963, two days after taking up the matter with Igino Cardinale, he did not put the patriarchate on the agenda.[103] But he did go on pressing the matter with the pope repeatedly in the next years, as he explained in an encyclical letter headed "A Message on the Matter of the Patriarchate of Kiev-Halyč" and dated 20/7 October 1971.[104] Thus he could write to Pope Paul VI on 18 March 1971, citing in support of the Ukrainian claims a historical monograph about the Ukrainian patriarchate that had just been prepared at his behest (and that was published in French).[105] But it was all to no avail. Together with a committee of cardinals, Pope Paul VI, in a seven-page solemn and official document, with all the seals and calligraphy attached, informed Slipyj: "We have regretfully come to the conclusion that it is impossible to proceed, at least at this time, to the establishment of a Ukrainian patriarchate." By

101. Slipyj, Tvory 12:89-90.
102. Slipyj to Amleto Cicognani, 9.ix.1963, Arch.Pat. 29:149.
103. "Udienza," 14.x.1963, Arch.Pat. 29:227.
104. Slipyj, Tvory 9:153-54.
105. Slipyj to Paul VI, 18.iii.1971, Arch.Pat. 40:48, enclosing and citing Madey (1971).

a grim irony that could hardly have been a coincidence, the document bore the dating: *"In festo SS. Cyrilli et Methodii."*[106]

During a visit to the United States in 1973, nevertheless, Slipyj discussed his recent audiences with Paul VI with the press, candidly acknowledging the existence of a "controversy between the Ukrainian Catholic bishops and the Vatican" over the patriarchate but closing with the declaration: "Our cause is God's cause, and with God's help we shall accomplish what we have undertaken to do. We shall win universal recognition that our Ukrainian Church is a patriarchate."[107] But Pope Paul went on speaking about *"le malaise diffuse de certaines communautés ukrainiennes et de leur pasteurs,"* and he rejected the interpretation that rejecting the patriarchate was a manifestation of papal insensitivity to the aspirations of Ukrainian Catholics.[108] When Karol Cardinal Wojtyła was elected pope as John Paul II, Slipyj, with his bishops joining in the appeal, almost immediately seized the occasion to request that, in accordance with *Cleri sanctitati*, he, as "patriarch or major archbishop," be declared to have authority over the Ukrainian Church both within and beyond Ukrainian territory.[109] And when Pope John Paul II on 19 March 1979 wrote to Slipyj (in Italian) about the need "to create a stable canonical form for the unity of the hierarchy of your church," Slipyj wrote back (in Polish) to say that "these words of Your Holiness implicitly contain the envisagement of a recognition [*przewidziane wyznanie*] of our patriarchate, and for this we are thankful from the bottom of our hearts"; and he enclosed copies of all his letters on the subject to the Holy See since 1963.[110] Implicit or not (and certainly not explicit), recognition of the Ukrainian patriarchate by Rome remained a vain hope to the end of Slipyj's life;[111] and Pope John Paul II, in his eloquent memorial tribute to Slipyj, avoided any reference—explicit or implicit—to the entire matter of the Ukrainian patriarchate.

Slipyj could, and did, address the specific needs of the Ukrainian Church in the exercise of his office as metropolitan. He could, and did, address the general needs of the Roman Catholic Church in the exer-

---

106. Paul VI to Slipyj, 7.vii.1971, *Arch.Pat.* 40:204-7.

107. Slipyj, *Tvory* 13:220-22.

108. *Oss.Rom.* 13.-14.xii.1976.

109. Slipyj and the Ukrainian Catholic bishops to John Paul II, 20.xi.1978, *Arch.Pat.* 118:58.

110. Slipyj to John Paul II, 7.ii.1980, *Arch.Pat.* 118:125-26.

111. Madey (1971) 227-43 was an earnest appeal on the basis both of historical and of contemporary considerations.

cise of his office as cardinal. But the years in which the title of "patriarch" came to assume such great importance to him were, not coincidentally, the years in which Slipyj's rôle as spokesman for the entire Christian East became a central part of the definition of his vocation. That rôle began to take on historic significance on the occasion of the Second Vatican Council, where Slipyj was in a position to interpret the Eastern tradition as it affected a great variety of issues on the conciliar agenda.[112] At the Second Vatican Council, in his felicitous phrase, the East was functioning "both as subject and as object [*jak pidmet i jak predmet*]."[113] Slipyj was still in prison when the Council opened and therefore, as he explained to the secretary-general of the Council, he had not been able to participate.[114] At the Council there were, it was reported, "present 15 Ukrainian bishops, but all originating from the emigration, and therefore not representing, in the strict sense of the word, the Church of Ukraine"; these included Ivan Bučko and Maxim Hermaniuk.[115] Metropolitan Hermaniuk had been a member of the Commission on Unity and, in a presentation noticed by a wider audience, had sought to explain in what sense it could be said that the guilt for the division between the Eastern and the Western Churches lay on both sides.[116] Slipyj fervently agreed with that assignment of guilt, and quoted Pope John XXIII in support.[117] He also acknowledged with thanks the part that Hermaniuk had played during his enforced absence.[118] But his own addresses to the Council—on 11 October 1963, 12 November 1963, 16 October 1964, 8 September 1965, and 1 October 1965—which have been collected in the critical edition of his works and from which this chapter quotes repeatedly, soon made up for lost time.[119]

At the heart of Slipyj's messages to the Council was the insistence on that truly comprehensive definition of "Catholicity" with which, as noted earlier, the tradition eloquently articulated by Metropolitan Šeptyc'kyj had been identified.[120] As a theologian who is both a scholar

112. Mončak (1965).
113. Slipyj, *Tvory* 12:78 (82).
114. Slipyj to Pericle Felici, 20.iii.1963, *Arch.Pat.* 28:185.
115. Movimento Cristiano Ucraino, *Notiziario*, 18.x.1962, *Arch.Pat.* 28:n.p.
116. Feiner (1967) 51.
117. Slipyj, *Tvory* 12:80 (84); he continued by applying to Pope John the words of John the Baptist about Christ in John 1:29: "Behold, the lamb of God, who takes upon himself the sin of the world!"
118. Slipyj, *Tvory* 13:108.
119. Slipyj, *Tvory* 12:86-90; 104-7; 152-53; 202-4; 205-8.
120. See chapter 4, pp. 53-54, and chapter 5, pp. 85-91 above.

of Šeptyc'kyj and a disciple of Šeptyc'kyj put it in a letter to Slipyj, discussing the Constitution of the Ukrainian Catholic Church, "in place of the term 'Catholic' it would perhaps be better to make use of the term 'Universal [vselens'ka],' for this distinguishes better between 'particular' and 'universal.' In the common parlance of the faithful, 'Roman' and 'Catholic' are synonymous terms. The Roman Church has neglected the Eastern tradition in its entirety, and is now imposing its own [tradition] on the entire church."[121] It was, as Slipyj too insisted, a disaster to use "Catholic" and "Latin" as synonymous terms.[122] He denounced the tendency to speak "only about the Catholic Church of the Latin Rite, but not about the total church of Christ."[123] Almost all of the fathers at the Council, he complained, "treat the issues from a Western point of view" rather than from a truly "Catholic" one.[124] Or, as he wrote to Pope Paul, quoting a priest whom he had met in India, "Catholic ecumenism in Rome ought to begin with dialogue, not between Catholics and non-Catholics (Protestants), but between Latin Catholics and the East."[125]

For him there was a simple rule, he told the Commission on the Eastern Church on 10 March 1964: "The welfare of the Eastern Catholic Church is the highest law. Everything that tends to its favor and welfare, in accordance with the Eastern tradition, is to be embraced; everything that is detrimental to it is to be eliminated."[126] The East, therefore, was "an important visible sign of unity [važlyvym vydnym znakom jednosti]" for the entire church, and one that had much to contribute to the Western Church.[127] When the West had neglected it, "compressing and narrowing the whole of the Christian life, both intellectual and practical, to the Latin mode," it had paid for its mistake with the tragedy of the Reformation.[128] Yet "the Byzantine traditions of culture are still very much alive" and well, Slipyj reported, also in those Western enclaves, such as Bari, where those traditions had deep medieval roots.[129] The same was true of Sicily, where Byzantium had once been dominant.[130] (Slipyj was able in that connection to refer to a visit he had made to Sicily a quarter

121. Lubomyr Husar to Slipyj, 21.viii.1972, Arch.Pat. 73:n.p. [3].
122. Slipyj, Tvory 13:37.
123. Slipyj, Tvory 13:287.
124. Slipyj, Tvory 12:205.
125. Slipyj to Paul VI, 26.xii.1964, Slipyj, Tvory 12:162.
126. Slipyj, Tvory 12:129.
127. Slipyj, Tvory 12:80 (84).
128. Slipyj, Tvory 12:152.
129. Slipyj to Paul VI, 21.v.1964, Slipyj, Tvory 12:144.
130. Slipyj to Paul VI, 6.ix.1963, Slipyj, Tvory 12:75-77.

of a century earlier.)[131] The Basilian monastery of Grottaferrata, to which Slipyj was brought after his liberation,[132] was, because of its long-standing Byzantine ties, "this Eastern temple."[133] Because of the decisive rôle of Cardinal Bessarion as a link between East and West, Slipyj sent out handsomely inscribed special invitations to the memorial liturgy observing the five-hundredth anniversary of Bessarion's death, which was celebrated at the Basilica of the Twelve Apostles in Rome (where Bessarion is buried) on Saturday, 18 November 1972, followed by a traditional Ukrainian "funeral banquet [*tryzna*]" at *UKU* on Sunday.[134] His homily on that occasion was a celebration of Bessarion.[135]

Everywhere during and after the Second Vatican Council, whenever the opportunity presented itself (and sometimes even when it did not), Slipyj was ready, as he put it somewhat ironically, "to say a few words about the East, because 'the exotic East' seems to have an enormous attraction for the mind of Westerners" in the church and beyond.[136] Of the multifarious Eastern concerns that he touched in his ceaseless probing and pleading, at least two must be examined, though all too briefly, even in a general "portrait" such as this: the revision of Eastern canon law and the renewal of Eastern liturgy and spirituality. Both were prominent items on the agenda of the Second Vatican Council. In Slipyj's treatment of them, moreover, they were directed simultaneously at the redefinition of Eastern church life as a whole, with special concern for its Ukrainian incarnation, and at what the Decree on Ecumenism called *Unitatis redintegratio*.

Despite his occasional repetition of the traditional expressions of the theologian's scorn for canon law and canon lawyers, Slipyj knew very well that (to paraphrase a bon mot of Whitehead) the only alternative to canon law was bad canon law. But he knew also that, in the words of a distinguished historian of canon law, "the legal institutions of the Slavic world . . . are not included under Roman jurisprudence," so that it was up to "our generation to create a new corpus of canon law" that would transcend its original Roman inspiration.[137] Yet Eastern scholars had not done very well at the task of investigating the distinctive elements of their own juridical tradition, leaving much of

131. See his report of that visit, Slipyj, *Tvory* 5:347-66.
132. Choma (1984) 341-43.
133. Slipyj, *Tvory* 12:198.
134. *Arch.Pat.* 41:235.
135. See chapter 4, pp. 64-65 above.
136. Slipyj, *Tvory* 13:121.
137. Kuttner (1967) 37-39.

that research to be done, if at all, by Western canonists in such collections of legal source material as the *Fonti della codificazione canonica Orientale*.[138] Without such research into Eastern law, however, the massive preponderance of Western legislation and of Western canonists threatened to swamp the Eastern ways of proceeding. Slipyj quoted Augustin Cardinal Bea as calling it "a blunder" to put out a Latin code of canon law for the Eastern Churches.[139] "The patriarch of Antioch and of all the East" was speaking for Slipyj and for all Eastern Rite Catholics when he expressed the fear that "the Eastern churches run the risk of never again being able to recover their true physiognomy in the new canon law."[140] But the only way to keep this from happening, Slipyj was convinced, was to issue two codes of canon law rather than to try to accommodate distinctively Eastern concerns in a code that was essentially Western and Latin.[141]

Certainly the most sensitive of all the problems associated with the difference between Eastern and Western canon law was clerical celibacy and the ordination of married men.[142] Along with the patriarchate, it was as well the problem on which Slipyj's efforts at resolution were the least successful.[143] "Married candidates for the priesthood, graduates of the Academy of L'viv" constituted an agenda item for one of his earliest interviews with a member of the Roman curia, but without immediate success.[144] At the Second Vatican Council, however, the discussions about the restoration of the married diaconate in the Western Church seemed to give some hope; for as Slipyj explained to the council, this had never disappeared in the East.[145] Ever since the early centuries, he insisted to the papal synod in 1971, there had been a *duplex praxis* in the church. He knew from his own experience that married priests had proved themselves faithful in persecution, and he urged that the rigid stance of the church be revised.[146]

138. See the acknowledgment of the most recent volumes: Slipyj to the Sacred Congregation for the Eastern Church, 10.iii.1964, *Arch.Pat.* 30:157.

139. Slipyj to Pericle Felici, 1.iv.1971, *Arch.Pat.* 40:73.

140. Memorandum of Paul Pierre Meouchi, 21.iv.1971, *Arch.Pat.* 40:108.

141. Slipyj to Commission on Canon Law, 26.xi.1965, *Arch.Pat.* 33:226.

142. Pospishil (1960) 67-70.

143. It goes without saying that for a traditionalist like Josyf Slipyj the question of the ordination of married men to the priesthood was totally unrelated to the question of the ordination of women, which was "to be rejected completely": Slipyj, *Tvory* 13:120.

144. Agenda of interview with Giovanni Battista Scapinelli, 4.v.1963, *Arch.Pat.* 28:299.

145. Slipyj, *Tvory* 12:89.

146. Slipyj, *Tvory* 13:117-19.

Recognizing the delicacy of the situation in Rome itself, Slipyj proposed to carry out the ordination of married candidates, alumni of L'viv, at the Studite monastery outside Rome.[147] The papal Secretary of State, in consultation with the Sacred Congregation for the Eastern Church, saw no impediment to Slipyj's proceeding with such an ordination.[148] A list of eight candidates was submitted and approved.[149]

The situation outside Rome appeared to be different. The Ukrainian Synod of Bishops continued to pass resolutions requesting that this be made a regular right of the Ukrainian Catholic Church throughout the diaspora, but the request was not granted.[150] Slipyj also raised the question of married Eastern Rite priests in Belgium.[151] He likewise joined in the recommendation that a married Orthodox priest in Canada who wanted to join the Catholic Church in his orders be permitted to do so.[152] And he asked publicly "that the prohibition of ordaining married priests in America be lifted."[153] Arguing that "a legal norm which produces an effect contrary to that envisioned by an enlightened legislator ceases to be reasonable and prudent and thereby stops to be law in accordance with basic principles well established in canon law and moral theology," a Ukrainian Rite scholar of canon law maintained in a journal article that as a result of its continued enforcement of that prohibition "the Roman Curia must *nolens volens* own up to the dubious merit of having presided over the creation of several Eastern Orthodox Churches in North America from Catholics who left the Church because of the refusal by Rome to permit the ordination of married priests."[154] Quoting that latter statement, Slipyj continued to press his case.[155] Various individual dispensations were granted, at least for a while, usually with a great amount of debate and after considerable hesitation. In Jugoslavia (and in L'viv itself) the ordination of married men is permitted; but the principle of "territoriality" precludes

---

147. Slipyj to Paul VI, 25.ix.1964, *Arch.Pat.* 31:409.

148. Angelo Dell'Acqua to Slipyj, 12.x.1964, *Arch.Pat.* 31:425.

149. Gustavo Testa to Slipyj, 25.xi.1964, *Arch.Pat.* 31:479a.

150. "Synod of the Episcopate of the Ukrainian Catholic Church under the Direction of His Beatitude, Major Archbishop Josyf Slipyj," 2.x.1969, *Arch.Pat.* 73:71; 89.

151. Interview with Mario Rizzi, 9.ii.1964, *Arch.Pat.* 30:88.

152. Slipyj to Alfredo Ottaviani, 28.ii.1966, *Arch.Pat.* 34:107-8; the recommendation had come in a letter from Maxim Hermaniuk to Gustavo Testa, 28.vii.1964, *Arch.Pat.* 34:109-10.

153. Slipyj, *Tvory* 13:117; 118-19.

154. Pospishil (1976) 149; 144-45.

155. Slipyj to Paul Philippe, 18.xii.1976, *Arch.Pat.* "Patriarchat 1963-1978": n.p.

it elsewhere, and there is in principle "no dispensation" from this provision of canon law.[156]

The revision of the ecclesiastical calendar was, at one level, also a matter of canon law; but as the appendix to the Constitution on the Liturgy entitled *"Sacrosancti Oecumenici Concilii Vaticani Secundi de Calendario Recognoscendo Declaratio"* suggests, it was as well one of the most delicate problems of liturgical reform, even within the Western Church. The problem became vastly more complicated for those Eastern churches that were still following the Julian calendar in the West. Slipyj suggested that the decree on the Eastern Churches should stipulate: "Particular churches may celebrate other festival dates in accordance with their venerable tradition."[157] Meanwhile in his own church throughout the diaspora, and especially in North America, the problem was growing more acute. Archbishop Ambrose Senyshyn of Philadelphia, a Basilian, supported the introduction of the Gregorian calendar, on the grounds that "95% of the parishioners were in favor of it."[158] The Ukrainian bishop of Chicago, Jaroslav Gabro, moved in the same direction, but his brother bishops urged him to address the concerns of those who wanted to retain the Julian calendar.[159] In an eight-page letter Slipyj denounced Gabro as "autocratic."[160] He claimed that he had received over a thousand telegrams from faithful in Chicago who objected to the change.[161] (There was, however, an eventual reconciliation with Bishop Gabro.)[162] For his own part, he made a point of still using the Old Style Julian calendar and then, not without condescension and a bit of ostentation, citing the "New Style" date according to the Gregorian.[163] He continued to regard "the introduction of the Gregorian calendar by force" as "truly a disaster for our church."[164] When the Council was over, he announced, he intended to stay with the Julian calendar.[165]

But the Eastern calendar was only one element—and, as Slipyj

156. Personal interview with Myroslav Ivan Cardinal Lubachivsky, 3.viii.1986, in Rome.

157. Slipyj to Amleto Cicognani, 9.ix.1963, *Arch.Pat.* 129:151.

158. Ambrose Senyshyn to Gustavo Testa, 7.iii.1964, *Arch.Pat.* 30:213-14.

159. "Conference of the Catholic Bishops of the Ukrainian Rite," 29.x.1965, *Arch.Pat.* 73:56; 18.xi.1965, *Arch.Pat.* 73:59.

160. Slipyj to Amleto Cicognani, 20.ix.1967, *Arch.Pat.* 32:292-97; see also Slipyj to Maximilian de Furstenberg, 8.ii.1968, *Arch.Pat.* 37:31-32.

161. Slipyj to Angelo Dell'Acqua, 26.v.1967, *Arch.Pat.* 36:170-71; Slipyj to Gustavo Testa, 2.vii.1967, *Arch.Pat.* 36:242-43.

162. Slipyj to Jaroslav Gabro, 1977, Slipyj, *Tvory* 14:307-8.

163. Slipyj, *Tvory* 9:37, 71, 123-26, 149; 12:47 (52); 13:229.

164. Slipyj to Amleto Cicognani, 16.ix.1964, *Arch.Pat.* 31:381-82.

165. Slipyj to Gustavo Testa, 2.i.1966, *Arch.Pat.* 34:1.

would have conceded, by no means the most decisive—in the total campaign for the preservation and restoration of authentically Eastern worship as expressed "in the old mosaics and icons."[166] What not only the Ukrainian Catholic Church, but all the Eastern churches needed most from the Council and from the Holy See was a bulwark against the peril of "Latinizing" the Eastern liturgy. Latinization presented the chief threat to the Ukrainian Catholic Church in North America, as well as throughout the diaspora, as Slipyj perceived it, and he had statistics to support that judgment.[167] There had developed in North America "a tremendous ritual confusion" whose result was "apostasy to Orthodoxy." Slipyj regarded the "exaggerated individualism" of that liturgical situation as "undoubtedly the greatest disaster in the history of the Ukrainian Church"[168]—greater, presumably, than any of the persecutions from East or West that it had undergone even in the twentieth century. The twin dangers of "deritualization" and "denationalization" were symptomatic of the church "in emigration."[169] Another formulation for these dangers was "deritualization and Americanization."[170] They were also evidence of the need for closer administrative scrutiny of the Ukrainian Church in North America, which implied of course the patriarchate.[171] Under American conditions, the requests of the children of Ukrainian immigrants for transfer to Latin Rite churches were on the increase.[172] Slipyj deplored this trend, lumping "Latin Catholics" and "non-Catholics" as the beneficiaries of such transfers.[173]

This was not in the first instance a matter of language, but of the integrity of the entire ritual, whatever its language. Five years before Slipyj's release from prison, "the Conference of Ukrainian Catholic Bishops" (as it was then called, and in Italian) had confronted the sobering reality that the second and third generations in the diaspora no longer understood Ukrainian, much less Church Slavonic; and it had

166. Slipyj, *Tvory* 12:211.
167. Slipyj, *Tvory* 12:153.
168. Slipyj to Amleto Cicognani, 8.ii.1965, *Arch.Pat.* 32:145-48.
169. Slipyj to Guglielmo Gaudreau, 1.iv.1963, *Arch.Pat.* 28:197-99; see also Slipyj to Ildebrando Antoniutti, 4.xi.1963, *Arch.Pat.* 29:276.
170. Slipyj to Gustavo Testa, 16.x.1963, *Arch.Pat.* 29:238.
171. Slipyj to Sacred Congregation for the Eastern Church, 11.v.1963, *Arch.Pat.* 28:307-8.
172. Jaroslav Gabro at "Synod of the Episcopate of the Ukrainian Catholic Church under the Direction of His Beatitude, Major Archbishop Josyf Slipyj," 2.x.1969, *Arch.Pat.* 73:70.
173. Slipyj, *Tvory* 12:128.

adopted the compromise of "observing and retaining the liturgical language [Church Slavonic] in liturgical services, but introducing in sermons the use of the language of the particular country."[174] But the situation continued to deteriorate, and subsequent sessions of "the Bishops' Synod" (as it was now called) continued to address it.[175] At the very least, the liturgical books had to be published in a translation from Church Slavonic into Ukrainian.[176] In North America, accordingly, they should appear in Church Slavonic and English, also as a defense against the Eastern Orthodox.[177] At the same time, it became part of the mission of UKU in its summer term to stem the tide by teaching Ukrainian to the children and grandchildren of the immigrants.[178] Slipyj watched the actions of the Second Vatican Council very closely for their bearing on this issue. Thus he found the draft decree on the Eastern Church objectionable because "a door is opened for the conversion of Eastern Rite Christians to the Latin Rite."[179] The Constitution on the Liturgy represented an important forward step, with its recognition that liturgy must be a living, developing reality, not a useless relic; but its lesson was also that "first of all we need to be absolutely vigilant in protecting our Rite—not the Bulgarian, not the Russian, not the Byzantine or any other, but our Ukrainian Rite."[180]

Underlying both the problem of the patriarchate within the context of Western canon law and the problem of the Eastern liturgy in its distinctness from the Roman rite, whether in Latin or in the vernacular, were in fact questions of doctrine that ran deeper than Slipyj sometimes appeared willing to recognize. To say as he did in 1973 that all of this controversy "does not involve dogmatic differences in any way"[181] was true, but only in the technical sense of the word "dogma." In a deeper sense, however, there were differences that went far beyond ecclesiastical titles or canon law or even liturgical ritual, and sometimes, especially in his late years, Slipyj admitted as much. Writing to the pope, he

174. "Conference of the Ukrainian Catholic Bishops," 2.-3.xi.1958, Arch.Pat. 73:3.
175. "Conference of the Catholic Bishops of the Ukrainian Rite," 13.ix.1964, Arch.Pat. 73:40; "Conference of the Episcopate of the Ukrainian Catholic Particular Church, under the Direction of His Beatitude, Patriarch Josyf," 10.xii.1976, Arch.Pat. 73:280-81.
176. "Synod of the Episcopate of the Ukrainian Catholic Church under the Direction of His Beatitude, Major Archbishop Josyf Slipyj," resolution 5, 1.x.1969, Arch.Pat. 73:67.
177. Slipyj to the Sacred Congregation for the Eastern Church, 11.v.1963, Arch.Pat. 28:307-8.
178. Slipyj, Tvory 13:111.
179. Slipyj to Amleto Cicognani, 9.ix.1963, Arch.Pat. 29:148.
180. "La costituzione sulla s. Liturgia," Arch.Pat. 30:182-85.
181. Slipyj, Tvory 13:222.

could assert that the differences between the Eastern (including Eastern Catholic) and the Western (Roman Catholic) Churches were of several kinds: theological; juridical-canonical; structural; ritual-liturgical.[182] Near the end of his life, writing to a Dominican cardinal, he could speak, in extraordinarily critical fashion, about "the Latin mentality" characteristic of members of the Western Church, with its heavy emphasis "on the law and on absolute obedience to the law,"[183] which he contrasted with the less legalistic attitudes of Eastern Christianity. Addressing the Second Vatican Council on 16 October 1964, he expressed the judgment that a constriction of Western theology and spirituality to the narrow Latin style had helped to bring on the Protestant Reformation of the sixteenth century.[184] And to a later session, on 1 October 1965, he quoted one of his fellow Eastern prelates about the excessively Western emphasis of manuals of moral theology, which desperately needed to be revised.[185]

Even earlier, shortly after his release from prison, he had already allowed himself the "audacious thought" that the Reformation seemed to have provoked Western Roman Catholic theology into various doctrinal overemphases, brought about by the neglect of the Eastern tradition, and that without a recovery of that Eastern tradition Latin theology would continue to be incomplete.[186] And appearing before the Commission on the Eastern Churches a year after his release, he warned against the excessive "formalism" to which the official language of the Western Church, especially at the Vatican, seemed to be prone.[187] Although he emphasized that "the dogmas of the faith are the same," he also urged that "the explanations and arguments for them can be many."[188] And the Roman Catholic West needed the East, also the doctrines of the East, if it was to become authentically Catholic.[189] When he overcame his Thomistic limitations and his diffidence toward the Holy See enough to speak that way, Slipyj, in his dual rôle as Roman cardinal and Eastern patriarch, became "a new and unexpected link between the logical West and the illuminated East."[190]

182. Slipyj, *Tvory* 14:123.
183. Slipyj to Paul Philippe, 18.xii.1976, *Arch.Pat. Patriarchat*:n.p.
184. Slipyj, *Tvory* 12:152.
185. Slipyj, *Tvory* 12:205.
186. Slipyj to Lucca Di Schiena, 24.viii.1963, *Arch.Pat.* 29:118-19.
187. Slipyj, *Tvory* 12:128.
188. Slipyj, *Tvory* 1:405.
189. Slipyj, *Tvory* 2:103-4.
190. M. West (1963) 142.

11

A New and Unexpected Link between East and West

When Josyf Cardinal Slipyj died on 7 September 1984 in Rome at the age of ninety-two, his long and eventful life reminded many, perhaps also himself,[1] of the "boast" of the apostle Paul to the Corinthians:

> . . . on frequent journeys, in danger from rivers, danger from rob-
> bers, danger from my own people, danger from Gentiles, danger
> in the city, danger in the wilderness, danger at sea, danger from
> false brethren; in toil and hardship, through many a sleepless
> night, in hunger and thirst, often without food, in cold and ex-
> posure. And, apart from other things, there is the daily pressure
> upon me of my anxiety for all the churches.[2]

But for others, it called to mind as well the familiar words of Matthew Arnold's apostrophe, by now almost proverbial, to the University of Oxford as a "home of lost causes, and forsaken beliefs, and unpopular names, and impossible loyalties." In some ways, however, the most trenchant epigrammatic description of his abiding significance comes neither from the New Testament nor from the English literary criticism of the nineteenth century, but from a novel of the twentieth century.

As its colophon indicates, Morris L. West's best-selling novel *The Shoes of the Fisherman* was written between March 1961 and August

---

1. See Slipyj, *Tvory* 14:209.
2. 2 Cor. 11:26-28.

1962, by which time Josyf Slipyj had been in Soviet imprisonment for seventeen years; and it was published in 1963, the year of Slipyj's release. Despite the author's conventional disclaimers about this being "a book set in fictional time, peopled with fictional characters, and no reference is intended to any living person, whether in the Church or out of it," it is in many ways a roman à clef. For example, no one can read Morris West's descriptions of the character named Jean Télémond—the controversial French Jesuit anthropologist whose foundational book, published only after his death, is entitled *The Progress of Man* and deals with the theme of the ultimate evolutionary "convergence" of human and cosmic reality—without being strongly reminded of Pierre Teilhard de Chardin, the controversial French Jesuit anthropologist whose foundational work on that very theme was entitled *The Phenomenon of Man* and was published only after his death.[3]

Even closer to a "living person," however, is the book's central figure, Kiril Lakota,[4] the Ukrainian cardinal, who is, as one scholar has put it, "a complete reproduction of the figure of His Beatitude" Josyf Slipyj, despite certain "weaknesses" in the characterizations and descriptions.[5] Kiril Lakota is introduced as the book opens, in a description much of which, as previous chapters of our portrait have shown, would fit Slipyj to the letter:

> When the war with the Germans was over, he had been named, in spite of his youth, Metropolitan of Lvov, successor to the great and saintly Andrew Szepticky, leader of all the Ruthenian Catholics. Shortly afterwards he had been arrested . . . and deported . . . , left alone, shepherd of a lost flock, to carry the Cross on his own shoulders.
>
> For seventeen years he had been in prison, or in the labor camps. . . . All that he could cling to of doctrine and prayer and sacramental formulae was locked in his own brain. All that he had tried to spend of strength and compassion upon his fellow prisoners he had to dredge out of himself and out of the well of the Divine Mercy.[6]

In this Ukrainian prelate, now elected pope of Rome as His Holiness Kiril I, the world and the church were to find what West calls "a new

3. M. West (1963) 112-14, 139, 194.
4. The name itself is taken from that of Slipyj's and Šeptyc'kyj's colleague, Bishop Hryhoriji Lakota; see Slipyj, *Tvory* 3/4:273.
5. Leonid Rudnytzky in Choma-Muzyčka (1984) 681-82.
6. M. West (1963) 20.

and unexpected link between the logical West and the illuminated East."[7]

Although Slipyj was not elected pope, he did become, and he still is, "a new and unexpected link" between East and West, and that for several reasons, all of which were new and unexpected—and in some sense were so even to him. The front façade of his Ukrainian Catholic University in Rome bears the inscription, printed in Latin and in Ukrainian: "Truth and the love of knowledge unites those who have been dispersed [*Veritas et amor scientiae unit dispersos; Istyna i ljubov nauky sobyraje v rozsijanni suščych*]."[8] In the first instance, this may be taken to refer to the Ukrainian Catholics of the diaspora, scattered by what Slipyj himself recognized as the "exigencies" of modern times.[9] And much of his ministry between his liberation and his death was devoted to the vocation of uniting those scattered members of his own flock, as becomes clear from the anguished words of his Testament:

> Foreseeing the end, I cannot refrain from expressing my bitter spiritual pain, which I experienced during my years in the West. This pain was born of the lack of unity among our bishops in the West. The lack of unity is, so to speak, the original sin [*pervorodnyj hrich*] which has imbedded itself in the soul of those who are supposed to be the bearers of light for others. This sin was like a thief who crept from the West into our suffering church in Ukraine.[10]

But the fundamental meaning of the inscription extended far beyond only Ukrainian Catholics, indeed far beyond only Ukrainians or only Catholics, to the scattered members of the flock of Christ throughout East and West. Soon after coming out of prison, he wrote a ten-page single-spaced letter on the division between Eastern and Western Christianity, concluding with the challenge: "And for all these reasons no one can be indifferent any longer to the unity of the church of Jesus Christ, above all in our times, in which what is at stake is the very being or nonbeing of every single religion and of every single form of faith in God. Above all, the strategy of today's religious spirit calls for unity."[11]

Eleven years later that challenge was still echoing: "We must hold the line of the unity of the church, and be prepared again and again to

7. M. West (1963) 142.
8. On this inscription, see Slipyj, *Tvory* 14:161.
9. *Arch.Pat.* 37:148; see chapter 9, pp. 174-75 above.
10. Slipyj, *Tvory* 14:483.
11. Slipyj to Lucca Di Schiena, 24.vii.1963, *Arch.Pat.* 29:124.

stake our lives on it. And Christ desired unity. Whether someone understands it or not, whether someone likes it or not, *the unity of the church must be achieved [jednist' cerkvy musyt' buty]*! One Shepherd and one flock."[12] In 1979 Slipyj complained that "our ecumenism is not making any headway."[13] In view of "the sad rôle"[14] of the Orthodox patriarchate of Moscow within the Soviet political-ecclesiastical structure, especially during the years after the Second World War and above all in its connivance at the so-called Synod of L'viv in 1946, it is difficult to imagine how the moral commitment of the metropolitan of the Ukrainian Catholic Church could have permitted Josyf Slipyj to take any other position toward official Russian Orthodoxy than he did. As one of his close associates has suggested, Slipyj, unlike Šeptyc'kyj, did not know very many Orthodox prelates whom he felt he could trust. But that experience did sometimes seem to overshadow the no less profound commitment to what Lubomyr Husar has called the ideal of "corporate union."[15] Slipyj had inherited this commitment from Metropolitan Šeptyc'kyj,[16] whom he described as a founder of modern ecumenism, also because of his participation in the Malines Conversations with Anglican theologians initiated by the Belgian archbishop and Thomist philosopher, Désiré Joseph Cardinal Mercier.[17] While Šeptyc'kyj did take a lively interest in dialogue with Anglicans and even with Protestants, it was above all the vision of Catholic-Orthodox reunion that impelled him all his life,[18] especially when, as a surprising consequence of the Russian Revolution of 1917 and of the emigration and Western exile of Orthodox theologians, "the theological discussion between East and West, interrupted in the fifteenth century, was at last resumed."[19]

The vision that Šeptyc'kyj had perceived had consistently been reaffirmed by Slipyj, perhaps most eloquently in his remarkable paper of December 1936: "Examination of the United and the Separated Churches of the East and of the Dogmatic Differences Dividing Them

12. Slipyj, *Tvory* 13:316; in the original Ukrainian the italicized words are printed in capital letters.
13. Slipyj, *Tvory* 14:177.
14. Slipyj, *Spomyny* 121.
15. Husar (1972) 862.
16. Baran (1947) 118-37 is a useful summary, also because of the documents he reproduces *in toto*.
17. Slipyj, *Tvory* 13:298 (303).
18. Minenko (1985) 15-23 describes the response of Orthodox bishops to Šeptyc'kyj's overtures for reunion.
19. Zernov (1963) 282.

[*Pohljad na zjedyneni j nezjedyneni cerkvy Schodu i dohmatyčni rižnyci meži nymy*]."[20] There he itemized the issues of dogma on which Eastern Orthodox and Catholic (including Eastern Catholic) teaching diverged: "purgatory, as defined at the Council of Trent; the Immaculate Conception, promulgated by Pope Pius IX; the infallibility and supreme jurisdiction of the pope, determined by the [First] Vatican Council; the canonicity of the so-called deuterocanonical books, also at the Vatican Council; and the indissolubility of wedlock, [declared] at the Council of Trent."[21] Although he conceded that some of the dogmatic differences, too, were primarily "of a speculative nature," he then went on to list other sources of difference that were not so much "dogmatic" as "theological": "theses that are based on Latin liturgical books; the scholastic frame of mind [*scholjastyčne unjattja*]; and *Codex iuris canonici*."[22] As he pointed out later, it was essential to distinguish between the official "dogmatic" differences and the unofficial "theological" ones.[23] The discussion of these differences, Rector Slipyj proposed, should be the business of "a future joint council [*majbutnij spil'nyj Sobor*]."[24]

It was with a clear-eyed awareness of all these differences that thirty years later Metropolitan Slipyj strove to lead his bishops, clergy, and people toward "the maximum ecumenical activity."[25] That would involve relations with all Christians, but above all with "our Orthodox brethren, [to whom] we are united by one Christian tradition, a common ecclesiastical and national tradition, a common culture going back two thousand years."[26] All of this was in keeping with the legacy of Metropolitan Andrej Šeptyc'kyj, who had "dedicated his entire life to the realization of the great idea of the unification of Christians."[27] "We are as Orthodox as you are Catholic! [*My taki Pravoslavni, jak vy Katolyky!*]" was Slipyj's message to the Eastern Orthodox in his encyclical letter under the title "Toward Unification in Christ" of 3 June 1976.[28] In that encyclical letter, as a contemporary response put it, Slipyj had set forth a "panorama" of the ecumenical church.[29]

20. Slipyj, *Tvory* 5:107-39.
21. Slipyj, *Tvory* 5:136.
22. Slipyj, *Tvory* 5:137.
23. Slipyj, *Tvory* 5:157.
24. Slipyj, *Tvory* 5:136.
25. "Conference of the Catholic Bishops of the Ukrainian Rite," 11.xi.1965, resolution 29, *Arch.Pat.* 73:57.
26. Slipyj, *Tvory* 14:483.
27. Slipyj, *Tvory* 9:117.
28. Slipyj, *Tvory* 9:265.
29. Hryn'och (1977) 55.

Josyf Slipyj's abiding significance as a link between East and West, as "a Confessor of the Faith and of the Unity of the Church Universal, but at the same time . . . the stout defender of the Christian East, [including] the dignity and rights of the Eastern Orthodox Churches,"[30] may well be summarized in the same four themes with which we began this portrait—but in reversed order.[31]

I.   He made it possible for Christians East and West to recognize the danger of equating Christian identity with the life-style of the Old World, at the eventual cost both of Catholicity and of particularity; and he helped to provide the means by which both East and West could overcome that danger by fostering the identity of the Eastern Church in its new (and New World) contexts.

II. Despite his emphasis on the profound affinity between cultus and culture, he emphasized no less vigorously the danger of a cultural impoverishment that neglects critical scholarship.

III. Because the typically Eastern danger of a ritualism that cannot distinguish between the important and the trivial was such a real one for him, he pointed to new and creative ways of reaffirming the centrality of liturgy.

IV. Having inherited a method of doing theology that ran the constant danger of a traditionalism in which creativity was stifled, Slipyj pointed to new ways of achieving the preservation of tradition in a creative tension with the development of doctrine.

Fortunately, we have in his Testament [*Zapovit*]—which was begun in 1970, signed on the eve of the Feast of the Immaculate Conception in 1981, published in booklet form soon after his death in 1984, and eventually included in the edition of his collected works—his own words on these very themes.[32]

I. The "exigencies" of the new situation into which the history of the twentieth century had thrust him and his Ukrainian Church, while unique in many respects, did have some parallels in the experience through which successive nationalities have passed during the nineteenth and twentieth centuries. Under the provocative title *Has the Immigrant Kept the Faith?* a pioneering study in the sociology of religion

---

30. Bilaniuk (1984) 42.

31. See chapter 1, pp. 13-22 above.

32. Slipyj, *Tvory* 14:471-87. The separate edition of 1984 also contained an English translation by Myroslaw Tataryn, which I have found helpful, although I have made changes of my own.

by Professor (later Bishop) Gerald Shaughnessy analyzed the statistical patterns of behavior from one generation to another among several groups of Roman Catholics who came from the Old World to the New.[33] Not surprisingly, the process of putting off the language, customs, and values of the mother country had frequently resulted in a defection from the church as well. In this sense Slipyj's equation of "Americanization" with "deritualization"[34] was an understandable reaction to the crisis of the Ukrainian diaspora, and one with firm grounding in the law of the church.[35] But Shaughnessy's study went on to show that, contrary to the prophecies of the doomsayers, members of the first and second generations born in the New World had often found, in community with other Catholic believers of other national backgrounds, a new dedication to the essential content of the faith, if not always to the specific ethnicity with which it had been identified by their parents and grandparents. For the Ukrainian diaspora throughout the world, but especially in North America, mobility and intermarriage posed the key problem of possible alienation from the Catholic faith altogether, but also presented a new opportunity. And it was to the churches of the Ukrainian diaspora that Slipyj in his Testament addressed some of his most impassioned pleas to stay loyal and not to forget their Ukrainian mother, pleas cast in the language of the opening chapters of the Revelation of Saint John the Divine and its letter to the seven churches.[36]

The loyalty expressed to Metropolitan Slipyj himself by the diaspora on his various journeys was in one sense the expression of a personality cult, a loyalty born of devotion and admiration for him as a confessor of the faith. But in a deeper sense it was as well an affirmation of the abiding worth of the principles that he embodied. Even and especially in "a mosaic of various cultures"[37] like Canada, therefore, those principles had held. Nevertheless, Slipyj's rather simplistic coupling of the threat of "deritualization," viz., the loss of Eastern Christian identity as a consequence of the position of his church between East and West, with the danger of "denationalization,"[38] viz., the loss of Ukrainian identity, did not represent his most profound thought on the ecumenical question. As he grew to recognize, though only gradually, the temptation of the New World could be transformed into

33. Shaughnessy (1925).
34. Slipyj to Gustavo Testa, 16.x.1963, *Arch.Pat.* 29:238.
35. Mudryj (1973) 102-7.
36. Slipyj, *Tvory* 14:485-86.
37. Vitošyns'ka (1972) 10.
38. Slipyj to Guglielmo Gaudreau, 1.iv.1963, *Arch.Pat.* 28:197-99.

an opportunity as well, but only if his cry, "Whether someone understands it or not, whether someone likes it or not, the unity of the church must be achieved!"[39] could take precedence over some of the particular forms in which he himself had articulated the stance between East and West.

For in the New World, and no less fundamentally in the new era in the Old World as well, Eastern Orthodoxy, too, had been undergoing "denationalization" and had known the perils of "deritualization." It had, however, begun to do so without the political involvement that had brought upon it, justly or unjustly, a reputation for "Caesaropapism." Slipyj knew, as early as his visit to Istanbul/Constantinople in 1934, that this political involvement had been both a support for the church and a burden to it.[40] Although he had other misgivings about the larger picture, he did quote with apparent approval the position of those who had, in the Czarist Russia of 1917, declared for "the total independence of the church from the state, but with the proviso that the legalization [of the church] is also necessary."[41] Yet in his position he could not have been expected to be fully conscious of the liberating force that the "denationalization" of Eastern Orthodoxy had set into motion, even and especially among those in the New World whose roots went back to Russian *Pravoslavie*, and of its corresponding need for cooperation with others who stood in the lineage of Eastern Christendom. For most Eastern Christians, whether Eastern Orthodox or "Greek Catholic," in the diaspora and no less in their respective Eastern homelands as well, the need to discover (or to recover) an authentically Eastern Christian life-style had begun to supersede the need to be merely Russian or Serbian or Greek—or even perhaps Ukrainian.[42] In the "post-Constantinian era," therefore, as Slipyj had discovered through his association with Eastern prelates from other traditions at the Second Vatican Council,[43] there was an increasing number of those who saw the real question for Eastern Christendom, including the Ukrainian Church in the diaspora and at home, as a choice between that Eastern life-style, as shared with all the other Eastern churches, and the loss of Eastern Christian identity altogether.

II. To prevent that loss, a massive scholarly effort was called for, and an effort which Eastern Christian theology could not go on expect-

39. Slipyj, *Tvory* 13:316.
40. Slipyj, *Tvory* 5:324-39.
41. Slipyj, *Tvory* 3/4:77.
42. Vasyl Markus in Magocsi (1979) 127-28.
43. See chapter 10, pp. 197-99 above.

ing Western scholars to supply. Slipyj frequently criticized Eastern scholarship for its neglect of the treasures in its own theological and artistic past and for its dependence on the West for studies of that past.[44] In his Testament he blamed the lack of church unity in the East upon "an inadequate theological knowledge, a product of being educated in foreign schools, the effect of a foreign environment, an ignorance of the history of our church."[45] On the other hand, he also criticized the supercilious assumption widespread throughout the Western Church that there was no decent scholarship in the East. Despite his own Western education, he was critical as well of Western-trained Eastern scholars who had become tone-deaf to the nuances of their own background. As early as 1929 he had voiced this criticism in a powerful analysis that deserves, despite its length, to be quoted in full:

> It would be a grave error to suppose that theological work in the East has to start entirely from scratch. Many things have been accomplished by Western scholars in the knowledge of Eastern theology. The task remains above all of organizing all of this into a system, of applying it to life, and then of carrying it further. For the individual investigations of Eastern theology carried out by Westerners have remained purely theoretical and have lacked a connection with actual life. On the other hand, as has been shown, Easterners trained in Latin seminaries lacked the necessary knowledge to continue their tradition. All of this, therefore, must be set aright.
>
> In addition, the education of Eastern scholars has been imperfect, and has at most been carried to the level of the doctorate. They lacked either the time or the will for deeper studies to be undertaken in the Oriental Institute or under the direction of some learned mentor. Half-baked scholars were brought to the point of admiring alien works, rituals, and discipline, but they were not qualified to undertake the analysis, criticism, and application of all of this in their own rite.
>
> Often, all too often, the more capable people have forsaken scholarly work because of administrative duties that were imposed upon them or because of high positions to which they were appointed. Finally, there has been no cultivation of a network among Eastern scholars in theology, to enable them to take joint counsel about the dissemination of their scholarly labors.[46]

44. Slipyj to Pope Paul VI, 26.xii.1964, Slipyj, *Tvory* 12:165.
45. Slipyj, *Tvory* 14:483.
46. Slipyj, *Tvory* 1:407.

The comment about "administrative duties" in the penultimate sentence of the quotation was, of course, autobiographical; as Slipyj once wrote to Pope Paul VI, his own scholarly work had been suspended as a consequence of the illness and eventual death of Metropolitan Šeptyc'kyj.[47]

More interesting still in the present context is the final sentence of the quotation. For it represented the felt need of an Eastern scholar and educational administrator, still in his middle thirties, for a "network [*nexus*] among Eastern scholars in theology." The training Slipyj had received at Innsbruck and at Rome had given him a scholarly equipment he was to cherish all his life.[48] As the preceding chapters of this book have suggested in considerable detail, Ukrainian culture has manifested a distinct identity that has doggedly refused to be subsumed under some other rubric, be it Austro-Hungarian or Polish or Russian. At the same time, as some interpreters of Slipyj have suggested, the prison experience made him much more of an "Easternizer [*Vostočnik* in Russian]" than he had been before 1945; and the two decades during which Slipyj as an exile in Rome battled against "the Latins" to articulate and preserve the identity of Ukrainian culture also impelled him more and more in the direction of assessing and appreciating its Byzantine roots. As a scholar, he had already analyzed these with sensitivity and skill in 1933, describing the way " 'Byzantinism' acquired a negative connotation in the eighteenth century" among Western thinkers influenced by the Enlightenment, who equated it with "archaism."[49]

The more conscious he became of the distinctiveness of the "Byzantine" cultural tradition and of its decisive meaning for his own cultural, spiritual, and Christian identity, the more vigorously he defended it against such canards. In turn, the need for such a defense made the absence of "a network among Eastern scholars in theology, to enable them to take joint counsel about the dissemination of their scholarly labors" all the more obvious and all the more painful. The primary motivation for the reunion of East and West in the church, Slipyj declared soon after his release and was to repeat many times, was the prayer of Christ "that they may all be one."[50] But the establishment of cooperation among Eastern scholars of theology, both Orthodox and Catholic, would be simultaneously a cause and an effect of such a reunion. As Slipyj said in his Testament,

47. Slipyj to Paul VI, 1.vii.1963, *Arch.Pat.* 29:4.
48. See his comments, as quoted on pp. 106-7 above.
49. Slipyj, *Tvory* 2:105.
50. Slipyj to Gustavo Testa, 20.iii.1963, *Arch.Pat.* 28:176 (quoting John 17:20).

Reflecting upon the meaning and value of learning [*nauka*], in the face of that eternity which is relentlessly approaching me, I bequeath to you:

Love learning, develop and enrich it with your work and your knowledge—be its servants! Raise temples of learning, burning with the spiritual strength of our church and of our people. Remember that the fullness of life in the church and in our people is not possible without our own indigenous scholarship. Learning is their breath of life![51]

This commitment to scholarship was the first and the most fundamental of all his bequests in that farewell.

III. Slipyj acknowledged, but he also sometimes exhibited, one of the problems with Eastern theological scholarship, both Orthodox and Catholic: its tendency to put all liturgical issues on the same level. For example, the right to retain the Julian calendar had indeed been one of the provisions of the Union of Brest establishing communion with Rome in 1596.[52] But for Slipyj to cling to the Julian calendar as tenaciously as he did in 1964, when he called its abolition in favor of the Gregorian calendar a "disaster,"[53] was a manifestation of that Eastern tendency, as well as of his own personal tendency toward a tenacity that was sometimes indistinguishable from stubbornness. As "the greatest disaster" of all for Eastern Christians in the twentieth century, "ritual confusion" did need to be confronted.[54] But the method of confronting it was not the one being espoused by those whom Slipyj, in a mood of what he himself described as "inconsolable depression," called "a few fanatic ritualists, who love 'the pure Eastern ritual' more than the very existence of our church.' "[55] Under his chairmanship, therefore, the Conference of Ukrainian Bishops approved various abbreviations of the liturgy.[56] And he lived to be able to announce, with obvious gratification, the appearance of a Ukrainian translation of the Liturgy of the Presanctified.[57] Yet as he knew all too well, moving the language of the abbreviated liturgy from Old Church Slavonic to Ukrainian would not meet the needs of the second and third generations in

---

51. Slipyj, *Tvory* 14:473.
52. See chapter 3, pp. 49-50 above.
53. Slipyj to Amleto Cicognani, 16.ix.1964, *Arch.Pat.* 31:381-82.
54. Slipyj to Amleto Cicognani, 8.ii.1965, *Arch.Pat.* 32:145-48.
55. "Nonnullae adnotationes," 4.ii.1968, *Arch.Pat.* 37:25-29.
56. "Conference of the Catholic Bishops of the Ukrainian Rite," resolution 2 at session of 23.iii.1965, *Arch.Pat.* 73:48-49.
57. Slipyj, *Tvory* 14:78-79, 190-92.

the emigration, upon whom everything depended;[58] for they were, gradually but steadily, losing their knowledge even of Ukrainian, not to mention Old Church Slavonic. Slipyj had some hope that summer courses at the Ukrainian Catholic University in Rome might reverse the loss of Ukrainian, but even if this worked it would help only a tiny minority.[59] Meanwhile, the Conference of Ukrainian Bishops had earlier sanctioned the use of the vernacular in sermons, while continuing to require Church Slavonic for the liturgy,[60] and the movement toward a Ukrainian liturgy moved irresistibly forward.

Nevertheless, Slipyj did recognize the peculiar dilemma posed by the language question: the transition from Ukrainian to English or Spanish could bring about a loss to the "Latin rite," especially as the several Western Roman Catholic churches were making their own transitions from Latin to the vernacular, in keeping with the legislation of the Second Vatican Council. On the other hand, the Orthodox claim to have "a great concern for the preservation of the purity of the ritual and of the Old Slavonic language in the liturgical books" seemed to argue for a retention of the ancient cultic language, supplemented by the preparation of Slavonic-cum-vernacular books for the people.[61] This was, of course, a dilemma being faced no less grimly by the Orthodox, and one that all those who shared the heritage of the Old Church Slavonic liturgy had to face together if any of them were to face it successfully. The evolution of an Eastern liturgy in English within the Orthodox Church of America was a major step in that direction, and one that could not go unheeded by Ukrainian Catholics. A special contribution of that Eastern Christian heritage to the ecumenical theological enterprise, as Slipyj often pointed out, was that "its scientific theology has often developed from a highly original point of view [because of its characteristic emphasis on] the contemplative life" and on the liturgy.[62] For the Eastern tradition, the liturgy was, as Slipyj put it in a message issued in January of the final year of his life, "the teacher of our faith."[63] And that was not an exclusively Ukrainian, much less an exclusively Ukrainian Catholic, contribution, as Slipyj had an opportunity to make clear when he was approached by the archbishop of

58. Slipyj, *Tvory* 14:99.
59. Slipyj, *Tvory* 13:111.
60. "Conference of the Ukrainian Catholic Bishops," 2.-3.xi.1958, *Arch.Pat.* 73:3.
61. Slipyj to Sacred Congregation for the Eastern Church, 11.v.1963, *Arch.Pat.* 28:307-8.
62. Slipyj to Lucca Di Schiena, 24.viii.1963, *Arch.Pat.* 29:122.
63. Slipyj, *Tvory* 14:78-79.

Zagreb for his views on the legitimacy of veneration addressed by Eastern Rite Catholics to Orthodox saints who had not received Western Catholic canonization.[64] He cited the precedent of the "Petersburg Synod" of Eastern Catholics held in 1917, which had approved such veneration.[65] Specifically, he took the position that the veneration of Saint Gregory Palamas was justifiable, even though he had not been canonized, and had indeed been condemned, within the Roman Catholic Church; Slipyj based this interpretation of Palamite theology on the works of the Orthodox scholars Georges Florovsky and John Meyendorff.[66] This was an authority and a precedent that he could well have invoked in many more places than he did.

IV. For what was finally at stake was in fact the Eastern Christian tradition itself, as well as the special Eastern Christian approach to the Christian tradition as a whole. Slipyj had once defined that approach in the formula: "The Eastern Church is the church of the seven [ecumenical] councils and of nine centuries of traditions."[67] When he spoke of "tradition," he was sometimes referring to "the traditions of our Church of Rus'-Ukraine."[68] He was committed to defending the particularity of these Ukrainian traditions against the encroachment of other Christian traditions, even of other Eastern Christian traditions, be they "Bulgarian or Russian or Byzantine or any other."[69] "The struggle for the fullest expression of our church life within a patriarchate," he affirmed, "goes hand in hand with the struggle for church unity among our Ukrainian people."[70] Nevertheless, one of the by-products of that campaign for the patriarchate, "the center of our present worldwide yearnings and strivings" as he was to call it,[71] was the realization that any such yearning and striving would stand or fall on the basis of its relation to the larger Eastern Christian tradition. It may have been a typical flight of rhetoric, but it was also a sincere expression of a deeply felt conviction when he affirmed his allegiance to that larger Eastern Christian tradition in the words: "The welfare of the Eastern Catholic Church is the highest law. Everything that tends to its favor and welfare, in accordance with the Eastern

64. Franciscus Seper to Slipyj, 30.iii.1971, *Arch.Pat.* 40:92.
65. Slipyj, *Tvory* 3/4:75-83.
66. Slipyj to Franciscus Seper, 6.iv.1971, *Arch.Pat.* 40:90-91.
67. Slipyj, *Tvory* 5:147.
68. "Message" of 18.ii.1981, *Arch.Pat.* 74:262.
69. Comments on "La costituzione sulla s. Liturgia," *Arch.Pat.* 30:182-85.
70. Slipyj, *Tvory* 14:482.
71. Slipyj, *Tvory* 13:107; further comments, pp. 108-9.

tradition, is to be embraced; everything that is detrimental to it is to be eliminated."[72]

The corollary of this Eastern Christian dedication to tradition was a tendency, which Slipyj noted in himself and in other Eastern theologians, to glorify the past, especially the Byzantine past, as some sort of theological golden age.[73] In a brief essay of 1929 entitled "Some Directions Looking to Theological Progress in the East," he had striven to counteract that tendency by invoking the principle of development of doctrine—although without direct reference to John Henry Newman.[74] While conceding that "Ukrainian and Russian culture would have achieved a higher level of development if the Latin rite had been introduced,"[75] he nevertheless argued that there were indigenous resources within the Eastern Christian tradition by which it could be renewed and enabled to develop further. He reviewed the various fields of theological thought—dogmatics, moral theology, canon law, ascetic teaching, mystical thought, homiletics, historiography, biblical study, and philosophy—to identify in each the presence of such resources as well as the reasons for the lack of such renewal and development.[76] If the interpretation suggested earlier[77] is defensible and Slipyj in his final years was developing from a less critical to a more critical attitude toward Thomism, it also seems fair to suggest that at the same time he was developing toward a more profoundly and more authentically Eastern position on many questions.

Those also happened to be the years in which, at the Second Vatican Council, such Eastern positions were receiving the attention of the Western Church as they had not since the patristic era. When the Council was in its early stages, Slipyj had seemed to be espousing "ultramontane" positions on such questions as collegiality, papal primacy, and the function of a church council,[78] positions that were eventually transcended by the Council itself. Therefore it seems to have come as something of a surprise to him when the Council moved toward positions both on church polity and on theology that were closer to the historic Eastern views than either ultramontanism or Thomism had been.[79]

72. Slipyj, *Tvory* 12:129.
73. Slipyj, *Tvory* 13:108.
74. See chapter 6, p. 121 above.
75. Slipyj, *Tvory* 1:397.
76. Slipyj, *Tvory* 1:402-5.
77. See chapter 6, p. 122 above.
78. Slipyj, *Tvory* 12:87-88.
79. See chapter 10, pp. 206-15 above.

An essential component of that development was a deepening Roman Catholic sympathy toward Eastern Orthodoxy. The embrace of Pope Paul VI and Patriarch Athenagoras of Constantinople was a symbol of a slow but steady shift. The situation of Ukrainian Eastern Catholics amid such a shift had to be a highly ambiguous one: they welcomed the new awareness in Rome of the traditions for which they had been raising a lonely voice for so many centuries, but they saw themselves in danger of becoming victims of their own success through being undercut by direct negotiations between Rome and Moscow. Thus Slipyj spoke near the end of his life about the Ukrainian Catholic Church as a bridge between East and West,[80] but at the very same time he was expressing his hurt at being told that this church had become an obstacle to ecumenism between East and West.[81] The proposal of a Ukrainian Roman Catholic Church, as part of an agreement with Moscow, was "a sentence of death."[82]

Such anxieties came out of the lifelong battle to preserve the unique vocation of the Ukrainian Church as simultaneously Catholic and particular. In a deeper sense, however, they could be said to belong to the short-term rather than to the long-term perspectives for which Slipyj stood. He was being sincere, but he was also being quite wary, when he said in July 1981: "We wish the Russian Orthodox Church holiness and spiritual growth in the spirit of the gospel of Christ."[83] For looked at in the longer term, this new openness of the West to Eastern Orthodoxy, fraught though it undoubtedly was with peril, could be viewed as potentially the fulfillment and the vindication of the very goals that Metropolitan Josyf Slipyj and Metropolitan Andrej Šeptyc'kyj before him had been laboring to achieve since the early years of the twentieth century. These were the goals of East-West reconciliation for which, since the Unions of Brest and of Užhorod and even since the Union of Florence, the "unionistic apostolate" in the East had been working and praying, but vainly, as its ultimate vision, beyond all the chauvinistic Western language about "converting" Eastern Christians.

In one paragraph of his own final Testament, Josyf Slipyj himself best summarized the significance of his lifework:

> This love for Christ; this love for the holy church, which is his mystical body; this love for our beloved Ukrainian Church, which is an integral part of the universal Christian family; this love for

80. Slipyj, *Tvory* 14:65.
81. Slipyj, *Tvory* 14:260 (263).
82. Slipyj, *Tvory* 14:269.
83. Slipyj, *Tvory* 14:259.

our beloved Ukrainian people, with their spiritual and material wealth of universal significance—this love has marked my life's task, my thoughts and my work, both in freedom and in prison.[84]

What Ralph Waldo Emerson once said of Michelangelo may be said of Josyf Slipyj as well: "He builded better than he knew." All of Christendom, East and West, continues to stand in his debt.

84. Slipyj, *Tvory* 14:471-72.

Bibliography

Abbott, Walter M., ed., *The Documents of Vatican II.* New York: The America Press, 1966.

Adeney, Walter Frederic. *The Greek and Eastern Churches.* New York: Charles Scribner's Sons, 1932.

Armstrong, John A. *Ukrainian Nationalism.* New York: Columbia University Press, 1955.

———. "Collaborationism in World War II: The Integral Nationalist Variant in Eastern Europe." *Journal of Modern History* 40 (1968): 396-410.

Aster, Howard, and Potichnyj, Peter J. *Jewish-Ukrainian Relations: Two Solitudes.* Oakville, Ont.: Mosaic Press, 1983.

Attwater, Donald. *The Christian Churches of the East.* 2 vols. Milwaukee: Bruce Publishing Company, 1947-48.

Baran, Stepan. *Mytropolyt Andrej Šeptyc'kyj: žyttja i dijal'nist'* [Metropolitan Andrej Šeptyc'kyj, his life and work]. Munich: Ukr. Vydavnyče Tovarystvo "Vernyhora," 1947.

Barry, Colman James. *Worship and Work: Saint John's Abbey and University 1856-1956.* Collegeville, Minn.: American Benedictine Academy, 1956.

Bartoszewski, Władysław. *The Warsaw Ghetto: A Christian's Testimony.* Foreword by Stanisław Lem. Translated by Stephen C. Cappellari. Boston: Beacon Press, 1987.

Bauer, Walter. *A Greek-English Lexicon of the New Testament and Other Early Christian Literature,* tr. William F. Arndt and F. Wilbur Gingrich. 2d ed. Chicago: The University of Chicago Press, 1979.

Baum, Gregory. *That They May Be One: A Study of Papal Doctrine (Leo XIII—Pius XII).* Westminster, Md.: Newman Press, 1958.

Beck, Hans-Georg. *Kirche und theologische Literatur im byzantinischen Reich.* Munich: C. H. Beck'sche Verlagsbuchhandlung, 1959.

Beck, Hildebrand. *Vorsehung und Vorherbestimmung in der theologischen Literatur der Byzantiner*. Rome: Pontifical Institute of Oriental Studies, 1937.

Beinert, Wolfgang. *Um das dritte Kirchenattribut: Die Katholizität der Kirche im Verständnis der evangelisch-lutherischen und römisch-katholischen Theologie der Gegenwart*. 2 vols. Essen: Ludgerus-Verlag, 1964.

Benz, Ernst. *Geist und Leben der Ostkirche*. 2d ed. Munich: Wilhelm Fink, 1971.

Berlin, Isaiah. *Russian Thinkers*. Harmondsworth and New York: Penguin Books, 1979.

Bilaniuk, Petro B. T. *The Fifth Lateran Council (1512-1517) and the Eastern Churches*. Dissertation, Free Ukrainian University of Munich. Toronto, 1975.

————. *Studies in Eastern Christianity*. 3 vols. Munich and Toronto: Ukrainian Free University, 1977-83.

————. "The Father of Modern Ecumenism: Patriarch Joseph Cardinal Slipyj (1892-1984): A Biblio-Biographical Sketch." *Bohoslovija* 48 (1984): 27-42.

Bilinsky, Yaroslav. *The Second Soviet Republic: The Ukraine after World War II*. New Brunswick, N.J.: Rutgers University Press, 1964.

Billington, James H. *The Icon and the Axe: An Interpretive History of Russian Culture*. New York: Vintage Books, 1970.

Blažejovskyj, Dmytro. *Ukrainian and Armenian Pontifical Seminaries of Lwiw (1665-1784)*. Rome: Analecta Ordinis Sancti Basilii Magni, 1975.

Bolshakoff, Serge. *The Doctrine of the Unity of the Church in the Works of Khomyakov and Möhler*. London: Society for Promoting Christian Knowledge, 1946.

Boorstin, Daniel J. *The Americans: The National Experience*. New York: Vintage Books, 1967.

Boreckyj, Izydor. "Pravna osnova Ukrajinskoji Cerkvy na patrijarše zaveršennja" [The legal foundation for the patriarchal polity in the Ukrainian Church]. *Bohoslovija* 34 (1970): 40-47.

Boshyk, Yury, ed. *Ukraine during World War II: History and Its Aftermath*. Edmonton, Alberta: Canadian Institute of Ukrainian Studies, 1986.

————, and Balan, Boris. *Political Refugees and "Displaced Persons," 1945-1954: A Select Bibliography and Guide to Research, with Special Reference to the Ukrainians*. Edmonton, Alberta: Canadian Institute of Ukrainian Studies, 1982.

Brezik, Victor B., ed. *One Hundred Years of Thomism: "Aeterni Patris" and Afterwards*. Houston: Center for Thomistic Studies, 1981.

Brostrom, Kenneth N., ed. *Archpriest Avvakum: The Life Written by Himself*. Ann Arbor, Mich.: Michigan Slavic Publications, 1979.

Buchsweiler, Meir. *Volksdeutsche in der Ukraine am Vorabend und Beginn des Zweiten Weltkriegs—ein Fall doppelter Loyalität?* Gerlingen: Bleicher Verlag, 1984.

Budorowycz, Bohdan. "Poland and the Ukrainian Problem, 1921-1939." *Canadian Slavonic Papers* 25 (1983): 473-500.

Casey, Robert Pierce. *Religion in Russia*. New York: Harper and Brothers, 1946.

Catton, Bruce. *Bruce Catton's Civil War: Mr. Lincoln's Army; Glory Road; A Stillness at Appomattox*. New York: Fairfax Press, 1984.

Choma, Ivan. "Ideja spil'noho synodu 1629 r." [The idea of a joint Catholic-Orthodox synod in the year 1629]. *Bohoslovija* 37 (1973): 21-64.

BIBLIOGRAPHY

———. "Dejaki z peršych instrukciji Kongregaciji pošyrennja Viry vidnosno cerkvy na Rusi-Ukrajini" [Various facts about the first instructions of the Congregation for the Propagation of the Faith in Rus'-Ukraine]. *Bohoslovija* 38 (1974): 93-121.

———. "Kyjivs'ka mytropolija naperedodni Berestja" [The metropolitanate of Kiev before the Synod of Brest]. *Bohoslovija* 40 (1976): 5-75.

———. "Sobory eksarchiv u L'vovi 1940-41" [Councils of exarchs in L'viv 1940-41]. *Bohoslovija* 44 (1980): 131-80.

———. "Ukraijinske posolstvo pry apostol'skomu prestoli 1919-1921" [The Ukrainian legation at the Apostolic See 1919-1921]. *Bohoslovija* 45 (1981): 3-65.

———, and Muzyčka, eds. *Intrepido Pastori: Naukovyj zbirnyk na čest' Blažennišoho Patrijarcha Josyfa v 40-littja vstuplennja na Halyc'kyj prestil* [To the intrepid pastor: A Festschrift in honor of His Beatitude Patriarch Josyf on the 40th anniversary of his accession to the See of Halyč]. Rome: Universitas Catholica Ucrainorum S. Clementis Papae, 1984.

———. "Šljachamy katorhy Blažennišoho Josyfa vid 11.IV.1945–27.I.1963" [Itinerary of the imprisonment of His Beatitude Josyf between 11 April 1945 and 27 January 1963]. *Bohoslovija* 49 (1985): 89-149.

Chubatyi, Nicholas D. "Russian Church Policy in the Ukraine." *Ukrainian Quarterly* 2 (Autumn 1945): 43-56.

Churchill, Winston Spencer. "The Sinews of Peace." In Robert Rhodes James, ed., *Churchill Speaks: Winston S. Churchill in Peace and War; Collected Speeches, 1897-1963*. New York and London: Chelsea House, 1980, pp. 876-84.

Cibulka, Josef. *Velkomoravský kostel v Modré u Velehradu a začátky křesťanství na Moravě* [The Greater-Moravian church in Modrá at Velehrad and the beginnings of Christianity in Moravia]. Prague: Československá Akademia Věd, 1958.

Congar, Yves M.-J. *Tradition and Traditions: An Historical and a Theological Essay.* Translated by Michael Naseby and Thomas Rainborough. New York: The Macmillan Company, 1966.

Conquest, Robert. *Harvest of Sorrow: Soviet Collectivization and the Terror-Famine.* New York: Oxford University Press, 1986.

Cousins, Norman. *Present Tense: An American Editor's Odyssey.* New York: Mc-Graw-Hill Book Company, 1967.

———. *The Improbable Triumvirate, John F. Kennedy, Pope John, Nikita Khrushchev.* New York: W. W. Norton and Company, 1972.

Cross, Samuel, ed. *The Russian Primary Chronicle: Laurentian Text.* Cambridge, Mass.: The Medieval Academy of America, 1953.

Dekan, Ján. *Moravia Magna: The Great Moravian Empire, Its Art and Times*, tr. Heather Trebatická. Minneapolis: Control Data Arts, 1981.

Dijannja Soboru Hreko-Katolyc'koji Cerkvy u L'vovi 8.-10. bereznja 1946 [Acts of the Synod of the Greek Catholic Church in L'viv 8-10 March 1946]. L'viv: Vydannja prezydiji soboru, 1946.

Dmytryshyn, Basil. "The Nazis and the SS Volunteer Division 'Galicia.'" *American Slavic and East European Review* 15 (1956): 1-10.

Dragan, A. *Our Ukrainian Cardinal*. Translated by Oksana Dragan. Jersey City, N.J.: Ukrainian National Association, 1966.

Dulles, Avery. *Models of the Church*. Garden City, N.Y.: Doubleday, 1974.

Dvornik, Francis. *The Photian Schism: History and Legend*. Cambridge: Cambridge University Press, 1948.

————. *The Idea of Apostolicity and the Legend of the Apostle Andrew*. Cambridge, Mass.: Harvard University Press, 1958.

————. *The Slavs in European History and Civilization*. New Brunswick, N.J.: Rutgers University Press, 1962.

————. *Byzantine Missions among the Slavs: SS. Constantine-Cyril and Methodius*. New Brunswick, N.J.: Rutgers University Press, 1970.

Dzwonyk, Danylo. *La mission de l'église dans l'apostolat unioniste de Metropolite Kyr André Szeptyckyj*. Unpublished dissertation, n.d.

Farmer, Kenneth C. *Ukrainian Nationalism in the Post-Stalin Era: Myth, Symbols, and Ideology in Soviet Nationalities Policy*. The Hague: Martinus Nijhoff, 1980.

Federici, Tommaso. "Due colonne della Chiesa Ucraina nel XX secolo." *Bohoslovija* 48 (1984): 9-26.

Fedunyk, A. "Mytropolyt Josyf—rektor Hreko-Katolyc'koji Bohoslovs'koji Akademiji" [Metropolitan Joseph as rector of the Greek Catholic Theological Academy]. *Bohoslovija* 21/24 (1963): 106-12.

Feiner, Johannes. "Kommentar" on "Dekret über den Ökumenismus." In Herbert Vorgrimler, ed. *Das Zweite Vatikanische Konzil: Dokumente und Kommentare*, 2:40-126. Freiburg: Herder, 1967.

Fireside, Harvey. *Icon and Swastika: The Russian Orthodox Church under Nazi and Soviet Control*. Cambridge, Mass.: Harvard University Press, 1971.

Florovsky, Georges V. *Ways of Russian Theology*. Translated by Robert L. Nichols. Belmont, Mass.: Nordland Publishing Company, 1979.

Fouilloux, Étienne. *Les catholiques et l'unité chrétienne du XIXe au XXe siècle*. Paris: Le Centurion, 1982.

Friedman, Philip. *Roads to Extinction: Essays on the Holocaust*. New York: The Jewish Publication Society of America, 1980.

Geanakoplos, Deno John. *Emperor Michael Palaeologus and the West, 1258-82*. Cambridge, Mass.: Harvard University Press, 1959.

————. *Greek Scholars in Venice: Studies in the Dissemination of Greek Learning from Byzantium to Western Europe*. Cambridge, Mass.: Harvard University Press, 1962.

————. *Byzantine East and Latin West: Two Worlds of Christendom in the Middle Ages and Renaissance*. New York: Barnes and Noble, 1966.

————. *Byzantium: Church, Society, and Civilization Seen through Contemporary Eyes*. Chicago: The University of Chicago Press, 1984.

Ghellinck, Joseph de. "La nouvelle constitution sur les études." *Nouvelle revue théologique* 58 (1931): 769-85.

Gibbon, Edward. *The Decline and Fall of the Roman Empire*, ed. J. B. Bury. 7 vols. London: Methuen, 1896-1900.

Gratieux, Albert. *A. S. Khomiakov et le mouvement slavophile*. 2 vols. Paris: Editions du Cerf, 1939.

Gregorovich, Andrew. *Ukraine, Rus', Russia and Muscovy: A Selected Bibliography of the Names.* Toronto: New Review Books, 1971.

Grekov, B. *Kievan Rus.* Translated by Y. Sdobnikov. Moscow: Foreign Languages Publishing House, 1959.

Grimsted, Patricia Kennedy. *Archives and Manuscript Repositories in the USSR: Moscow and Leningrad.* Princeton: Princeton University Press, 1972.

————. *Archives and Manuscript Repositories in the USSR: Estonia, Latvia, Lithuania, and Belorussia.* Princeton: Princeton University Press, 1981.

————. "The Archival Legacy of Soviet Ukraine: Problems of Tracing the Documentary Records of a Divided Nation." *Occasional Papers of the Kennan Institute for Advanced Russian Studies,* number 203. Washington: Woodrow Wilson International Center for Scholars, 1985.

Halecki, Oskar. *From Florence to Brest.* Rome: Sacrum Poloniae Millennium, 1958.

Harnack, Adolf von. *Aus der Werkstatt des Vollendeten.* Edited by Axel von Harnack. Giessen: Alfred Töpelmann, 1930.

Herbigny, Michel d'. *Vladimir Soloviev (1853-1900): un Newman russe.* 3d ed. Paris: G. Beauchesne, 1934.

Heuser, Herman Joseph. "Greek Catholics and Latin Priests." *American Ecclesiastical Review* 4 (1891): 194-204.

————. "Decretum de sacerdotibus Ruthenis." *American Ecclesiastical Review* 7 (1892): 66-67.

————. "The Appointment of a Greek Catholic Bishop in the United States." *American Ecclesiastical Review* 37 (1907): 457-67.

Holl, Karl. *Gesammelte Aufsätze zur Kirchengeschichte: Der Osten.* Tübingen: J. C. B. Mohr (Paul Siebeck), 1928.

Holowackyj, Romanus R. *Seminarium Vilnense SS. Trinitatis (1601-1621)* [The Seminary of the Most Holy Trinity at Vilno (1601-1621)]. Rome: Analecta Ordinis Sancti Basilii Magni, 1957.

Horak, Stephan M. *Ukraine in der internationalen Politik, 1917-1953.* Munich: Verlag Ukraine, 1957.

Hordyns'kyj, Svjatoslav. "Ukrajins'ki cerkvy" [Ukrainian churches]. *Bohoslovija* 33 (1969): 74-90.

Hrushevsky, Michael. *A History of Ukraine.* Edited by O. J. Frederiksen. New Haven: Yale University Press, 1941.

Hryn'och, Ivan. "Poslannja Patrijarcha Josyfa pro pojednannja v Chrysti: Sproba interpretaciji" [The message of Patriarch Joseph on reunion in Christ: An attempt at an interpretation]. *Bohoslovija* 41 (1977): 11-72.

————. "Vidhomin Kyrylo-Metodijivs'koji ideji na II Vatykans'komu Sobori" [Echo of the Cyrillo-Methodian ideal at the Second Vatican Council]. *Bohoslovija* 44 (1980): 181-87.

Hugo, Victor. *Les Misérables* (1862). Translated by Charles E. Wilbour. New York: The Modern Library, n.d.

Hunczak, Taras, ed. *The Ukrainian Revolution: Documents, 1919-1921.* New York: The Ukrainian Academy of Arts and Sciences in the United States, 1984.

————. "Ukrainian-Jewish Relations during the Soviet and Nazi Occupations." In Yury Boshyk, ed. *Ukraine during World War II: History and*

Its Aftermath, pp. 39-57. Edmonton, Alberta: Canadian Institute of Ukrainian Studies, 1986.

Husar, Lubomyr. "Andrej Sheptycky, Metropolitan of Halych 1901-1944, A Pioneer of Ecumenism." Dissertatio in Lauream in Sacra Theologia Consequendam. Pontificia Universitas Urbaniana, 1972.

Ikonostas Soboru Svjatoji Sofiji v Rymi [The iconostasis of the Church of Saint Sophia in Rome]. Rome: Santa Sofia, 1979.

Isajiv, Petro. "Memorandum Mytropolyta Andreja Šeptyc'koho do urjadiv Central'nych Deržav 3-15 serpnja 1914" [Metropolitan Andrew Sheptytsky's memorandum of 15 August 1914, to the Central Powers]. *Bohoslovija* 32 (1968): 30-74.

Jáki, Stanislas. *Les tendances nouvelles de l'ecclésiologie.* Rome: Herder, 1957.

James, Robert Rhodes. *Anthony Eden: A Biography.* New York: McGraw Hill, 1987.

Janiv, Volodymyr, ed. *Bibliografija prac' Kardynala Josyfa Slipoho* [Bibliography of the works of Cardinal Josyf Slipyj] (1966). Revised as: "Bibliographie der Werke des Kardinals Josyf Slipy." In: *Studien und Beiträge zur neueren Geschichte der Ukraine.* Munich: Ukrainische Freie Universität, 1983.

————, ed. *Cerkva i relihija v Ukrajini: 50 lit pislja žovtnevoji revoluciji (1917-1967)* [The Church and religion in Ukraine fifty years after the October Revolution 1917-1967]. Munich: Ukrainische Freie Universität, 1984.

Jedin, Hubert. "L'importanza del decreto tridentino sui seminari." *Seminarium* 15 (1963): 396-412.

Kamenetsky, Ihor. *Hitler's Occupation of Ukraine, 1941-1944: A Study of Totalitarian Imperialism.* Milwaukee: Marquette University Press, 1956.

Karlinsky, Simon, and Appel, Alfred, Jr., eds. *The Bitter Air of Exile: Russian Writers in the West 1922-1972.* Berkeley and Los Angeles: University of California Press, 1977.

Kimball, Warren F., ed. *Churchill and Roosevelt: The Complete Correspondence.* 3 vols. Princeton: Princeton University Press, 1984.

King, John Joseph. *The Necessity of the Church for Salvation in Selected Theological Writings of the Past Century.* Washington: Catholic University of America Press, 1960.

Knowles, M. David. *Great Historical Enterprises.* New York: Nelson, 1963.

Kohn, Hans. "The Historical Roots of Czech Democracy." In Robert J. Kerner, ed. *Czechoslovakia: Twenty Years of Independence,* pp. 91-105. Berkeley and Los Angeles: University of California Press, 1940.

Kononenko, Konstantyn. *Ukrajina i Rosija: socijalno-ekonomični pidstavy ukrajins'koji nacional'noji ideji, 1917-1960* [Ukraine and Russia: Socio-economic foundations of the Ukrainian national idea, 1917-60]. Munich: Ukrajins'kyj technično-hospodars'kyj instytut, 1965.

Korolevskij, Cyrille (Jean François Joseph Charon). *Metropolite André Szeptyckyj 1865-1944.* Rome: Opera Theologicae Societatis Scientificae Ucrainorum, 1964.

Kosyk, Wolodymyr. "Ukraine's Losses during the Second World War." *The Ukrainian Review* 33-2 (Summer 1985): 9-19.

Krawchenko, Bohdan. *Social Change and National Consciousness in Twentieth-Century Ukraine*. London: Macmillan, 1965.

Krčméry, Štefan. "Ozvena Veľkej Moravy v slovenskej literatúre" [Echoes of Great Moravia in Slovak literature], in Ján Stanislav, ed. *Ríša Veľkomoravská: sborník vedeckých prác* [The Greater Moravian Empire: A collection of scholarly studies], pp. 411-39. 2d ed. Prague: L. Mazáč, 1935.

Kritzeck, James. *Peter the Venerable and Islam*. Princeton: Princeton University Press, 1964.

Kubijovyč, Volodymyr, ed. *Ukraine: A Concise Encyclopaedia*. 2 vols. Toronto: University of Toronto Press, 1963-67.

Kuttner, Stephan. "Il codice di diritto canonico nella storia." *Commemorazione del cinquantesimo anniversario della promulgazione del "Codex Iuris Canonici" celebrata all'augusta presenza del Santo Padre Paolo VI il 27 maggio 1967*, pp. 17-39. Vatican City: Tipografia Poliglotta Vaticana, 1967.

Laba, Vasyl'. "Mytropolyt Kyr Josyf, hidnyj perejemnyk velykoho Mytropolyta Kyr Andreja na Halyc'komu mytropolyčomu prestoli" [Metropolitan Kyr Joseph, a worthy successor of the great Metropolitan Kyr Andrej in the see of Halyč]. *Bohoslovija* 36 (1972): 5-12.

———. *Patrolohija* [Patrology]. 1st ed. L'viv: Greek Catholic Theological Academy, 1931-34. 2d ed. by Josyf Dačkevyč. Rome: Ukrainian Catholic University of Pope Saint Clement, 1974.

Lacko, Michael. *The Union of Užhorod*. Cleveland and Rome: Slovak Institute, 1966.

Lampe, Geoffrey W., ed. *A Patristic Greek Lexicon*. Oxford: Oxford University Press, 1961.

Lelouvier, Yves-Noël. *Perspectives russes sur l'église: Un théologien contemporain, Georges Florovsky*. Paris: Le Centurion, 1967.

Lencyk, Vasyl'. "Ideja cerkovnoji jednosty u Mytropolyta Šeptyc'koho" [The ideal of church unity in Metropolitan Šeptyc'kyj]. *Bohoslovija* 35 (1971): 175-201.

Levi, Virgilio, ed. *The Common Christian Roots of the European Nations: An International Colloquium in the Vatican*. 2 vols. Florence: Le Monnier, 1982.

Lewin, Kurt I. "Archbishop Andreas Sheptytsky and the Jewish Community in Galicia during the Second World War," *Unitas* (Summer 1960): 137ff.

Likowski, Edward. *Unia brzeska (r. 1596)* [The Union of Brest in 1596]. 2d ed. Warsaw: Skład główny Gebethnara i Wolffa, 1907.

Lopuchin, Aleksandr Pavlovič, and Glubokovskij, Nikolaj Nikaronovič, eds. *Pravoslavnaja bogoslovskaja enciklopedija ili bogoslovskij enciklopedičeskij slovar* [Eastern Orthodox theological encyclopedia or theological encyclopedic dictionary]. 9 vols. in 12. Petrograd: Strannik, 1900-1911.

Lozovei, P. *De metropolitarum Kioviensium potestate*. Rome: Analecta Ordinis Sancti Basilii Magni, 1962.

Lužnyc'kyj, Hryhor. *Ukrajins'ka Cerkva miž schodom i zachodom: Narys Istoriji Ukrajins'koji Cerkvy* [The Ukrainian Church between East and West: Outline of the history of the Ukrainian Church]. Philadelphia: "Providence" Association of Ukrainian Catholics, 1954.

McGrath, Margaret. *Étienne Gilson: A Bibliography*. Toronto: Pontifical Institute of Mediaeval Studies, 1982.

Macha, Joseph. *Ecclesiastical Reunification*. Rome: Orientalia Christiana Analecta, 1974.

Madey, Johannes. *Kirche zwischen Ost und West: Beiträge zur Geschichte der Ukrainischen und Weissruthenischen Kirche*. Munich: Ukrainische Freie Universität, 1969.

———. *Le patriarcat ukrainien vers la perfection d l'état juridique actuel*. Rome: Praci Ukrajins'koho Bohoslovs'koho Naukovoho Tovarystva, 1971.

———. *Das Zweite Vatikanische Konzil und die Revision des Rechtes der Ostkirchen*. Rome: Bohoslovija, 1978.

Magocsi, Paul Robert, ed. *The Ukrainian Experience in the United States*. Cambridge, Mass.: Harvard Ukrainian Research Institute, 1979.

———. *Galicia: A Historical Survey and Bibliographic Guide*. Toronto: University of Toronto Press, 1983.

———. *Ukraine: A Historical Atlas*. Toronto: University of Toronto Press, 1985.

Makarij of Moscow. *Istorija Kievskoj akademij* [History of the academy of Kiev]. St. Petersburg: Konstantin Žerpakov, 1843.

Markham, James Joseph. *The Sacred Congregation of Seminaries and Universities of Studies*. Canon Law Studies, vol. 384. Washington: The Catholic University of America, 1957.

Martinos, Athanasios, ed. Θρησκευτικὴ καὶ Ἠθικὴ Ἐγκυκλοπαιδεία [Encyclopedia of religion and ethics]. 12 vols. Athens: A. Martinos, 1962-68.

Marusyn, Myroslav. "Pohljad na vychovannja kandydativ duchovnoho stavu na Ukrajini" [An examination of the education of candidates for the priesthood in Ukraine]. *Bohoslovija* 21/24 (1963): 40-94.

Masaryk, Tomáš Garrigue. *Světová revoluce*. Prague: Orbis, 1925. (English translation: *The Making of a State: Memories and Observations 1914-1918*, tr. Henry Wickam Steed. London: George Allen & Unwin Ltd., 1937.)

Merkle, S. *Das Konzil von Trient und die Universitäten*. Würzburg: H. Stürtz, 1905.

Migovič, I. I. *Prestupn'ij al'jans: O sojuze uniatskoj cerkvi i ukrainskogo buržuaznogo nacionalisma* [Unholy alliance: the union between the Uniate Church and Ukrainian bourgeois nationalism]. Moscow: Izdatel'stvo Političenskoj Literatury, 1985.

Milaš, Nikodim. *Pravoslavno crkveno pravo* [Eastern Orthodox church law]. 3d ed. Belgrade: Izdavačka knjižarnica G. Kona, 1926.

Minenko, Tymofiji. *Vidpovid' pravoslavnych ukrajinciv na zaklyk Mytropolyta Andrija Šeptyc'koho v 1941-42 rohach do pojednannja ukrajinskych cerkov* [Ukrainian Orthodox Reply to an Appeal of Metropolitan Andrew Sheptytsky in 1941-42 for Reunion of the Ukrainian Churches]. Winnipeg: Ecclesia, 1985.

Mončak, Ihor. "Vatykans'kyj Sobor pro Schidni Cerkvy" [The Vatican Council on the Eastern Churches]. *Bohoslovija* 29 (1965): 132-86.

———. "Rozvytok synodal'nosty v Ukrajins'kiji Katolyc'kiji Cerkvi" [The development of the synodical structure in the Ukrainian Catholic Church]. *Bohoslovija* 47 (1983): 41-72.

————. *Florentine Ecumenism in the Kyivan Church*. Rome: Universitas Catholica Ucrainorum S. Clementis Papae, 1987.

Motyl, Alexander J. *The Turn to the Right: The Ideological Origins and Development of Ukrainian Nationalism, 1919-1929*. Boulder, Colo.: East European Monographs, 1980.

Mudryj, Sophronius S. *De transitu a rito Byzantino-Ucraino ad ritum Latinum*. Rome: Pontificia Università Lateranense, 1973.

Müller, Ludolf, ed. *Die Werke des Metropoliten Ilarion*. Munich: W. Fink, 1971.

Murray, John Courtney. *The Problem of God Yesterday and Today*. New Haven: Yale University Press, 1964.

Muzyčka, Ivan. "Počatky ukrajinskoj bohoslovskoj nauky v dvadcjatomu stolittju i Blažennišyj Patriarch Josyf" [The beginnings of Ukrainian theological education in the twentieth century and His Beatitude Patriarch Josyf]. *Bohoslovija* 41 (1977): 73-146.

————. "Ekumenična dijaľnisť Mytropolyta Andreja Šeptyc'koho v Rosiji v 1914-1917 rokach" [The ecumenical activity of Metropolitan Andrej Šeptyc'kyj in Russia during the Years 1914 to 1917]. *Bohoslovija* 47 (1983): 3-39.

————. "Mytropolyt Andrej v časi nimec'koj okupaciji" [Metropolitan Andrej during the time of the German occupation]. *Bohoslovija* 51 (1987): 1-15.

Mykula, Wolodymyr. *The Gun and the Faith: Religion and the Church in Ukraine under the Communist Russian Rule*. London: Ukrainian Information Service, 1969.

Nahajevs'kyj, Isydor. *Kyrylo-Metodijinske Chrystyjanstvo v Rusi-Ukrajini* [Cyrillo-Methodian Christianity in Rus'-Ukraine]. Rome: Analecta Ordinis Sancti Basilii Magni, 1954.

————. "Sv. Kyrylo i Metodiji v svitli novych doslidiv" [Saints Cyril and Methodius in the light of new research]. *Bohoslovija* 31 (1967): 180-97.

Nazarko, Irynej. *Kyjivs'ki i Halyc'ki Mytropolyty: Biohrafični narysy (1590-1960)* [Metropolitans of Kiev and Halyč: biographical sketches (1590-1960)]. Rome: Analecta Ordinis Sancti Basilii Magni, 1962.

Nemec, Ludvik. *Antonin Cyril Stojan: Apostle of Church Unity*. New Rochelle, N.Y.: Don Bosco Publications, 1983.

Nichols, Robert, and Stavrou, Theofanis George, eds. *Russian Orthodoxy under the Old Regime*. Minneapolis: University of Minnesota Press, 1978.

Nicol, D. M. "The Fourth Crusade and the Greek and Latin Empires, 1204-61." *The Cambridge Medieval History*, vol. 4, 2d ed., pp. 275-330. Cambridge: Cambridge University Press, 1966.

O'Connor, Edward Dennis, ed. *The Dogma of the Immaculate Conception: History and Significance*. Notre Dame, Ind.: University of Notre Dame Press, 1958.

O'Donohue, J. A. *Tridentine Seminary Legislation: Its Sources and Its Formation*. Louvain: Bibliotheca Ephemeridum Theologicarum Lovaniensium, 1957.

Patrylo, Isydor. *Archiepiscopi Metropolitani Kievo-Halicienses attenti praescriptis M. P. [Motu Proprio] "Cleri sanctitati"* [The metropolitan archbishops of Kiev-Halyč in accordance with the prescriptions of the motu proprio *Cleri sanctitati*]. Rome: Analecta Ordinis Sancti Basilii Magni, 1962.

Pekar, Basilius. *De erectione canonica eparchiae Mukačoviensis (an. 1771)* [The canonical establishment of the eparchy of Mukačevo (in the year 1771)]. 2d ed. Rome: Analecta Ordinis Sancti Basilii Magni, 1956.

Pelikan, Jaroslav. *Obedient Rebels: Catholic Substance and Protestant Principle in Luther's Reformation.* New York: Harper & Row, 1964.

———. *Development of Christian Doctrine: Some Historical Prolegomena.* New Haven: Yale University Press, 1969.

———. *The Christian Tradition: A History of the Development of Doctrine.* 5 vols. Chicago: The University of Chicago Press, 1971-89.

———. "Introduction" to George C. Berthold, ed., *Maximus Confessor: Selected Writings,* pp. 1-13. "The Classics of Western Spirituality." New York: Paulist Press, 1985.

———. *The Mystery of Continuity: Time and History, Memory and Eternity in the Thought of Saint Augustine.* Charlottesville, Va.: University Press of Virginia, 1986.

Petryshyn, Roman W., and Chomiak, Natalia, eds. *Political Writings of Post–World War Two Ukrainian Émigrés: Annotated Bibliography and Guide to Research.* Edmonton, Alberta: Canadian Institute of Ukrainian Studies, 1984.

Philippou, Angelos James, ed. *The Orthodox Ethos: Essays in Honour of the Centenary of the Greek Orthodox Archdiocese of North and South America.* Oxford: Holywell Press, 1964.

Polons'ka-Vasylenko, N. *Istoryčni pidvalyny UAPC* [The historical foundations of the Ukrainian Autocephalous Orthodox Church]. 2d ed. Rome: Analecta Ordinis Sancti Basilii Magni, 1964.

Popov, Andrej Nikolaevič. *Istoriko-literaturnyj obzor drevnerusskich polemičeskich sočinenij protiv Latinjam* [Historical-literary survey of ancient Russian polemical works against the Latins]. Moscow: Tip. T. Ris', 1875.

Popova, Olga. *Russian Illuminated Manuscripts.* Translated by Kathleen Cook, Vladimir Ivanov, and Lenina Sorokina. New York: Thames and Hudson, 1984.

Pospishil, Victor J. *The Law on Persons (in the Oriental Code).* Ford City, Pa.: St. Mary's Ukrainian Catholic Church, 1960.

———. *Der Patriarch in der serbisch-orthodoxen Kirche.* Vienna: Herder, 1966.

———. *Divorce and Remarriage: Towards a New Catholic Teaching.* New York: Herder and Herder, 1967.

———. "Compulsory Celibacy for the Eastern Catholics in the Americas." *Diakonia* 11 (1976): 133-56.

Prokop, Myroslav. *Ukrajina i ukrajins'ka polityka Moskvy* [Ukraine and the Ukrainian politics of Moscow]. 2d ed. 2 vols. Munich: Sučasnist', 1981.

Prokoptschuk, Gregor. *Metropolit Graf Scheytyćkyj: Leben und Wirken des großen Förderers der Kirchenunion.* 2d ed. Munich: Verlag Ukraine, 1967.

Prus, Edward. *Władyka Świetojurski: Rzecz o arcybiskupie Andrzeju Szeptyckim (1865-1944)* [The prelate of Saint George's: A discussion of Archbishop Andrej Šeptyc'kyj]. Foreword by Ludwik Bazylow. Warsaw: Instytut Wydawniczy Zwiazków Zawodowych, 1985.

Rackl, M. "Eine griechische Abbreviatio der Prima Secundae des hl. Thomas v. Aquin." *Divus Thomas* 9 (1922): 50-59.

Riasanovsky, Nicholas V. *A History of Russia*. New York: Oxford University Press, 1963.

Rizzi, Marius. "De archiepiscopi maioris iuridico fundamento in Ecclesia Catholica" [On the legal foundations of the office of major archbishop in the Catholic Church]. *Bohoslovija* 25/28 (1964): 121-24.

Rostovtzeff, Michael. *Skythien und der Bosporus*. Berlin: H. Schoetz, 1931.

Rudnyc'ka, Milena. *Nevydymi Styhmaty* [The invisible stigmata]. Rome: Society for the Promotion of the Patriarchal System in the Ukrainian Catholic Church, 1971.

Rudnytsky, Ivan L., ed. *Rethinking Ukrainian History*. Edmonton, Alberta: Canadian Institute of Ukrainian Studies, 1981.

Rudnytzky, Leonid. "Obraz Patrijarcha Josyfa v literaturi" [The image of Patriarch Josyf in literature]. In *Choma-Muzyčka* (1984): 681-89.

Runciman, Steven. *A History of the Crusades*. 3 vols. Cambridge: Cambridge University Press, 1951-54.

Schmemann, Alexander. "On Solzhenitsyn." In John B. Dunlop, Richard Haugh, and Alexis Klimoff, eds. *Aleksandr Solzhenitsyn: Critical Essays and Documentary Materials*. Belmont, Mass.: Nordland Publishing Company, 1973.

———. "The Problem of the Church's Presence in the World in Orthodox Consciousness." In Savas Chr. Agouridés, ed., *Deuxième congrès de théologie orthodoxe*, pp. 236-49. Athens: Savas Chr. Agouridés, 1978.

Shaugnessy, Gerald. *Has the Immigrant Kept the Faith?* New York: The Macmillan Company, 1925.

Shifrin, Avraham. *Četvretoe izmerenie* [The fourth dimension]. Frankfurt am Main: Posev, 1973.

———. *The First Guidebook to Prisons and Concentration Camps of the Soviet Union*. Uhldingen/Seewis: Stephanus Edition, 1980.

Sobieski, Jacques. "Saint Cyrille et Saint Méthode et l'actualité de leur oeuvre." *Bohoslovija* 30 (1966): 83-103.

Solzhenitsyn, Aleksandr I. *The Gulag Archipelago 1918-1956: An Experiment in Literary Investigation*. Translated by Thomas P. Whitney. 3 vols. New York: Harper & Row, 1973-78.

Southern, R. W. *Western Views of Islam in the Middle Ages*. Cambridge, Mass.: Harvard University Press, 1962.

Stasiw, Myron. *Metropolia Haliciensis, eius historia et iuridica forma* [The Metropolitanate of Halyč, its history and juridical form]. 2d ed. Rome: Analecta Ordinis Sancti Basilii Magni, 1960.

Stehle, Hansjacob. *Eastern Politics of the Vatican, 1917-1979*. Translated by Sandra Smith. Athens, Ohio: Ohio University Press, 1981.

Sysyn, Frank E. *Between Poland and the Ukraine: The Dilemma of Adam Kysil, 1600-1653*. Cambridge, Mass.: Harvard Ukrainian Research Institute, 1985.

Tappert, Theodore G., Pelikan, Jaroslav, Fischer, Robert H., and Piepkorn, Arthur C., ed. and tr. *The Book of Concord: The Confessions of the Evangelical Lutheran Church*. Philadelphia: Muhlenberg Press, 1959.

Thomson, S. Harrison, ed. *Magistri Johannis Hus Tractatus de Ecclesia*. Cambridge: Cambridge University Press, 1956.

Vasilij, Diakon. *Leonid Fedorov: žizn' i dejatel'nost'* [Leonid Fedorov: his life and work]. Rome: Studion, 1966.

Vishnevskaya, Galina. *Galina: A Russian Story*. Translated by Guy Daniels. New York: Harcourt, Brace, Jovanovich, 1984.

Vitošyns'ka, Ol'ha. *Podoroži Blažennišoho Kyr Josyfa VII 1968-1970 u svitli čužoji presy* [The travels of His Beatitude *Kyr* Josyf VII 1968-1970 as reflected in the foreign press]. Rome: Opera Theologicae Societatis Scientificae Ucrainorum, 1972.

Wallace, Lew. *Ben Hur*. Wallace Memorial Edition. New York: Harper and Brothers, 1908.

Welykyj, Athanasius G., ed. *Documenta unionis Berestensis eiusque auctorum (1590-1600)* [Documents of the Union of Brest and its authors (1590-1600)]. Rome: Analecta Ordinis Sancti Basilii Magni, 1970.

Weres, Roman. *Ukraine: Selected References in the English Language*. Chicago: Ukrainian Research and Information Institute, 1974.

West, Morris L. *The Shoes of the Fisherman*. New York: William Morrow and Company, 1963.

West, Rebecca. *Black Lamb and Grey Falcon: A Journey through Yugoslavia*. New York: Penguin Books, 1982.

Wiwčaruk, Stephanus. *De synodo provinciali Berestensi anno 1765 non celebrata*. 2d ed. Rome: Analecta Ordinis Sancti Basilii Magni, 1963.

Wojnar, Meletius Michael. "Projekt konstytuciji patriarchatu Ukrajns'koji Cerkvi" [The projected constitution for the patriarchate of the Ukrainian Church]. *Bohoslovija* 34 (1970): 5-39.

Wolff, R. L. "Politics in the Latin Patriarchate of Constantinople, 1204-1261." *Dumbarton Oaks Papers*, 7 (1954): 225-304.

Yuzyk, Paul. *The Ukrainian Greek Orthodox Church of Canada (1918-1951)*. Ottawa, Canada: University of Ottawa Press, 1981.

Zernov, Nicolas. *Eastern Christendom*. New York: G. P. Putnam's Sons, 1961.

———. *The Russian Religious Renaissance of the Twentieth Century*. New York: Harper & Row, 1963.

Index

(Several names—notably, Metropolitans Josyf Slipyj and Andrej Šeptyc'kyj, and the patriarchates of Rome and Constantinople—appear so often throughout the book that they are not included in the index.)

Seymour, Horatio, 154
Shaughnessy, Gerald, quoted, 221-22
Sheen, Bishop Fulton J., 188
Shifrin, Avraham, 166-68
Sobieski, Jacques, quoted, 30n.54
Soloviev, Vladimir, 37, 42, 50, 67-72, 164
Solzhenitsyn, Aleksandr, 163-64
Spasskij, A. A., 18-19
Spellman, Francis Cardinal, 192
Stalin, Joseph, 73-74, 146, 150-51, 153, 159, 160, 168
Steed, Henry Wickham, 40
Stojan, Archbishop Anton Cyril, 25
Strossmayer, Bishop Josip Juraj, 68, 71
Studites, xii, 18, 126-27, 175, 186-89, 211
Šuchevyč, General Roman, 8, 152-53
Sysyn, Frank, quoted, 10n.20, 66n.85
Szeptycki, Jan, 76

Tarnopil'skyj, Volodymyr, 104-5
Tass, Soviet News Agency, 146-47
"Tatjana [Romanov]," 80
Teilhard de Chardin, Pierre, 217
Testa, Gustavo Cardinal, 189, 204
Theodore of Studios, St., 18, 86, 113-14, 189
Thomas à Kempis, St., 177
Thomas Aquinas, St., 5, 52, 62, 65, 76-77, 84, 86, 99, 103-22
Tisserant, Eugène Cardinal, 11, 130, 172, 192
Treadgold, Donald W., quoted, 161 n.111
Trent, Council of, 16, 35, 81, 220

Ukrainian Autocephalous Orthodox Church, 38-39, 88-89

Ukrainian Catholic University of Pope St. Clement (UKU), 4, 24, 26, 124-25, 134-45, 169-70, 175, 177-78, 182, 214, 218, 227
Ukrainian Insurgent Army (UPA), 8, 152-53
Ukrainian National Council, 79, 154
"Ukrainian National Republic," 7-8
Ukrainian Scientific Theological Society, 10, 124, 131-33, 137, 139, 141, 143
Urban VIII, Pope, 205

van Straaten, Werenfried, 181-82
Velehrad, union congresses of, 25-26, 197
Verbites, 186
Villot, Jean Cardinal, 193
Vincenzi, 108
Vishnevskaya, Galina, quoted, 153 n.45
Vitošyns'ka, Ol'ha, quoted, 176-77, 222n.37
Vladimir (Volodymyr), St., 5, 23, 24-25, 130, 192

Wallace, Lew, quoted, 165n.147
West, Morris L., 215n.190, 216-18
West, Rebecca, quoted, 71
"West Ukrainian People's Republic," 7-8
Wilhelm, Archduke, 89
Woytyła, Karol. See John Paul II
Wrocław (Breslau), University of, 74
Wycliffe, John 48
Wyszynski, Stefan Cardinal, 185-86

Zagreb, University of, 131
Zernov, Nicholas, quoted, 219
Zhukov, General, 165-66, 170, 172
Ziegler, Adolf W., quoted, 78